# WOMEN IN SOCIETY
## A Feminist List edited by
## Jo Campling

*editorial advisory group*

The 1970s and 1980s have seen an explosion of publishing by, about and for women. This new list is designed to make a particular contribution to this process by commissioning and publishing books which consolidate and advance feminist research and debate in key areas in a form suitable for students, academics and researchers but also accessible to a broader general readership.

As far as possible books will adopt an international perspective incorporating comparative material from a range of countries where this is illuminating. Above all they will be interdisciplinary, aiming to put women's studies and feminist discussion firmly on the agenda in subject-areas as disparate as law, physical education, art and social policy.

# WOMEN IN SOCIETY
## A Feminist List edited by Jo Campling

# Women and Social Policy

*A Reader*

*Edited by*

## Clare Ungerson

MACMILLAN

First published 1985

Published by
Higher and Further Education Division
MACMILLAN PUBLISHERS LTD
Houndmills, Basingstoke, Hampshire RG21 2XS
and London
Companies and representatives
throughout the world

Filmsetting by Vantage Photosetting Co Ltd,
Eastleigh and London

Printed in Great Britain, at the
University Press, Oxford

British Library Cataloguing in Publication Data
Women and social policy.—(Women in society)
1. Women—Great Britain—Social conditions
I. Ungerson, Clare    II. Series
305.4'2'0941    HQ1593
ISBN 0-333-36725-1
ISBN 0-333-36726-X Pbk

# Contents

# Preface

While preparing a course on 'Women and Social Policy' at the University of Kent I realised that the literature in this area of Social Administration and Women's Studies was still widely scattered across a range of journals, government reports and books (fiction and non-fiction), such that it was practically impossible for any student, let alone teacher, to find everything they needed for an adequate grasp of the issues across all the social services. This book is designed to bring some of those scattered readings together in such a way that the relationship between women and each of the five social policy areas, namely social security, housing, education, health and the personal social services, is clarified. Each section of the book deals with one of these five areas. The final section deals with women's relationship to the fast-growing area of social service provision in the voluntary and informal sectors.

The sections of the book (and the two sub-sections) are each prefaced by a short introduction written by myself. These introductions are designed to do three things: first, to make sense of the particular readings I have chosen for the section; second, to introduce the literature pertinent to each policy area; and third, to outline some – though by no means all – the issues that arise out of each set of readings. Since each of the introductions is specifically designed to introduce further reading on the topic, readers should use the full bibliography at the end of the book to build up their reading lists. Where I have been unable to weave all the important and relevant reading into the thread of the argument, I have appended a brief note on additional reading to each of the introductions.

It is my hope that each section will spark off far more ideas than I have had the space to develop here. It is partly for that reason that most of the introductions are deliberately left open-ended. But there is also an intellectual reason: it seems to me that there are dilemmas for women contained within each social service area which are extremely difficult to resolve. Again, I hope that the posing of unresolved questions will lead to further discussion among students and teachers alike. There are also two issues which, for reasons of space, have not been discussed at length. Class relations and race relations form much of the context for discussion of the relationship between women and social policy, but to cover them fully would have needed a second book.

I first started to think about teaching a course on 'Women and Social Policy' arranged in this way when, in 1981, I spent a semester at the Department of Political Science at the University of Massachusetts, Amherst. My grateful thanks are due to the small group of students who attended that embryonic course and who, with their enthusiasm, convinced me that here was a course that was worth developing. Subsequently, at the University of Kent, I have taught a course of that name on the MA in Women's Studies and on the undergraduate degree in Social Administration. Members of the Women's Studies Committee, particularly Mary Evans and Janet Sayers, have been of immense help to me in very many ways, both as colleagues and as friends. Sarah Carter, Assistant Librarian at the University of Kent, recognised in its very early days the great importance of academic feminism, and, largely through her efforts, the University now has an excellent collection of feminist writing which I have found invaluable. Members of the Board of Studies in Social Policy and Administration, particularly John Baldock, Nick Manning and Peter Taylor-Gooby, each of whom have contributed to the course, have also been extremely helpful. And, last but not least, I must thank, for their responsiveness and confidence, the MA students and undergraduates at the University of Kent who have taken this course over the past three years.

A number of people have helped me directly with this book by commenting on the introductions. They are: David Donnison, Vic George, Hilary Land, Nick Manning, Chris Pickvance, Marion Roberts and Janet Sayers. I am very grateful to all of them; they are, of course, not responsible for what remains. Jo Campling, the editor of this list, was always at the end of the telephone with supportive and soothing words. Finally, I am deeply grateful to William Fortescue for all his support – practical and otherwise.

CLARE UNGERSON

# Acknowledgements

The author and publishers wish to thank the following who have kindly given permission for the use of copyright material:

Edward Arnold for an extract from 'In Practice Supported, In Theory Denied' by Hilary Rose in *International Journal of Urban and Regional Research,* Vol. 2, No. 3 (1978).

Helen Austerberry and Sophie Watson for 'A Woman's Place: A Feminist Approach to Housing in Britain' first published in *Feminist Review,* No. 8 (1981).

The British Sociological Association for extracts from 'Notes on Patriarchy, Professionalization and the Semi-Professions' by Jeff Hearn which first appeared in *Sociology,* Vol. 16, No. 2 (1982).

Cambridge University Press for an extract from 'The Working of the 1967 Abortion Act in Britain' by M. Potts, P. Diggory and J. Peel in *Abortion* (1977); and an extract from 'Community Care and the Family: A Case for Equal Opportunities?' in *Journal of Social Policy* by J. Finch and D. Groves (Vol. 9, Part 4, October 1984).

Carfax Publishing Company Ltd for an extract from 'State Policy and Ideology in the Education of Women, 1944–1980, by Rosemary Deem in *British Journal of Sociology of Education,* Vol. 2, No. 2 (1981).

Critical Social Policy Ltd for an extract from 'Women, Health and the Sexual Division of Labour' by Lesley Doyal in *Women's Health Movement, Critical Social Policy,* Issue 7 (1983).

Croom Helm Ltd for an extract from *Women's Welfare, Women's Rights* by Hilary Land; and an extract from *Single and Pregnant* by Sally McIntyre.

André Deutsch Ltd for an extract from *The Women's Room* by Marilyn French.

A. M. Heath & Co. Ltd on behalf of Zoë Fairbairns for 'The Cohabitation Rule' first published in *Women's Studies International, Quarterly,* Vol. 2 (1979).

Heinemann Educational Books Ltd for an extract from *Change, Choice and Conflict in Social Policy* by P. Hall, H. Land, A. Webb and R. Parker.

The Controller of Her Majesty's Stationery Office for an extract from the evidence submitted by the Family Allowances Campaign to the Select Committee on Tax Credit (1973).

Hutchinson Ltd for an extract from *Gender and Schooling* by Michelle Stanworth (1981).

Martin Robertson & Co. Ltd for an extract from 'The Politics of Poverty' in *Women and Social Policy* by David Donnison (1982).

Spokesman for an extract from *Poverty: The Forgotten Englishmen* by Ken Coates and Richard Silburn.

Margaret Thatcher for an extract from her speech to the WRVS National Conference (1981).

Virago Press Ltd for an extract from *Benefits: A Novel* by Zoë Fairbairns.

Every effort has been made to trace all the copyright holders, but if any have been inadvertently overlooked the publishers will be pleased to make the necessary arrangements at the first opportunity.

# I

# Women and Social Security

# A. Motherhood

## Introduction

Family Allowance, or Child Benefit as a modified version of it is now known, has not always had the unequivocal support of the entire women's movement. This is despite the fact that it is the only universal non-contributory benefit payable to all mothers on behalf of their children, and thus guarantees mothers at least some income for which they do not have to ask their husbands or cohabitees.

Both before the adoption of the principle in the 1945 Family Allowance Act and for at least a decade after its implementation, some women's organisations were either positively hostile or distinctly lukewarm in their attitudes. As Hilary Land reminds us in another article (Land, 1980) Ada Nield Chew, a radical suffragist, wrote that women should eschew the role of the 'domestic tabby cat' and that 'marriage and motherhood should not be for sale. They should be disassociated from what is for sale – domestic drudgery.' Similarly, after the implementation of the allowances, the Cooperative Women's Guild, an organisation of working-class women within the Cooperative Movement which had originally been among the strongest supporters of the campaign for family allowances (Lewis, 1980), defeated a resolution calling for an increase in the amount of the allowance at their annual Congress in 1951 (Gaffin and Thoms, 1983, p. 161). Indeed, Frank Field claims that the Child Poverty Action Group, which since its foundation in 1965 has consistently and somewhat single-mindedly campaigned for the extension of and increases in family allowance, was positively hindered by the latent opposition of women to the scheme (Field, 1982).

3

It would be wrong, however, to exaggerate the extent of women's opposition to this benefit. As on so many issues both now and in the past, the pre-war women's movement was neither homogeneous nor united. On the whole socialist feminists were suspicious of allowances on the grounds that they would undermine male wage-bargaining and preferred to argue, like Ada Nield Chew, for services in kind to support mothers in the 'drudgery' of child care; Fabian women preferred direct payment to mothers in order to maintain their economic independence from their husbands and free them from the need to take on paid work which would distract them from their primary task of mothering (Alexander, 1979). Middle-class feminists, particularly members of the National Union of Societies for Equal Citizenship, of which Eleanor Rathbone was the President, strongly supported family allowances largely on the grounds that it would undermine the concept of the family wage and thereby (a rather optimistic thought) pave the way for equal pay for equal work. Working-class feminists put rather more of their energies into campaigns for better maternity and child welfare services than for cash in hand.

However, as is generally the case with most benefits hard won from the state, once implemented the recipients unite in defence of it when it appears to be under threat. In 1972 the then Conservative government proposed to reform and unite the entire tax and social security system into a scheme of combined benefits and tax reliefs to be known as 'tax credits'. It was therefore proposed that family allowances and child tax allowances should be folded up into one new benefit to be known as the 'child tax credit'. In the Green Paper that presaged the proposed reforms it was suggested that, logically, the new benefit should be payable to the father through his pay packet rather than, as had been the case with family allowances, to the mother through the post office. There was no question of the principle of a universal state benefit to supplement the incomes of families with children being abandoned; what was at issue was consistency within the scheme, as opposed to the maintenance of mothers' rights and minimal independence. There was an immediate outcry from the women's movement, particularly women prominent in the so-called 'wages for housework' campaign that was very active at the time (Malos, 1980). The more active occupied some post offices and gave evidence to the House of Commons Select Committee, part of which is reproduced here (Fleming,

1973). But the issue touched many more than just the activists in the women's movement: a petition demanding that the allowance 'be given to every mother for every child' was presented to Parliament with 300 000 signatures (Fleming, 1973; Castle, 1976).

Other powerful allies emerged, amongst them the Child Poverty Action Group and the Trade Union Congress (House of Commons (HOC), 1973, Vol. II). The support of the TUC for payment of the child tax credit to the mother rather than the father was something of a change of heart. As Hilary Land points out in the first of her articles reproduced here, the TUC had been ambivalent and suspicious about the introduction of family allowances throughout the 1930s. Moreover, the new credits entailed a transfer from husbands to wives or, as the issue came to be known, from 'wallet to purse', and hence one might have expected the male-dominated TUC to be opposed to them. The reason the TUC gave for supporting payment to mothers was an interesting one: they argued that 'in most cases mothers have the major responsibility for the family budget', but little or no independent income (HOC, 1973, Vol. II, p. 258) – in other words mothers should have the wherewithal to carry out a household chore. In one sense the Child Poverty Action Group (CPAG) was also a surprising ally: since its inception it had captured the idea that family allowances were a bulwark, not so much against women's economic dependence on men, but rather against the exigencies of low pay. The needs of children rather than the needs of mothers were, and to some extent remain, the chief focus of its attention. However, by the time the CPAG came to give evidence to the Select Committee it had taken on board the idea of women's financial dependency in marriage and had carried out a survey to discover the extent of mothers' dependence on family allowance for their own and their children's survival, irrespective of the level of their husbands' earnings. As they told MPs, they had found that 34 per cent of mothers interviewed in their survey had failed to receive any increase in their housekeeping allowance in the previous year, while prices had risen 7 per cent over the same period (HOC, 1973, Vol. II, p. 318).

The campaign to get the new 'child tax credit' payable to mothers was eventually a successful one: while the tax credit scheme as a whole was abandoned, the child benefit, combining family allowance and child tax allowance and payable to the mother for all her children including the first, rose like a Phoenix from the ashes, in the form of the Child Benefit Act, 1975. Nevertheless, at one point the Phoenix was very nearly shot down; the new Labour Prime Minister (Jim Callaghan) and the Chancellor of the Exchequer (Denis Healey) decided that a transfer 'from wallet to purse' was a certain vote loser, and they managed to play on old trade union antagonisms and Cabinet confusion such that the benefit was seriously delayed and nearly abandoned (Land, 1977a; Field, 1982). But a 'mole' leaked Cabinet minutes to CPAG (*New Society*, 17 June 1976) and the resulting furore meant that Child Benefit was rescued. It was introduced in embryonic form for all children in 1976, and child tax allowances disappeared altogether over the next two years. (However, the Married Man's Tax Allowance has been increased to compensate – see p. 45.)

The three excerpts reproduced here demonstrate the complexity of the issue of family allowance or child benefit, and the mixture of motives and alliances that have in the past, and may in future, be generated by it. At the root of many of the dilemmas and contradictions is that while mothers gain a great deal materially from these benefits, they run the risk, at an ideological level, of merely confirming the link between being a woman and necessarily, therefore, becoming a mother. Not only that: benefits for children tend to confirm the link between biological mothering and social mothering. If mothers receive a benefit which they are expected and indeed do spend to service the needs of their families, then this re-confirms them as the day-to-day managers of household finances, which for millions of women is not only a chore but also a source of considerable anxiety (McClelland, 1982). In contrast, of course, stand the words of mothers themselves. As Mrs A. of Milton Keynes wrote to the *Sun* newspaper: 'Although the benefit is only a pittance, it does enable the women of this country to struggle through until pay day with a little pride and dignity' (quoted in McClelland, 1982).

The eugenicist strand in the argument, which is based on an assumption of hereditary social characteristics, is brought out in the pieces by Land and Fairbairns. But one does not have to go so far as to support child benefit for the *qualitative* demographic effect it may or may not have. Many countries, including France in the capitalist West and almost all the more developed countries of the Eastern bloc, pay large child benefits on the assumption that this will have a *quantitative* demographic effect (see, for example, Scott, 1976). In other words, women are being offered a considerable financial inducement to turn themselves into 'walking wombs'.

The eugenicist and pro-natalist arguments are in abeyance at the moment in this country although there is always a latent undercurrent that ebbs and flows. Of far greater importance is the argument in favour of child benefit as the most efficient way (so far) devised to maintain male work incentives. The piece by Hilary Land shows how this argument was used in the 1920s and 1930s. It has taken present-day governments some time to understand that a universal benefit is a bulwark against the disincentive effects of a largely means-tested system, and that, given that the benefit is paid irrespective of whether the household head is in or out of work but is nevertheless deducted from supplementary benefit, it helps maintain a difference between income in paid work and income on the dole. Political leaders do now understand this (Lister, 1980), and as a result child benefit is generally increased every year. This is no victory for women, even though it is of very important material benefit to them. As soon as government discovers an alternative way of maintaining an incentive to work, such as reducing unemployment and supplementary benefits to below subsistence level, then child benefit will once more be at risk. Present discussions about overhauling the entire social security and tax systems may well presage such changes (writing in April 1984). The following excerpts may not clarify the best form of action should that occur, but they do at least point up some of the dilemmas.

**Additional reading**

Apart from the books and articles cited above, John Macnicol's book, *The Movement for Family Allowances 1918–1945* (1980) is a full and useful treatment of the period covered in the article by Hilary Land. The writings of Ada Nield Chew, a working-class feminist who, between 1894 and the First World War, wrote many newspaper articles on women's issues and was hostile to the idea of family allowances, have recently been collected together in *Ada Nield Chew: The Life and Writings of a Working Woman* (1982). Among the works referred to in this introduction, the other important historical study is that by Jane Lewis in *The Politics of Motherhood* (1980). Elizabeth Wilson's now classic *Women and the Welfare State* (1977) remains an important and stimulating overview of the historical relationship between perceptions of the needs of mothers and their children and the general development of social policy. For further reading on present-day debates readers should refer to the works cited in this introduction, and there is also a very useful and stimulating article by Fran Bennett in Lynne Segal (ed.) *What is to be Done about the Family?* (Bennett, 1983). For really serious students, the reports of and evidence to the *House of Commons Select Committee on Tax Credit* is a very rich source indeed (HOC, 1973).

# The Introduction of Family Allowances: an Act of Historic Justice?*

## HILARY LAND

The idea of paying family allowances in recognition of the need to adjust family income to family size is a very old one. Evidence of such allowances comes to us from the time of Augustus Caesar. In this country family allowances were paid in some areas in Tudor times, and at the end of the eighteenth century William Pitt made serious proposals for a national scheme of cash allowances for children. Apart from the system of Speenhamland, which was judged a disastrous failure in Britain, little thought was given again to the idea until the turn of this century when proposals for family allowances were being seriously discussed by a variety of left-wing political and feminist groups. From 1908 onwards successive governments made adjustments to the income of some groups of parents in the light of their responsibilities (for example, servicemen, the unemployed, widows and some income tax payers). However, the Family Allowances Act 1945 marked the first scheme of allowances to benefit *all* families with two or more children irrespective of the employment status of either mother or father and without proof of need or evidence of contributions.

The acceptance of such a scheme meant that the government had accepted, albeit for economic and demographic reasons, the princi-

*Source*: 'The Introduction of Family Allowances: an Act of Historic Justice', in Phoebe Hall, Hilary Land, Roy Parker and Adrian Webb, *Change, Choice and Conflict in Social Policy* (Heinemann, 1975), pp. 157–230.

* *Editor's note*: for reasons of space, many of the footnotes in Hilary Land's original article have had to be omitted or shortened. Readers are encouraged to read the original article for the full evidence and analysis.

ple that 'society should include in its economic structure some form of direct financial provision for the maintenance of children, instead of proceeding on the assumption that, save in cases of exceptional misfortune, this is a matter which concerns only individual parents and should be left to them because normally men's wages or salaries are, or ought to be and can be made to be, sufficient for the support of their families' (Rathbone, 1940). Few supported this principle as a means of reducing inequality between rich and poor, or between men, women and children; many did so as a means of achieving other objectives. The story of how such a principle was accepted by a war-time coalition government and why it was implemented in the form that it was in advance of all the other social security changes, is a useful illustration of the ways in which particular problems gain the attention of governments and how one social policy can be seen and adopted as at least a partial solution to those problems.

THE EARLY CAMPAIGN FOR FAMILY ALLOWANCES

The variety of the sources of support for a national scheme of family allowances are an important feature of the story of how the scheme was accepted and implemented. Initially, discussions about the state sharing with parents the cost of maintaining their children took place predominantly among socialists or left-wing groups who supported the principle as a worthy end in itself. Others only backed the idea as a means to other ends. During the 1930s, for example, family allowances were seen by increasing numbers of people as a method of combating the falling birth rate which had given rise to widespread fear of an ever declining population. By 1942, when family allowances were debated for the first time in Parliament, the principle had acquired supporters of most shades of political opinion.

**The principle and practice of state maintenence of children, 1900–20**

During the decade prior to the First World War there was some discussion of proposals for the state maintenance of children. These discussions took place in the context of widespread doubts about

Britain's 'national efficiency'; doubts which had arisen largely from our military incompetence during the Boer War. While such concern gained support for the provision of rate-financed school meals, proposals for *full* state maintenance had far less backing.

On 20 January 1905, for example, the Trades Union Congress, the London Trades Council and the Social Democratic Federation (a Marxist organisation) arranged a conference on the state maintenance of children. The conference was chaired by the former Conservative MP Sir John Gorst and held at the Guildhall. Will Thorne, leader of the Gas Workers' Union, moved a resolution:

> that this conference ... declares in favour of state maintenance of children as a necessary corollary of Universal Compulsory Education and as a means of partially averting that physical deterioration of the industrial population of this country which is now generally recognized as a grave national danger. As a step towards this, local authorities should provide meals for children attending 'common schools' to be paid for by the National Exchequer. (Trades Union Congress 1905, p. 15)

While the conference unanimously supported Treasury or rate-financed school meals, only a minority was prepared to let the state share parental responsibilities more fully. Indeed, it was claimed that such 'a wide and vague expression as "State maintenance" would excite great prejudice and alarm' (Report, 1905, p. 7). Ramsay MacDonald and Mrs Pankhurst, leading members of the Independent Labour Party, were among those who were opposed to the proposal on the grounds that it would seriously weaken the family as an institution. School meals, however, were acceptable because 'the common meal will be regarded as a ceremony of the greatest educational value' (MacDonald, 1909, p. 151).

The Fabians also discussed 'motherhood endowment' during this period. They were concerned about the status of mothers and children and wanted to reduce women's economic dependence on their husbands. However, they too were disturbed about the physical efficiency of the population and proposed that motherhood should be specially encouraged among the middle and upper classes in which the birth rate was declining. The eugenists also argued, on the assumption that the working classes were made up of less intelligent and less healthy stock, that if their birth rate remained higher than that of the middle and professional classes then the physical and intellectual standards of the British population must decline. In 1907 Sidney Webb, in a tract entitled (significantly) *The Decline in the Birth Rate*, wrote: 'In order that the population may be recruited from the self-controlled and foreseeing members of each class, rather than those who are feckless and improvident, we must alter the balance of remuneration in favour of the child-producing family', and therefore he concluded that 'we shall indeed have to face the problem of the systematic "endowment of mother-hood" and place this most indispensable of all professions upon an honourable economic basis' (Webb, 1907). Other leading Fabians, including H. G. Wells, Beatrice Webb and George Bernard Shaw, made similar proposals during this period and after.

Meanwhile the government, in addition to allowing local authorities to provide school meals from 1906, had recognised the parental responsibilities of certain income tax payers and men in the armed forces. In 1909 a direct graduation in the rates of tax had been established by imposing a super tax on large incomes in addition to ordinary income tax and by taxing small earned incomes at a lower rate than the larger earned incomes. At the same time a tax allowance in respect of children of married taxpayers whose annual incomes were less than £500 was introduced.[1] At first the allowance was £10 for each child under sixteen years of age, but this and the income limit were raised during the First World War, and later, in 1919, the age limit for the child was abolished provided he or she was still in full-time education. The following year, on the recommendation of the Royal Commission on Income Tax (1920), the child allowance was increased to £30 and the income limit removed altogether on the grounds that 'in all ranges of income some regard should be had to the taxpayers' marital and family responsibilities' ... and that 'rates of tax should be so adjusted that the taxation to be borne by each class should be redistributed among the individual taxpayers in that class with due recognition of family obligations' (Section VIII).

Only two members of the Royal Commission (William Knowles and J. Walter Clarke) were concerned with redistribution *between* income groups. Their reservation stressed that 'while a bounty should be given in aid of the maintenance of children it should be given to *all* parents for *all* children and the income tax is not the place in which to make a gift to one special minority of relatively well-to-do persons while refusing the gift to the great mass of poor parents who need it most'. Although their views appeared to carry little weight, they had raised a fundamental question about the relationship between tax allowances and cash allowances which remains a controversial issue. In addition, the existence of tax allowances for children was seen by others, including Beatrice Webb (1919, p. 307) and Seebohm Rowntree (1918, p. 141), as an important precedent to be used in the argument for extending the state's recognition of parental responsibilities by the introduction of cash family allowances.

Another form of child allowance was introduced during the First World War. This was incorporated in the separation allowance paid to the wives of men in the armed forces. It was based on the number of dependent children in the family and was provided largely because it was found difficult to recruit men without ensuring some financial security for their families.[2] These allowances were increased during the war, and by 1918 were worth four shillings for the first child, decreasing to one shilling each for fourth and subsequent children. Towards the end of the war separation allowances were extended to the families of commissioned officers.[3]

The payment of these separation allowances, which Eleanor Rathbone called 'the largest experiment in the State endowment of maternity the world has ever seen' (Rathbone, 1917; p. 55), was important in two respects. First, it demonstrated that the adjustment of family income to family size had beneficial effects on the family's health and standard of living. Advocates of family allowances later used this as evidence in support of their case (Rathbone, 1949; p. 48–51). Second, and more crucial, the principle of paying dependants' allowances to the wives of men in the armed forces was carried over, albeit by a very reluctant government, into unemployment benefit.

When servicemen were demobilised in 1918 they were given a free unemployment insurance policy which entitled them to an 'out-of-work-donation' for a maximum of twenty-six weeks during the first twelve months following their demobilisation. This was intended to help them return to civilian life until they found employment and, to conform with the allowances they had received in the services, this sum included additions for dependants. The donation was similar to unemployment benefit and from November 1918 was available for periods up to a maximum of thirteen weeks to all the unemployed covered by the 1911 insurance scheme, to ex-servicemen, civilians, insured and non-insured alike. Because of continuing unemployment, the out-of-work donation was subsequently extended for further periods although the amounts paid were lower after November 1920, by which time only ex-servicemen were eligible. The scheme for civilians ended in November 1919, but some unemployed ex-servicemen continued to receive the donation until March 1921.

After November 1919, therefore, all the unemployed except the ex-servicemen lost their dependants' benefits and this loss was not offset by the slight increase in the basic unemployment benefit rate made in December that year. In 1920 the unemployment insurance scheme was extended to cover all workers except those on the land, in domestic service or in the civil service. Ex-servicemen lost their dependants' allowances along with their donation the following year and in June 1921, when the number of registered unemployed stood at over two million, unemployment benefit rates were cut. However, in November that year, the government was obliged to restore small dependants' allowances in unemployment benefit as a 'temporary measure' lasting six months. They have never been withdrawn since.

**Table 1**  *Change in benefits for the unemployed, 1918–22 (amounts in shillings)*

|  | Out-of-work donation | | | Unemployment insurance benefit | | | | | | Poor law relief |
|---|---|---|---|---|---|---|---|---|---|---|
|  | Nov 1918 | Dec 1918 | Nov 1920 | Nov 1918 | Dec 1919 | Nov 1920 | Mar 1921 | July 1921 | Nov 1921 | Jan 1922 |
| Men over 18 | 24 | 29 | 20 | 7 | 11 | 15 | 20 | 15 | 15 | 15 |
| Women over 18 | 20 | 25 | 15 | 7 | 11 | 12 | 16 | 12 | 12 | 15 |
| Wife | — | — | — | — | — | — | — | — | — | 10 |
| First child | 6 | 6 | 6 | — | — | — | — | — | — | 6 |
| Each additional child | 3 | 3 | 3 | — | — | — | — | — | 1 | 5* |

* Subsequent children received slightly less than five shillings.
*Source:* Ministry of Labour, *Report on National Unemployment Insurance to July 1923; with a short account of the out-of-work Donation Scheme,* 1923.

While it was true that the experience of dependants' benefits demonstrated to the Ministry of Labour that 'not in a few cases they enabled respectable and industrious men and women to avoid having recourse to the Poor Law' (Ministry of Labour, 1924, p. 10), the restoration and continuation of dependants' allowances and the establishment of uniform minimum scales of Poor Law outdoor relief in January 1922 owed much to the activities of the National Unemployed Workers' Movement, which organised protests nationally as well as against local Boards of Guardians.[4] In 1921 the government was clearly still fearful of social unrest. Unemployment was proving to be an intractable problem; the successful Russian Revolution was not long passed, and although the police were controlling mass demonstrations of the unemployed, using violence on occasion, they too had gone on strike in August 1918.

For the next twenty years the number of unemployed never fell below a million. As later discussion will show, the existence of a large group of men who received an income from the state which took account of their family size considerably strengthened the case for family allowances to be paid irrespective of the employment status of the parents. In addition, the principle 'that relief given under the Poor Law should be sufficient for the purpose of relieving distress, but that the amount of relief so given should of necessity be calculated on a lower scale than the earnings of the independent workman' (Ministry of Health, 1921, p. 47) still stood. This made comparisons between the circumstances of the families of the unemployed and those in work unavoidable.

**The Family Endowment Society**

The campaign for a national scheme of cash family allowances began in earnest with the formation of the Nineteen Seventeen Committee which became the Family Endowment Society a year later in 1918. Describing this first committee, Eleanor Rathbone wrote that they 'had been brought to the idea [of family allowances] partly by the experience of the admirable effects of war-time separation allowances [and] partly by the difficulty of otherwise reconciling the claims of equal pay for equal work with the needs of mothers and children' (Rathbone, 1940, p. 68). In the words of another founder member, Mary Stocks, the committee 'had its roots in the women's suffrage movement, but its personnel was definitely left-wing' (Stocks, 1949, p. 98). They were all agreed that the provision of family allowances would enhance the status of women not only as mothers but as workers because 'it would strike at one of the main popular objections to "equal pay for equal work", i.e. the plea that a man requires a family wage whereas a woman requires only an individual subsistence wage' (NUSEC, 1920, p. 3). They also wished to achieve some redistribution of income in favour of families, particularly poor families. But even at this early stage they were unable to agree on the primary objectives of a scheme of family allowances (NUSEC, 1918).

The majority were concerned only with the redistribution *between* income groups. They were convinced that equal allowances, financed out of general taxation so that the rich contributed more than the poor, should be given in all income groups because the responsibility of motherhood and the value of the child were the same whatever the status of the parents. The minority, including Eleanor Rathbone, while not opposed to the redistribution of income in favour of the poor (Rathbone, 1949, p. 29), argued that they should also be aiming at the redistribution of income in favour of those with family responsibilities *within* each income group. Eleanor Rathbone firmly believed that the only way to remove a major barrier against equal pay in professions such as teaching would be to take account of the differences in standards of living reflected in the higher costs of bringing up children in the higher income groups. 'The fact remains', she wrote, 'that differences in status exist, and as long as they exist it is practically impossible, since the lives of children cannot be separated from those of their parents, to secure to all children a uniform standard of living' (Rathbone, 1949, p. 233). Acknowledging that it would appear unjust to pay higher allowances out of taxation to the middle classes, she argued that it would only be possible if the higher allowances were paid for by the income groups or occupations which benefitted from them. She therefore concluded that 'it may be necessary to make the State system a flat rate one and secure the necessary gradation by supplementary allowances from an occupational pool for all the higher grade occupations' (Rathbone, 1949, p. 236).

The Family Endowment Society widened the basis of its support in the 1920s because 'family allowances could be approached from so many directions with such an infinite variety of emphasis and application. It could be handled as a problem of vital statistics, housing administration, minimum wage legislation, child nutrition, national insurance, teachers' salary scales, coal mining economics, feminism, social philosophy or pure finance' (Stocks, 1949, p. 102). As a result the society became less specifically a group of the left. It was 'committed to the principle of direct provision for the family, but to no specific scheme – concerning which there was indeed much difference of opinion among the advocates of the principle' (Stocks, 1949, p. 99). Indeed, by the end of the 1920s there were many schemes under discussion. Professor Fisher, who followed the family allowance debate closely,[5] said: 'It will be seen that the economic methods of establishing Family Allowances are very various. According to your political colour you can arrange the scheme to cost the Treasury £100 000 000 a year, or, by a re-allocation of wage and salary payments to cost not a penny' (Fisher, 1932).

**The status of mothers and children**

In 1925 (the year in which Eleanor Rathbone became its president) the National Union of Societies for Equal Citizenship (a suffragette organisation) passed a resolution in favour of a state-paid scheme of flat rate family allowances. A year later the National Labour Women's Conference adopted a similar resolution. It was clear that the supporters of the scheme were concerned with the status of mothers and children just as the early members of the Family Endowment Society had been. The idea of endowment paid to a mother 'on account of her motherhood and on behalf of each of her children ... is', it was asserted, 'entirely opposed to the idea of relief of distress or poverty, because it implies a universal national provision and not a means of making up deficiencies in the incomes of particular families'. (Labour Party/TUC, 1922, p. 4).

Opinion in both these movements, however, was as strongly divided as it had been among the trade union movement and the Independent Labour Party twenty years before. Only two years earlier, in 1923, the National Labour Women's Conference had rejected a resolution supporting the idea of cash family allowances. Some members believed the establishment of universal health and education services, together with improved housing provision, was more important because these services would benefit everybody, not only those with children. Linked with this idea was the belief that the economic structure of society must be changed first. In addition, some were convinced that family allowances would result in lower wages, although the danger of that happening was thought to be considerably less if they were financed by the state and not by employers' contributions. Others, including Dame Millicent Fawcett, never supported the idea of family allowances because, like Ramsay MacDonald, she feared they would have a detrimental effect on parental responsibility.

The majority of women's organisations, even those representing employed women, have never (until very recently) made family allowances one of their major preoccupations, although equal pay has (and still is) an issue of vital concern. Neither have women's organisations been particularly concerned with occupational schemes of family allowances. This is perhaps a little surprising, for in the 1920s and 1930s one of the main arguments against giving women equal pay in the professions was that men have families to support whereas women do not and therefore it was only proper to pay men a higher salary.

## The living wage policy

The Labour Party and the trade union movement considered family allowances again in 1926. Unlike the discussions that had taken place twenty years earlier, the wide and vague principle of state maintenance of children was superseded by more precise details and exposition. Nonetheless, varying degrees of commitment became evident but no unequivocal support for family allowances emerged.

The Independent Labour Party at its annual conference in 1926 adopted a 'living wage' policy. This meant the provision of a wage large enough for the needs of a man and wife supplemented by a state-paid system of allowances for all children. They had realised, as William Pitt had done, that minimum wage legislation, even if it were based on a family with three children, was not enough to meet the need of all families. 'Provision would be made for over sixteen million phantom children in the families containing less than three children, while those in excess of that number, over 1¼ million in all in families containing more than three children would still remain unprovided for.' (Rathbone, 1949, p. 15). One of the ostensible purposes of the ILP policy was the redistribution of income in favour of children, particularly children of the lower income groups. As one of their members, Hugh Dalton (who was to be Chancellor of the Exchequer when family allowances were first paid in 1946) wrote in an article advocating family allowances: 'We would raid the luxuries of the rich to give a chance of life to children of the poor' (New Leader 29 January 1926). For just this reason the only scheme of family allowances acceptable to the Labour movement as a whole was one financed out of general taxation. Contributory or employer-financed schemes, it was feared, might only help the worker with children at the expense of the childless worker. This might also weaken solidarity between workers. Even if the workers themselves made no contribution to the scheme it was argued that the cost of family allowance schemes to the employers would be used by them as an excuse to reduce wages or at least hold back wage increases[6] or to put up prices. The latter would handicap British exports and in either case the benefit to the workers would be illusory.

Therefore when, in 1926, the Royal Commission on the Coal Industry (largely at the instigation of William Beveridge, one of its members)[7] recommended the introduction of a system of children's allowances financed by the mining industry itself but with a hint that it might be accompanied by a reduction in wage rates, the Miners' Federation was only prepared to accept the proposal if financed out of general taxation. In the event the issue was largely forgotten in the upheaval following the General Strike in 1926, although the Miners' Federation was from that time on a strong supporter of a national non-contributory scheme of family allowances.

Family allowances have never enjoyed unanimous support in the Labour movement. When, as a result of the Independent Labour Party's adoption of a 'living wage' policy, a joint committee of the Labour Party and Trades Union Congress examined the question in 1928 and again in 1929, two reports were issued. The majority report recommended that cash allowances financed by the state should be paid in respect of children whose parents were not subject to income tax. Those paying income tax were excluded on the grounds that their income was already adjusted to family size. There was no suggestion that children's tax allowances should be abolished.'*In our view the principle of making an allowance for each child of the income tax payer is a sound one*, in practice the middle class parent who pays income tax receives a family allowance from the state. We do not see why the advantages should not be extended to working class people whose wages are too low to bring them within income tax limits' (my italics) (Labour Party/TUC, 1929, para. 4). Any kind of contributory scheme was firmly opposed. The minority report recommended that the social services should be developed first and accorded less priority to family allowances.

At the TUC annual conference in 1930 the General Council recommended that the minority report be accepted. Their reasons for doing so were based on several fears: that family allowances would weaken the trade union movement by driving a wedge between the interests of single and married men and that they could interfere with wage negotiations to the detriment of wage rates. Looking at foreign experience, as the Royal Commission on the Coal Industry had also done, it was argued that the trade unions were weak in countries with family allowances and strong in countries without them. As well as these apprehensions it was also considered that the extension and development of the social services was more in keeping with collectivist principles and would not restrict benefit to families with children. Moreover, it was impractical, they concluded, to advocate cash allowances faced with the prospect of reductions in public spending. The conference adopted the minority report and family allowances were not discussed formally at an annual conference again until 1941.

**The birth rate**

Discussions about family allowance schemes have always involved some consideration of their impact on the size and structure of the population. In the early stages of their campaign in the 1920s, supporters of family allowances were concerned lest fear of over-population militated against their proposals. During this period there was a considerable body of opinion, particularly among economists, which held that the country was over-populated. Partly in this belief the government was actively encouraging emigration. The provision of family allowances, which could have been interpreted (at least indirectly) as encouraging people to have more children, hardly commended itself.

By the mid-1930s the Malthusian revival of the previous decade was over and opinion changed with the widely publicised discovery that the country faced the prospect of a declining population. A leading article in *The Times* in September 1936 noted that: 'last year the population of our country probably reached its peak. It may increase slightly but if fertility continues to decline at the present rate that is unlikely. From now on we can only look back' (*The Times*, 28 September 1936). Calculations based on the assumption that the fertility and mortality rates of 1933 would remain unchanged showed that the population of this country would be halved in the course of a century. On the assumption that they would continue to fall at the same rate as in the first half of the decade, it was estimated that the population would be only one tenth of its size in a hundred years time.

The international implications were clearly disturbing. Yet another leading article in *The Times* drew attention to other countries, notably Germany and Italy, which were adopting pro-natalist policies with a small measure of success.[8] 'There will be problems of defence, of transport and building, adjustment of Imperial policy confronted with the growing population of Asia and the reluctant birth-rate of the Dominions.' But, continued *The Times*, 'it may be argued that if the same thing is happening everywhere there is no need to worry. But that is not the case. Apart from the fact that Asiatic birth rates flourish and will continue to flourish, that the population of Russia may double itself to over 320 000 000 before decline begins, there is evidence of resistance [to a declining birth rate] in Germany and Italy.' (*The Times*, 29 September 1936).

The government reacted to the growing concern about population trends by establishing a Population Investigation Committee in the autumn of 1936 and included an examination of family allowances in its terms of reference. At the Conservative Party conference in October 1936 there was much discussion about the need for greater physical fitness, but no mention of family allowances. In his budget speech Neville Chamberlain had justified a £10 increase in the tax allowance for second and subsequent children by saying that he saw a time not too far distant 'when countries of the British Empire will be crying out for more citizens of the right breed, and when we in this country shall not be able to supply the demand. I think that if today we can give a little help to those who are carrying on the race the money will not be wasted,' (House of Commons Debate, Vol. 300, col. 1634). Family allowances did not figure in his plans. The government appeared to take little interest in the schemes of the Family Endowment Society.

There was another aspect of the population question which also caused concern. The age structure of the population was changing. By 1975 it was estimated that seven per cent of the population would be under fifteen and thirty per cent would be over sixty, compared with twenty-five per cent and twelve per cent respectively in 1938, (Charles, 1935). The increasing number of old people had been noted by politicians during the 1920s, mainly because of the increased cost of pensions, but now, against the background of a declining population, this trend seemed more alarming. Duncan Sandys summarised the situation in this way: 'a declining population must inevitably involve a deterioration in the whole standard of life of our people. With a population whose numbers are declining, and where average age is rising, we shall be faced with the situation of a smaller and smaller proportion of active workers having to support an ever increasing proportion of old people,' (Sandys, 1937).

There was a further feature of the birth rate problem which had concerned the eugenists in particular for many years. This was an anxiety about the steady increase of fertility down the social scale. During the 1920s this fact had been used against universal family allowances because, it was claimed, they would have the 'dysgenic' effect of encouraging the idle and the feckless to have more children (Gray; 1927; McDougall, 1921). Although there were, of course, counter arguments, it was not until a rapidly declining population became an acknowledged fact that the case for excluding certain groups from family allowances lost its force. By the end of the 1930s, sociologists and demographers could forcefully press the need to increase the birth rate among the working classes as well (Glass, 1936).Thus the existence of different birth rates between classes could be used against the idea of *universal* family allowances when prevailing opinion feared over-population. When, during the 1930s and 1940s, the concern was with the *quantity* as much as with the *quality* of population this particular objection carried little weight, although being drawn upon as a reason for not restricting a national scheme of family allowances to the working classes alone. Moreover, of course, the case for occupational family allowances and child tax allowances has always gained in strength from the existence of differential birth rates, the argument being that the more prosperous parents warranted special encouragement (e.g. Fisher, 1932). During the 1920s and 1930s interest in occupational family allowances grew but the impetus to introduce them came largely from individuals. In 1924 William Beveridge established a scheme of family allowances for the staff of the London School of Economics, of which he was the Director. Eleanor Rathbone also campaigned for their introduction whenever the opportunity arose and by 1936 Leo Amery, one of the first Conservative members of the front bench publicly to support family allowances, was recommending occupational schemes to leading industrialists.[9] He introduced a scheme in a firm which he was a director.

## Poverty and malnutrition

During the 1930s the inadequacies of the wage system in meeting family needs were tellingly exposed by the growing knowledge of the extent of poverty and malnutrition in the population, particularly among children. Seebohm Rowntree, in his second study of poverty in York in 1936, found that half the children in working-class families were born into poverty-stricken homes and lived below the level of 'dietetic and health efficiency' during the first five years of their lives. Other surveys, including those carried out in relatively prosperous areas such as Bristol made similar estimates. It was undeniable that low wages as well as unemployment were a major cause of poverty. Although definitions of 'poverty' and adequate nutrition were (and are) debatable, the accumulation of these findings did make an impression and convinced more people of the need for family allowances, particularly when viewed against the background of a declining population at home and the pronatalist policies of our competitors abroad.

As the 1930s drew to a close and the shadow of war fell across Europe, a concern about 'the state of the nation' was clearly detectable. In 1938 Leo Amery expressed it in this way: 'when we are faced with the competition of a people who lay stress on the healthy development of their young manhood and womanhood, how can we afford a situation in which something like twenty-five per cent of the children of our country are growing up undernourished and likely to belong to the C3 rather than the A1 type when they grow up. How can we, confronted by dangers not of today and tomorrow, but of the generations which lie ahead, contemplate with equanimity the prospect of our population, already small compared with some of our competitors, steadily dwindling, above all in the younger spheres of life?' (*House of Commons Debates* Vol. 341, Col. 574). Amery was convinced of the need to introduce a scheme of family allowance even if, in the interest of economy, it was limited to third and subsequent children; and now he was finding more support for that view from the Conservative benches as well as from other parties.[10] However, his suggestions concerning family allowances were 'duly ignored in Ministerial replies' (Amery, 1955, p. 206) and he did not succeed in persuading Neville Chamberlain to have the question studied by the party research department until after the war began. Meanwhile, in spite of increasing requests in Parliament for at least an inquiry into family allowances schemes, the government did nothing, on the grounds that they 'were not aware of the widespread desire among [employers and workers] for a system of this kind' (*House of Commons Debates,* Vol. 345, col. 40).

Outside Parliament, an all-party Children's Minimum Campaign Committee had been formed in 1934 'to ensure that no child shall by reason of the poverty of its parents be deprived of at least the minimum food and other requirements for full health'. All organisations working for the welfare of children were invited to affiliate. 'The Ministry of Health, the Milk Board, the Board of Education, the Statutory Committee on Unemployment Insurance and the Unemployment Assistance Board all felt the impact of its activities. Memoranda issued from it; conferences were called by it; deputations proceeded from it; researches into nutritional standards and the incidence of malnutrition were stimulated by it' (Stocks, 1949). The Campaign Committee used the evidence of nutritional studies not only to show the inadequacies of the wages system but also to emphasize that provisions for children in the form of school meals and milk were not sufficient in themselves to eradicate malnutrition.

Nonetheless welfare provisions for school children had made progress during the 1930s although because of the frequent economic crises this progress had been rather erratic. Local authorities, moreover, had encountered difficulties in selecting children for these various benefits. School meals and milk as well as education maintenance allowances increasingly came to be regarded as *complements* to a universal scheme of family allowances by its advocates rather than alternatives as had been argued, for example, at the Trades Union Congress in 1930.

## Unemployment insurance and wage levels

The great depression of the 1930s during which unemployment never fell below nine per cent and at one point exceeded twenty-two per cent, meant that a large section of the population was dependent on insurance and assistance benefits. It became increasingly difficult to pay insurance and assistance benefits and at the same time keep them below the level of wages. Although the system of relief under the Poor Law had changed when the Boards of Guardians were disbanded in 1929 and changes had been made in the unemployment insurance scheme, the principle of not allowing unemployment benefit to exceed a man's wages was by no means abandoned. By 1938 the Unemployment Insurance Statutory Committee admitted that it could not increase dependants' benefits without pushing the level of unemployment benefit for the family man above the level of many workers earnings. In its annual report of 1938 the Committee stated that 'the existing scale of benefits cannot be regarded as so fully meeting needs as to make it undesirable to raise them further' and continued, 'if ... the wage system made allowance for dependency, the main objection to further increase in the rates of benefit would be removed' (Quoted in Green, 1938).

William Beveridge, who was a member of the Committee from its inception in 1934 until 1944, was keenly aware of this problem of less eligibility and was convinced that a scheme of family allowances could help to overcome it. This conclusion was obvious to others besides Beveridge. An interesting change of ground was occurring. The problem revealed by the Unemployment Insurance Statutory Committee led unquestionably to a view of family allowances as incentives to work rather than an encouragement to depend unduly on unemployment benefit. If family allowances were available to the man in work, his advantageous economic position in relation to the unemployed would be better secured. (see, for example, The Times, 4 March 1938). Mary Stocks later wrote that 'this was a solemn thought for opponents who had formerly visualized family allowances as a threat to the wage earner's incentive . . . it was her [Eleanor Rathbone's] turn to talk of economic incentive now'. (Stocks, 1949, p.182).

The Labour movement was not, however, convinced by these arguments: rather it continued to oppose family allowances. For example, in a debate on Unemployment Assistance in July 1938, Clement Attlee described proposals for family allowances as attempts to keep down wages. This 'determined hostility of the Socialist Party generally and of the Trade Union movement in particular' which Leo Amery later described as a 'curious feature' (Amery, 1955, p. 206) of the movement for family allowances can perhaps be explained by two factors.

First, the Conservatives who were in favour of family allowances mostly advocated contributory or employer-financed schemes, and the grounds for the Labour movement's opposition to such schemes, which they had voiced in the 1920s, were still valid. Indeed, the fact that Conservatives now supported such schemes heightened their suspicions. As Ellen Wilkinson (who in the 1920s had been among the first women in the Labour Party to support family allowances) wrote in 1938: 'what the Amery type want is to feed the existing and potential cannon-fodder with the greatest economy and lack of waste. Pay the money for the upkeep of each child, don't give it to the individual workman who may have few or no children. In short apply the means test to wages' (*Tribune*, 8 July 1938).

The second reason for the Labour movement's hostility was that the trade unions had still to be convinced that their strength had increased sufficiently to risk reconsidering the position as declared at their annual conference in 1930. Achieving better wages had a much higher priority. It was not until the war brought about radical changes in the strength and the economic position of the trade unions that the majority of the Labour movement felt able to accept a scheme of family allowances without fearing a serious loss of bargaining power.

**The end of the first stage of the campaign for family allowances, 1920–39**

By the end of the 1930s the idea of a national scheme of family allowances had gained support in many quarters, although opinion was divided about the most appropriate kind of scheme. 'This support', wrote Eleanor Rathbone, 'comes from sections of opinion otherwise widely divided, from employers and trade unionists, from economists, sociologists and experts on population, from parents and would-be parents of all classes, from organizations of women and leaders of religious thought' (Rathbone, 1940, p. xi). These new converts to the cause of family allowances were different from the feminist and 'living wage' advocates of the previous decade because their primary concern was not to improve the status of women or redistribute income from rich to poor, though these aims might incidentally be attained. The main objectives were now to abolish poverty among children and halt the decline in the birth rate. Nevertheless, family allowances had yet to become an integral part of the programme of either major political party and the trade unions remained, in the words of Elanor Rathbone, 'suspicious and aloof'.

It was only when the war created new economic and social needs and highlighted existing problems that a universal scheme of family allowances gained sufficient additional support to be accepted and implemented. Most important of all, family allowances were seen to be relevant to the government's *economic* policy. As Maynard Keynes explained when he proposed a national scheme of family allowances in 1940: 'at first sight it is paradoxical to propose in time of war an expensive social reform which we have not thought ourselves able to afford in time of peace. But in truth the need for this reform is so much greater in such times that it may provide the most appropriate occasion for it' (Keynes, 1940, p. 32).

## Notes

1. Explaining this new measure, Lloyd George said:'There is no class in the community which has a much harder struggle or a more anxious time than that composed of the men whose earnings just bring them within the clutches of the income tax collector ... When they have a family dependent upon them the obligation to keep up the appearance of respectability of all their dependants is very trying. I am strongly of the opinion that they deserve special consideration in the rearrangement of our finances,'(*House of Commons Debates*, Vol. 4, col. 508). William Pitt had included tax allowances in respect of children when he introduced income tax in 1976 but they were abolished in 1806 partly because of fears of over population and partly because of fraud.
2. During a debate on the progress of recruiting Sir Ivor Herbert said: 'In

all my experiences of the last few weeks I have found hesitation as to whether to enlist or not arising from one cause, and one cause only, a doubt in the mind of the man as to whether his family was adequately provided for' (*House of Commons Debates*, Vol. 64, col. 674). Debates concerning the level and method of payment of separation allowances filled many columns of *Hansard* between 1914 and 1918.

3. Eleanor Rathbone maintained that while commissioned officers were excluded from separation allowances many able non-commissioned officers with large families were prevented from accepting commissions because to do so would have resulted in a reduction of income. This, she argued later, was a good reason for making a state scheme of family allowances universal and not restricting it to the lower income groups. (Rathbone, 1949, p. 230).

4. Some Boards of Guardians were sympathetic. In September 1921, George Lansbury and his fellow councillors in Poplar were gaoled for six weeks for over-spending on outdoor relief. A lively account of the campaign against cuts in unemployment benefit can be found in the writings of one of the leading members of the NUWM (Hannington, 1936.)

5. Professor Fisher did much work on the hereditary aspects of intelligence and later became a well-known advocate of 'the inverted birth-rate theory' (which much impressed William Beveridge).

6. In France there is clear evidence that employers increased family allowances in preference to making general wage increases in the 1920s and 1930s. There were also examples of employers using family allowances as an extra means of control over their workers. For example, some employers would not pay family allowances to workers if their older children did not go to work in their firm.

7. William Beveridge was one of Eleanor Rathbone's most important and successful converts. Her book, *The Disinherited Family*, published for the first time in 1924, made a considerable impression on him. Before this time he had no interest in the subject. In the epilogue to the second edition of her book he wrote: 'I read this book ... and suffered constant and total conversion. Till that time in concentration upon other problems of unemployment, population and so forth, I had been apt to regard her [Eleanor Rathbone] and the Family Endowment Society as slightly tiresome creatures with a particularly loud bee in each of their bonnets' (Rathbone, 1949, p. 270).

8. In 1933, for example, Germany had passed an Act providing loans for young couples wishing to marry. The loans were interest-free and a quarter of the loan was cancelled with the birth of each child. In addition to encouraging marriage and children, they were also intended to reduce male unemployment, for the loan was given to women who had been working for at least nine months of the previous two years on condition that they ceased work on marriage. Germany's concern for her population certainly had military overtones. In March 1937 the Fascist Grand Council stated that 'the demographic problem, being the problem of life and survival, is in reality the problem of problems, for without life there is neither youth, nor military power, nor economic expansion, no sure future of the Fatherland'.

9.  By 1939 about two dozen firms, including Cadburys and Pilkingtons, had introduced family allowance schemes. Most excluded the first child.

10.  During 1938 Conservative members, Robert Boothby, Duncan Sandys and Lord Pilkington, a Labour member, David Adams, in addition to Leo Amery and Eleanor Rathbone asked for a Committee or Commission to investigate the question of family allowances (Eleanor Rathbone had been elected MP (Independent) for the combined Universities in 1929).

# Family Allowance*

## The Family Allowance Campaign

Family Allowance as it stands at present is for many women the only money we have which belongs to us by right. The importance of this cannot and must not be underestimated. Family Allowance is universal, there are no special qualifying conditions, it is paid to *every* mother with two or more children. It is not means-tested and is paid to women in all circumstances. As soon as a child is born entitlement begins and is never questioned until the child itself attains economic independence. There is little need for contact with the Department of Health and Social Security because payment is made through the Post Office; there is therefore no requirement to beg or argue one's case. We don't have to ask our husbands for the money, we know it is paid to us because we have the day-to-day responsibility for our children. We receive Family Allowance merely because we have children.

The actual method of payment, the book of orders cashable at the Post Office, is one of the most important factors. The possession of the book establishes our entitlement. We have the money for the

*Source:* 'Memorandum by the Family Allowance Campaign', evidence to the *House of Commons Select Committee on Tax-Credit*, 17 April 1973 (House of Commons, 1973), Vol. II, pp. 380–90.

* *Editor's note:* this extract is taken from the written evidence of the Family Allowance Campaign. For the true flavour of maximum feasible misunderstanding, readers should look at the oral evidence taken when the Select Committee examined members of the Campaign (HOC, 1973, Vol. II, pp. 385–90).

current week and for future weeks in our hands, we know come what may we can rely on our Family Allowance.

In many cases the man's pay packet is swallowed up at the weekend, when rent and other bills are paid and weekend food is bought, so the Family Allowance paid on Tuesdays provides some food for the family until the next pay day. We always know we can get this money on Tuesday and this is especially important if in any week the paypacket is depleted or non-existent.

Many women use the Family Allowance book as a way in which to save for more expensive essential items. We can delay cashing orders whenever the need arises and we have complete control over them and how much we save depending on the particular needs of the children at a particular time. (An unofficial survey conducted in Cheltenham showed that 48 per cent of women receiving Family Allowance saved in this manner.)

The security of possession of the Family Allowance book is in some cases the final consideration which enables a woman, with the help of friends and relations, to end an intolerable marriage. It is the financial life-line in times of marital crisis and breakdown.

Family Allowance is not related to the man's wage, it is paid when there is no wage, whatever the circumstances may be, it is paid when there is no man to support the children. In this society where women hold the ultimate responsibility for the welfare of children, it is vital that money paid for the children is paid to the mother on that basis alone, in order to avoid real hardship particularly in times of crisis.

Even if 'tax credits' were paid to the mother this would fall far short of the advantages of Family Allowance and would be completely unacceptable to women.

For women receiving Supplementary Benefit the thought of having their money 'cut-off' (e.g. through the cohabitation ruling) or of Giro orders being delayed or stolen is a constant worry. Tax credits would not be paid to women receiving Supplementary Benefit. If Supplementary Benefit is the only source of income, dependence on Supplementary Benefit is increased.

We need some money we can be sure of, some money we do not have to ask for either from men or from the Department of Health and Social Security. Some money we collect each week from the Post Office.

The emphasis of the 'tax credit' would be towards a form of tax relief rather than a payment of benefit. The position of the mother would be one of even greater dependence than exists at the moment. The dangers of a system where those who have care of children are completely dependent on another person are obvious. The man may or may not be earning a wage; he may not understand the particular needs of the children.

Women, in order to have any financial independence, are forced to work outside the home as well as in it, often to take unsuitable jobs, working in all up to sixteen hours per day. The Green Paper mentions the need for married women to join the labour force and talks about 'incentives' (paragraph 79). When, however, a woman is doing the important and demanding work of child care, taking a further job must be a matter of choice and not of financial necessity. A woman must not be made financially dependent because she is involved in child care, nor must this work be regarded as socially unimportant.

# The Wrong Rats

## ZOË FAIRBAIRNS

And the dying welfare state brought its own newspeak as well: governments' failure to link child benefit, unemployment pay and so on to the cost of living was *the fight against inflation*; putting children on half-time schooling was referred to as *giving parents a free hand*; closing hospitals and dumping dying patients on the doorsteps of unwarned and distant relatives was *community care*; and a new political movement that saw remedies to the whole predicament, if only the nation's women would buckle down to traditional role and biological destiny, was known quite simply as FAMILY.

FAMILY'S enemies (and it had many, most notably among feminists) were fond of equating its origins with movements of the seventies such as the anti-abortion campaigns, the racialist right and the pro-censorship lobby, and certainly it had drawn members from all these. But it was not the same as any of them, and could not seriously be dismissed as anti-black or anti-woman by anyone who took the trouble to find out the facts; after all, as FAMILY was fond of pointing out, one of its founders was a woman of Pakistani origin!

Rashida Patel was not its chief publicist, however. That task fell to the strictly British Mrs Isabel Travers, who never needed any encouragement to explain how FAMILY was born. 'We were chatting in Sainsbury's, Mrs Patel and I, rather more years ago than I care to remember. I do remember saying that these Asian women had a lot to teach us about family life. She replied that that might be

*Source:* Zoë Fairbairns, *Benefits – a novel* (Virago, 1979).\*
\* *Editor' note:* most of this novel is set in the future, some time after 1984. . .

33

so, 'but maybe in her community women didn't stand up for themselves quite as much as they should.' Mrs Travers seemed to think that said it all. Alan Travers had risen to prominence in his wife's organisation and was now one of the Family Party's two members of parliament.

The other MP, David Laing, was a younger man, around forty, with a passionate hatred of feminists. He shared this with many other members of the party, but not Isabel Travers. In fact, she was fond of saying that FAMILY and the women's liberation movement were both on the same side if they did but know it.

'How can you say that, Mrs Travers?' interviewers liked to ask. Mrs Travers was a delight to interview. Always blonde and cool and pretty and respectful. Always informal and chatty but never waffly. She tempered her approach to each medium like a professional: for newspaper journalists she spoke slowly in short, simple generalities; on television she smiled a lot and complimented her opponents on the intelligence of their remarks; on radio she allowed herself to be profound, even vulnerable. Yet in essence what she said was always the same.

'I say that because the true liberation of women will never come about until proper respect and value is placed upon their role as nurturers.'

Mrs Travers and Mrs Patel had shown flair for public relations from the beginning; and the beginning for them had been shortly after the famed conversation in Sainsbury's, when they organised a summer procession in honour of family values in a South London borough particularly hard hit by both government spending cuts and feminists insisting that 'family values' were a euphemism for women doing the housework. When she wasn't explaining that she and the libbers were on the same side really, Mrs Travers took pains to point out that FAMILY had no quarrel with the poor or socially inadequate; it was just that she wanted to pay tribute to the unsung millions of women (and men) who lived normal lives, did not swap roles, get divorces or abortions, become homeless or batter their children (or their wives); people who faced misfortune with re-sourcefulness and courage and without recourse to public funds. When a national newspaper first published Mrs Travers' views, the response was so great that a whole page had to be given over to readers' letters.

'My fiancée and I have a simple answer for homeless families. We won't be getting married until we've saved enough for our deposit. And we're old-fashioned enough to believe that children come after marriage, not before.'

'So sickness benefit is going up again! I have kept myself fit all my life, avoiding infections, abstaining from drink, tobacco and hazardous pursuits. Now, it seems, I am to be out of pocket . . .'

'Very nice to be an unmarried mother and live on social security. As a mere wife, I live on what my husband chooses to give me . . .'

The newspaper became embarrassed; so much so that they ran a follow-up feature called 'Lest We Forget'. Amid all the tales of scroungers, it said, let us not forget the deserving poor; and its journalists located hardship cases with impeccable credentials. The single mother who was a rape victim (*you have no excuse whatever,* the judge had told the culprit); the family whose home was struck by lightning the day after their insurers went broke; the legless man who packed cosmetics at home because he liked to feel he was paying his way.

'These are difficult times for all of us,' thundered the editorial, 'and will continue to be so until we are reaping the full benefits of North Sea oil. But let us not forget the reputation for compassion in which Britain still leads the world . . .'

Mrs Travers made one of her television appearances. 'Is it not remarkable,' she said, her pretty brows arched in bewilderment, 'that an organisation set up in support of the family is thereby assumed to be against the welfare state? Are the two incompatible? I hope not.'

Even the weather collaborated on the day of that first FAMILY procession. Sun shone through a gentle breeze. Crowds waited outside the town hall for three o'clock. A clash of cymbals struck the hour, trumpets and trombones burst into 'The British Grenadiers', the gates opened and the procession began.

Musical families from all over the borough formed the brass band. Their instruments gleamed with polish and sunshine, the players – men, women, children – were spotless in their white shirts and jeans. They sweated and marched, played and smiled. Their banner proclaimed, 'Families in Harmony'.

Cars followed. The mayor, the mayoress and an obscure royal rode in the first sleek open limousine. It was not an official visit by royalty. But it was rumoured that the Palace was enchanted by what it had heard of the planned event and wished to make a noncommittal gesture of support while not embroiling itself in politics. The mayor, who had a reputation for trendiness, wore a pale yellow suit under his chain of office; his lady was in pink flowers and a wide-brimmed white straw hat; the royal relative was orange from head to foot. The three dignitaries waved stiffly.

The second car carried Mrs Travers and Mrs Patel, respectively clothed in pale and deep green. There was no awkwardness in their greeting to the crowd; Mrs Travers' arm, pale and silk-gloved to the elbow, waved like the sail of a windmill, while Mrs Patel, shyly confident, gave little intimate grins and shook her wrist in short bursts. Watchers assumed they were film-stars or monarchs, but looked in their programmes and found each woman self-labelled as an ordinary housewife.

After the cars came representatives of the caring professions and local charities. There were few official delegations, but small contingents were present from most groups. 'Family Doctors for Family Life' handed out information on how mothers could treat colds at home without medical supervision. A few middle-aged social workers walked together with prim pride, while younger colleagues had leaflets: 'Lack of proper funding is making our job more difficult. But we're here to help families, and we'll help you all we can.' Nuns and priests had organised a float whose theme was the Holy Family.

Then came the families themselves. The Tynes, perched in their multitudes on the hand-carved cart that had lain cherished and unused in their garage. The cart, the programme explained, had been in the Tyne family for generations. Carpenters since the sixteenth century, the Tyne males now sat benignly sawing wood while the women and children did intricate carvings and played with sawdust. Then a family of writers: father published thick texts on the future of man, mother contributed to magazines, and the tall, serious children persistently took prizes in essay contests. Mr Meat the butcher (it actually was his name) with a pig's head on a tray, garlanded with strings of sausages carried by his wife and two sons. An income tax inspector (anonymous) on a rather flippant float, looking grimly into the crowd and singling out strangers. 'I want *your* money', he roared, while his wife brought him piles of paper and the children sat at his feet counting money into a piggy bank.

Fairytale characters mingled with the children in the crowd, giving them toys and bits of fruit: Mary Poppins, Mother Hubbard, the Old Woman Who Lived in a Shoe. Then came the International Section: an Indian family on the back of a lorry with a stove, the mother cooking real curry that you could smell in the air; an Irish group, parents with bagpipes and children dressed as leprechauns; a steel band from Trinidad.

Suddenly the section of the audience that was laughing at Italian children flinging spaghetti realised that everyone else had fallen silent. Their shouts died in mid-air; the procession had changed.

Discussing it afterwards, many people said it was too abrupt, but Mrs Travers and Mrs Patel defended it. These were just as much a part of family life as the healthy, celebrating adults and children earlier in the procession.

The afflicted families. Fathers pushing wheelchairs containing smart, vacant-eyed teenagers. Mothers with odd, floppy babies. Senile old folk in the passenger seats of cars, their younger relatives smiling bravely.

The spectators lowered their eyes and consulted their programmes.

'Mr and Mrs J's son Alex was born with spina bifida. "We were offered a special school" says Mrs J, "but it was so far away, we just couldn't." At thirteen Alex is very intelligent; he reads avidly (the Famous Five are a special favourite!) and is always cheerful. COPING AWARD: a local laundry has offered Mrs J vouchers to cover fifty per cent of the cost of washing bed-linen over the next six months.'

The spectators swallowed hard and stood very still.

'The W family have just welcomed their son home from Borstal. He is determined to make good and they are determined to help him. COPING AWARD: A local supermarket will give him a month's trial as a shelf-filler. After the month, he will be paid. The supermarket prefers to remain anonymous.'

'Miss Joanna G is one of hundreds of single women in the borough who have sacrificed career and marriage to care for elderly parents at home. Says Miss G: "Mother and I get on very well. I don't regard it as a sacrifice." COPING AWARD: Twelve double tickets for matinees at any local cinema.'

The sun beat down on the discomfort of the watchers, wondering if they were meant to clap or what.

The procession wound through the town, heralded by music and laughter, leaving perplexity and sadness in its wake. Only from the

windows of a derelict tower block squatted by women was there any
deliberately hostile response.

Each of the wide windows facing the road had been blocked with
a sheet of paper. And each of these placards bore a stark message,
white on black or black on white.

'Stop the cuts'
'More hospitals'
'More home helps'
'More nurseries'
'Better schools'
'Women can't do it all'
'Women won't do it all'

And so the lines had been drawn for the battle that still raged,
feminists and FAMILY glaring balefully at each other over the dying
body of the welfare state. Each held its demonstrations, its counter-
demonstrations; each established its model communities. It was a
new dichotomy, to confuse and criss-cross the older ones of class
and party. 'The state is responsible', asserted the feminists from
their squatted communes, their women-only states-within-a-state,
when truant children ran wild and delinquent, and old folk died
neglected; 'No, we women are responsible', crooned the green-
uniformed women stewards of FAMILY, running courses in domestic
skills and home nursing, and publishing books called *Play His Game
in the Marriage Bed* and *You Promised to Obey*. The feminists had
marched in thousands when David Laing MP, in his maiden speech,
urged married women to give up their jobs because 'there is so much
to do at home'; they sabotaged a cricket pitch (cricket being 'male
idleness elevated into a religion') etching into the grass with acid
their crudest symbol: a round-cornered diamond to represent a
vulva, with a large clitoris and no opening.

They ran health centres (offering a mixture of self-help, herbal-
ism, old wives' tales and orthodox medicine) for women finding to
their cost that FAMILY had a stronghold in the dwindling official
health services; they dug up neglected laws on sex equality and
fought hopelessly to get them obeyed. Women on the way to
FAMILY'S housework classes would be stopped by feminists and
asked if they would like to do karate or woodwork instead; new
fiancées would receive congratulatory cards in the post, enclosing
leaflets outlining the legal rights of wives, while their startled
boyfriends got anonymous warnings to behave. And at mid-day on

Sundays, when streets in which FAMILY had worked to re-establish
the day of domestic togetherness were fragrant with the smell of
cheap meat roasting, shrill voices would be heard through letter-
boxes: 'When's Mum's day off, then?' (And it was not unknown,
FAMILY learned to its regret, for the woman in the kitchen, hearing
this, to respond: 'Good question', and abandon her pans.)

Unemployment was at a record high, particularly among men.
Heavy industry was quailing before foreign competition, but the
decline in traditional female areas of work was less steep. Women
were cheaper, some firms preferred them. North European
businesses found it satisfactory to farm out big clerical jobs to
London agencies, and international corporations making domestic
appliances found the nimble-fingered women of the North and
Midlands surprisingly to their taste. FAMILY knew of whole streets
where women went out to work and men stayed at home and
neglected the children.

FAMILY'S anxiety was shared by industry. Today's children were
tomorrow's workers. Besides, women workers might be cheaper,
but too many depressed breadwinners could damage national
morale, and morale needed to be high for what was coming. The
country had been the sick man of Europe for too long, and Europe
suspected hypochondria. What was needed was nothing less than a
new industrial revolution.

The suspension of all social security payments was only to be
temporary, part of a national effort to restore confidence in the
pound.

The fact was, the beleaguered prime minister explained to a
restive House of Commons, that when it came to income maintenance, history had turned the welfare state on its head.

He made moving reference to its founding philosophy. It was, he
recalled, that people should first and foremost fend for themselves.
Merciful provision must be made for those who failed to do so, but
the failures must never be better off than the successes. Unfortunately, years of inflation, pay curbs and good intentions had taken
their toll; and social security payments were outgrowing wages.

'In our mad pursuit of fairness, we have forgotten equity. Our
British sense of fair play has recoiled from the prospect of anyone
starving or suffering, even through his own fault – but where is the
fair play when hospitals must close to put money in the pockets of
the workshy? Where is equity when the idle are better off than the

diligent? There have to be further cuts – on that we have no choice. But this we *can* choose: either to break faith with millions of decent, proud, hardworking citizens, or to look with more realism on the others: the tramps, the ne'er-do-wells, the offenders, the improvident – '

The Commons ceased to be merely restive, and erupted. House procedures used once to be compared by class-conscious critics to a public school debating chamber; these days it was more like breaktime in a comprehensive. No longer did MPs defer to the Speaker, grant courtesy titles or bow when they left; these days it was the loudest voice that got a hearing.

A socialist youth was on his feet, roaring with all the force and outrage of his years. The working class were not going to fall for this one, and neither were their wives. It was quite obvious what was going on. Foreign industry saw unemployment pay – meagre as it was – as the last obstacle before this country became a handy offshore pool of cheap labour. It wasn't a question of social security payments being too high, it was a question of wages being lower than even government estimates of subsistence! Offer jobs to the unemployed; then the prime minister would see who was workshy and who was not. If people lived mean, dirty, anti-social lives it was their mean environments, made by dirty, anti-social government policies, that made them so. There had to be cuts, did there? Then cut profits, cut arms spending, abolish the monarchy.

He was howled down by monarchists of right and left, and the house switched its attention to another speaker. David Laing did not have a loud voice; but newness was on his side, the novelty value of the Family Party. His appearance compelled the kind of attention a mouse gives a snake: in his late thirties, he looked shrivelled and ageless, anxious and ill. He was unmarried, lived alone, and, it was said, ate rarely and eccentrically, needing much of his salary to feed his addiction to coffee. The world shortage and price rises had made it a rare delicacy for ordinary citizens, but David Laing liked to sip and swig constantly. A beaker and a flask steamed on the bench beside him as he spoke.

All around, honourable members lounged on benches in shirts, slacks and occasional frocks of Olex, the new, cheap, crepey material being manufactured in the Far East out of North Sea oil byproducts. It came in two colours, medium brown or medium grey; it shone with a slightly oily sheen. Laing made it clear that he despised his fellow MPs for affecting the common touch and wearing Olex; he himself never appeared in the house without a worsted suit and a carnation. His hair was very short, the back of his neck shaven and stubbly. He wore thin-rimmed spectacles.

His narrow tongue flicked once across each dry lip. He glared at the prime minister.

'May I remind you that one of the largest groups receiving social security are receiving it not because they are neglecting their duty, but because they are doing it? I refer, of course, to unsupported mothers, women who have neither shirked their obligation to have children, nor left them to seek jobs, nor abandoned them to the tender mercies of the social services –'

The house sighed, wishing it had not let him start. The trouble with pressure-group MPs was that they were bores. Fanatics. They brought their favourite subject into every damn debate, relevant or not. With Laing it was mothers. Single mothers, married mothers, he didn't care. Just women who had babies and looked after them properly. Funny bloke. Unmarried, but didn't look queer. A Sunday newspaper had once revealed that he'd wanted to marry a feminist and she'd run off with a lesbian, which was why he had it in for both. That was before he became an MP. He'd been a social worker, then a deputy director of social services – he'd been fired after the famous 'babyswap' scandal, but that was how he came to be taken up by FAMILY. Some woman journalist friend of his had a handicapped daughter and found she was entitled to virtually no help looking after her, whereas if she fostered someone else's kid she got any number of handouts. Laing had worked some fiddle and hadn't minded being caught; he said he'd proved that the state only acknowledged the work of mothers when they didn't do it...

The prime minister was smiling indulgently.

'As I have said, the suspension of payments will be only temporary, and when the social security system has been overhauled, special consideration will be given to deserving groups. But in any case . . .' The prime minister's smile spread even further in the slightly crooked way it had when he thought he had an opponent hoist with his own petard. 'There are ways, are there not, of avoiding becoming an unsupported mother, just as there are ways of avoiding becoming unemployed? The Family Party above all would not wish us to place a premium on unorthodox styles of living...'

Alan Travers, the other FP member, took over from David. He

was past fifty, tall and straight, lean-faced, with large handsome features. He dressed more casually, in a green suit; he liked to play the calm paternal figure to David's impetuous youth.

'Isn't this the point we're always making? We fail so utterly to reward responsible married women that if we give anything at all to single mothers we appear to be placing a premium – '

Something seemed to explode behind Alan Travers. David Laing had leapt to his feet again, spraying his neighbours with cold coffee. He seemed to be having some kind of fit. His eyes stared, his mouth spat.

'Yes!' he cried, 'Yes! Exactly! The prime minister dares – *dares* – to talk about unorthodox styles of living in a society that actually penalises motherhood, so much so that virtually the only women who'll take it up are those capable of nothing else! Who's having all the big families today? Social classes four and five, the filth, the dregs, the dross of society. The better females are too busy working, or seeking work, or fighting for their rights – and who in honesty can blame them? Who can blame a liberated woman for not settling for slavery? So they leave it to the ones who don't recognise degradation when they see it – I've been a social worker, I know about these people – women too stupid and disorganised to – '

Alan Travers grabbed his arm. 'Sit down, Laing.' David wrenched free and went on furiously: 'Those women whose homes are sties, whose habits are bestial, who couldn't raise a guinea-pig never mind a child – ' he drew a deep, shuddering breath to steady himself, then continued more slowly. 'Do you remember – it seems a century ago – we used to worry about being overrun by blacks? Send 'em home, some of us said, stop 'em breeding. Who but the lunatic fringe thinks colour is the issue now – as we look at the decaying bones of our great compassionate nation, gnawed by whining, idle, dirty, anti-social *rats* of all colours . . .' His voice had sunk to a piercing whisper. 'The wrong rats are breeding. Maybe we can't stop that,' he hissed, 'but we'd better make maternity a better deal for the others, or we're going to be overrun.'

The house dissolved in uproar. Police had to be brought in to protect Laing from the outraged violence of some of his hearers. But when he made his appearance in the members' bar a few hours later, there were others happy to shake him by the hand and talk with him far into the night.

The debate was resumed. The house would not approve the

prime minister's plans for scrapping the social security system. The
pound fell and fell on the foreign exchange markets. The government lost a vote of confidence. A general election was called. It was
late summer.

# B. Marriage

## Introduction

For the last ten years or so, feminist commentators on social policy have remarked upon two particular features of the British social security system: first, that it is based on clear and consistent views about the nature of marriage and the economic and social relationship between husbands and wives (Land and Parker, 1978; O'Donovan, 1979); and secondly, despite considerable changes in the position of women in society since the principles of the modern social security system were laid out in the Beveridge Report (Beveridge, 1942) and consolidated in post-war legislation, the system itself and its principles have remained obstinately impervious to change (Land, 1975).

The article by Hilary Land reproduced here indicates that some changes in the social security system are now taking place. The rigid view of the sexual division of labour previously contained within the system is being diluted, to be replaced by a scheme which assumes that women will both want and need to switch from home to paid work and back again, particularly as the special demands of dependants such as children and the elderly – for whom the system still assumes women are primarily responsible – come and go. There nevertheless remain some aspects of the scheme which demonstrate how difficult it seems to be for government to jettison the original ideas of the Beveridge Report; for example, the Invalid Care Allowance (ICA), which was introduced as recently as 1976, is not payable to married women on the grounds that they are likely to be at home anyway and hence not in need of compensation for giving up paid work in order to care for a chronically sick person in their household (Groves and Finch, 1983); the tax system (which is not under detailed discussion here) still assumes that all men need an additional allowance to help pay for the cost of 'keeping' a wife. Indeed, the Married Man's Tax Allowance has recently been re-confirmed despite strong criticism of it (for example, Equal Opportunities Commission, 1982b): in the March 1984 budget the allowance went up so that in real terms it is now higher than at any time since the war (*Financial Times*, 14 March 1984).

The women's movement and the Equal Opportunities Commission have assiduously pointed out unequal treatment of men and women in the marriage relationship when and where it occurs. But as Fairbairns points out, there has been some disagreement as to where the solutions to the subordinate position of women lie. There are basically two kinds of argument and constellations of opinion. First, one of the most important conceptual changes brought about by the most recent wave of feminism is the general recognition that housework is *work* in all the conventional senses, except that it is unpaid. Indeed, as Fairbairns points out, both in this article and in her novel *Benefits*, when a houseworker fails to carry out her domestic duties 'properly' someone else (usually another woman) is brought in by the state and *paid* to do the identical job. If the conceptual boundaries between unpaid housework in the home and paid work in the labour market have been broken down, then it seems demonstrably unfair that housewives are not paid for the work they currently carry out for nothing. Thus some feminists have argued that there should be wages for housework. However, if the husband were forced to pay, this would create havoc in the labour market, and would introduce an employer/employee relationship into marriage, thus exacerbating existing dependencies and ine-qualities of status between husbands and wives. Thus they argue that the state should pay these wages out of public expenditure. This would be asking rather more of the social security system than exists under the present arrangements, for this payment would be made, not on the grounds of 'need' as with existing Supplementary Benefits (SB), nor on grounds of compensation, as with ICA, nor on the grounds of purchased 'rights' as in the case of insurance benefits, but on grounds of work carried out. Housewives would have the same relationship to the state as public employees, except that the services they render would be allocated to an unchanging unit in an unchanging place – namely, their own families in their own homes. Thus this set of arguments takes the four roles of women – wives, mothers, daughters and paid workers – and elevates the first two for special treatment and recognition. It problematises housework, and suggests a form of positive discrimination in favour of housewives and mothers. (For a critique of the 'wages for housework' campaign, see Freeman, 1980, and McIntosh, 1981).

The second constellation of arguments is not an argument for positive discrimination: instead, it is an argument for the equal treatment of women and men irrespective of their relationship to each other. In other words, it is based on what Land calls 'economic individualism' and its point of reference is not the home and unpaid housework, but the labour market and paid work. It problematises inequality of treatment. Within this set of solutions women would be treated as workers rather than as housewives and mothers. They would be able to claim benefit in their own right and for their husbands as their dependants. They would become subject to the same conditions of claiming benefit as men: for example, it would be a matter of discretionary decision on the part of the allocators of SB as to whether the existence of children or other dependants at home would relieve them of the need to register for work (DHSS, 1978a, p. 95). If they fail to find work and the Department of Employment considers it to be available, then their benefit would be cut in exactly the same way that men's benefit is presently reduced or taken away altogether (DHSS, 1978a, p. 92). In short, women claimants would find themselves in a system that assumes they are alienated workers rather than – as the present system assumes – scrounging mistresses or 'walking wombs'. Mary McIntosh would support such changes; writing about the process of achieving socialist social policy, she argues that economic individualism would lead to a unity of working-class men and women:

> the wage system is fundamental to capitalist society, so that despite all the disadvantages of wage work, the way forward must be through furthering the process of proletarianisation of women and rescuing women from preproletarian dependence. The struggle to end capitalist wage labour cannot be helped by women opting out and can only be undertaken by a working class that is

less divided by male domination than the present one. (McIntosh, 1981, p. 40).

The difficulty with both these kinds of argument is that they emphasise only one or, at the most, two aspects of women's lives. However various kinds of feminists might wish it otherwise, women play a mix of roles in present-day British society: they are wives, mothers, daughters *and* paid workers, and they somehow juggle all these roles together, largely by taking on part-time work which, as Land points out, is seriously marginalised when it comes to occupational benefits. Arguments around the issue of housework fail to take account of the fact that large numbers of married women with children spend large amounts of their working days outside the home in paid work. In their study of *Women and Employment: a lifetime perspective*, Martin and Roberts found that, in 1980, 65 per cent of married women and 56 per cent of women with dependent children under the age of 16 were, in Great Britain, 'economically active' (Martin and Roberts, 1984). If their roles as housewives in general and mothers in particular are emphasised in social policy to the exclusion of consideration of their other roles, then this would reinforce their marginality in the labour market both ideologically and materially. Similarly, if women's role as workers is emphasised to the detriment of consideration of their role as housewives and – more particularly – their role as mothers, then the 'proletarianisation' of women could confine them and their children to dependence on means-tested state benefits and/or low pay from part-time 'women's work'. In short, they and their children would be condemned to grinding poverty and, if their income comes from the state, to permanent state surveillance, not in this case for cohabitation but for 'scrounging'.

Both Fairbairns and Donnison, for their different reasons and from very different political perspectives (the former a radical feminist largely concerned with relations between men and women, the latter a left-of-centre policy-maker and academic, largely concerned with social inequality and the alleviation of poverty), understand and accept that, at least in the short run, women are going to continue their multiple roles. Both of them take the present sexual division of labour as given and understand that this has important implications for women in their search for an income. They identify the central issue as that of dependency: given the sexual division of labour, women, unlike men, have dependants who need them for their very survival. As Donnison says, 'The crucial needs arise from an unavoidable responsibility for caring for someone who depends on you'; as Fairbairn says, 'Dependency is the key to women's oppression. And child care is the key to dependency, for the very simple reason that it takes a lot of time and is unpaid'. As a result of women's 'unavoidable' domestic responsibilities, women are extremely disadvantaged in the labour market. (For a fuller discussion of this point, see Land, 1981). Neither of them, though, want to see women given an income simply because they are wives: for Donnison, this would be massively expensive, degrading to women as a whole, and unreasonably generous to the rich man's wife; for Fairbairns, payment for 'skivvying for a demanding but fit husband' would be payment for work that is 'unnecessary and demeaning'. But if wives, as wives, are unable to generate a reasonable income for themselves and their children either from the state or from the labour market, then it has to be assumed that their husbands will 'keep' them. If that is the case, then the cohabitation rule is unavoidable.

The answer to this dreadful conundrum, for both Donnison and Fairbairns, is to elevate the central issue of women's dependants and to increase benefits for them such that, where women do have dependants – be they very young or very old – women also have a considerable income. For Fairbairns this would be payment for hard work; for Donnison this would be protection for both the woman carer and her dependants – in other words, maintenance of, and provision for, family relationships. But whatever the reasoning behind these considerably increased benefits for women carers, the result would be that a woman with 'dependants' would have a reasonable income, *whether she is married or not.* There would be two effects: the dependent financial relationships between husbands and wives would be considerably loosened, and unmarried women with dependants would have a substantial non-means-tested income as of right. Thus simultaneously the justification for and effect of the cohabitation rule would be radically undermined.

But we have come full circle: by sliding from discussion of women as wives to a discussion of women as mothers and carers, we are once more caught up in the dilemmas about benefits for children outlined in the previous section. The tentacles of the labour market (capitalism) and of the sexual division of labour (patriarchy) are long, clinging, and extremely hard to untangle!

**Additional reading**

Fran Bennett's article on 'The State, Welfare and Women's Dependence' (Bennett, 1983) gives an excellent account of the different strands within the contemporary women's movement and their views about the appropriate source of an income for women. There is an increasing amount of empirical work being done on the allocation of resources within marriage; in this country Jan Pahl (1980, 1983) and Anne Gray (1979) have concentrated particularly on the distribution of household income between marriage partners. For more theoretical work on the marriage relationship and how far marriage is at the root of the oppression of women, readers should refer to the work of Christine Delphy – a French radical feminist – whose work has recently been collected together in *Close to Home: a materialist analysis of women's oppression* (Delphy, 1984); her work has been directly criticised from a socialist perspective by Michele Barrett and Mary McIntosh (Barrett and McIntosh, 1979).

# Who Still Cares for the Family? Recent Developments in Income Maintenance

## HILARY LAND

The world as it is at present is divided into two services; one the public and the other the private. In one world the sons of educated men work as civil servants, judges, soldiers and are paid for that work; in the other world the daughters of educated men work as wives, mothers or daughters . . . but the wives and mothers and daughters who work all day and every day without whose work the State would collapse and fall to pieces, without whose work your sons, sir, would cease to exist, are paid nothing whatever. (Virginia Woolf, 1930)

So wrote Virginia Woolf nearly fifty years ago in her brilliant and witty, feminist polemic *Three Guineas*. Then women, especially married women, were less visible in the public world and were discriminated against in it in many more explicit ways than is currently the case. However, although women are no longer as exclusively confined to the private world of the family, it does not mean that their work within the family is valued any more highly or indeed that there is less of it. The rhetoric of the Right in recent years, is that women have acquired rights and opportunities in the public world, especially in the labour market, but this, it is alleged has been at the expense of their families. This is an undesirable state of affairs so women must once again be taught, persuaded and encouraged to give priority to their families, and in future social

*Source*: extracted from Hilary Land, 'Who Still Cares for the Family? Recent Developments in Income Maintenance, Taxation and Family Law', in Jane Lewis (ed.), *Women's Welfare, Women's Rights* (Croom Helm, 1983), pp. 64–83.

policies should be developed, or indeed not developed, with this aim in mind. Individualism is not a creed to be adopted by women. Such a view assumes that as wives, mothers and daughters, women care less for their families because they are more active outside the home. It also presupposes that the assumptions upon which social policies have been based in the past have changed in recent years in order to facilitate women's participation in activities outside the home. Neither supposition is correct. Not only do women still provide nearly all the care for the old, the sick and the young (and most of it still unpaid), but also social policies are still framed, allocated and delivered on the assumption that they do so.

In this paper I want to examine recent developments in three areas of social policy: income maintenance, taxation and family law,* exposing the assumptions made about the division of responsibilities within the family on which debates and changes have been based. Although these three key areas of state activity were excluded from the Sex Discrimination Act 1975, as we shall see, the rhetoric surrounding the changes proposed, and already made, included greater concern than in the past to treat women as individuals rather than as dependants on men. However, this has been done in ways which least disturb the traditional division of labour between men and women within the family.

I shall therefore examine the assumptions about the economic relationship between men and women within the family, together with assumptions about the division of labour within it. These are intimately bound up together, not least because of the way in which the marriage contract is defined. The marriage contract still has different meanings for men and women and, although unwritten in Britain, it cannot be altered. Men take on an obligation to maintain their children and their wives, and refusal to take paid employment in order to do so can in the last resort lead to imprisonment. (It is an obligation therefore concerned as much with male work incentives as with the welfare of their families.) Women, however, take on an obligation to care for children, sick and elderly relatives and their able-bodied husbands. This is expected to take precedence over their paid employment and their leisure. Failure to provide this care will not lead to imprisonment unless there is evidence of criminal

*Editor's note*: in this extract, the discussion is largely limited to income maintenance. For discussion of taxation and family law, readers should look at the original article.

neglect, but may well reduce or remove their claim to maintenance on their husbands. This is very important, because married women still have fewer claims than men to maintenance from the state. Moreover, they have a much weaker foothold in the formal labour market than men, not least because there is a conflict between their family responsibilities and their paid employment, whereas for men there is no conflict.

Attempts to improve women's opportunities and pay within the labour market can therefore only have a limited success as long as women within the family continue to undertake most of the work of caring. The processes of production and reproduction have to be analysed and understood in relation to each other. This has exciting theoretical consequences, for in trying to do this, feminist analyses are attempting to fill huge lacunae left by most economists and sociologists, including Marx. On the practical level, changes in social policies which reduce women's claims to maintenance on men but do not recognise that changes in the division of responsibilities for caring between men and women within the family and between the family and the wider community are also required, may in the end be counter-productive as far as women are concerned.

The history of the development of state systems of income maintenance for men is bound up with the development of wage-labour and the separation of men and women from direct and independent access to the means of subsistence. Formal labour markets in capitalist economies have never been able to provide paid employment for everyone who needed it, and short of allowing wage-labourers and their families of future wage-labourers to starve, either individual capitalists or the state on their behalf had to provide alternative means of support. Paradoxically, this provided for the possibility of voluntary unemployment, an anathema to the capitalist class, and so the conditions under which men's claims to maintenance from the state were met were such as to weaken male work incentives as little as possible, and ideally to discourage men from making a claim at all, except in the direst circumstances. The subsequent development of state contributory systems of income maintenance, although to some extent building on the systems of mutual support developed by some trade unions and friendly societies, which were informed by a collective ideology and embodied the concept of the right to support, has also been constrained by the desire to maintain male work incentives.

Women's claims to maintenance from the state have been subject to different constraints. Although the old and the young have been gradually denied access to the formal labour market and hence to wages, they have acquired increased rights to sources of income independent of their families. Since 1948, for example, the elderly have no longer been deemed to be the financial responsibility of their adult children or grandchildren. Women's claims to maintenance, however, are still derived less from their labour-market activities or the state and more from the men to whom they are married (or with whom they cohabit). The growth of individualism has weakened the economic relationships between the generations to a far greater extent than that between the sexes within the family. The conditions under which women, particularly married women, acquire maintenance from the state are determined not by a desire to maintain their incentives to take waged work, but by a concern that they will continue their unwaged work for caring for their families. This is still evident in the latest policy developments and debates.

## Income maintenance

The British social insurance system was reformed in certain important respects in the legislation passed in 1975. Under the Social Security Pensions Act there was an attempt to change what Barbara Castle, then Secretary of State to the Department of Health and Social Security, described as a situation in which women were 'Second class citizens entitled to third class benefits' (*House of Commons Debates*, 1974). However, the changes were not a complete break with the past.

The Beveridge Report, which formed the basis of much of the post-war social security legislation, contained certain features which in part led to the need to reform the pension system. These features profoundly affected the shape and priorities of the new scheme, although not all were carried over into it. They included different retirement ages for men and women; the choice offered to married women, including those in paid employment, of opting out of paying full contributions and relying instead on their husbands' contributions (this is known as 'the married woman's option'); and flat-rate benefits in return for flat-rate contributions.

The first – unequal retirement ages – has been incorporated into the new scheme. Since 1940, the retirement age for women has been 60 years, five years earlier than for men. Prior to that time retirement ages for men and women were the same, and this meant that a man retiring at 65 often had to support himself and his wife on a single-rate pension, because on average women were younger than their husbands. This could cause considerable hardship. The 1946 legislation introduced dependency benefits for wives, irrespective of age, provided they were not earning. This removed one of the major justifications for different retirement ages; nevertheless they have remained. As a result the effects of differential mortality rates for men and women are exacerbated. Women currently outlive men by about six years, so that as they retire five years earlier they can expect on average to spend twice as long as men in retirement. The capital value of a flat-rate pension for a woman, paid from the age of 60, is about twice as much as that of the same pension for a man paid from age 65. When paid from the same age the difference in capital value is 10 per cent.

Mortality rates are still expected to improve and, if anything, the gap between men and women is likely to widen rather than narrow. The life expectancy of a baby born in 1975 is estimated to be 71.9 years if male and 78.6 if female. This compares with an average life expectancy in 1975 of 69.1 years for males and 75.2 years for females. A higher proportion of men and women are marrying than among the generation who are currently retired, and married men and women have lower mortality rates than single men and women. Marital status has a greater impact on the mortality rates for men than those for women (see Table 1).

**Table 1**    *Standardised mortality rates at ages 15–84 by sex and marital status, England and Wales, 1965–7*

| Marital status | Male | Female |
| --- | --- | --- |
| Single | 110 | 104 |
| Married | 92 | 89 |
| Widowed | 128 | 109 |
| Divorced | 116 | 94 |

*Source*: Office of Population Censuses and Surveys, *Registrar General's Statistical Review of England and Wales for the year 1967*, Part III Commentary, p. 136.

In particular, widowhood has a more dramatic effect on men than on women. Thus survivors' pensions are of greater concern to women than to men. If equal treatment is defined to mean that the same level of contribution must earn the same level of weekly or monthly pension, and if the notion of survivors' pensions is retained, then in these circumstances women are likely to get more in total from their own contributions than men and more out of their husband's contributions as their survivors. But because they retire earlier and live longer they need more.

There has been a considerable debate about equalising retirement ages for men and women in the state scheme. The Trades Union Congress and the Labour Party support a common pension age of 60 years. However, they give priority to providing an adequate state contributory pension which does not require a means-tested supplement. The Occupational Pensions Board, which was set up under the 1973 Social Security Act to monitor and establish minimum standards for private occupational pension schemes, was asked to consider the question of equal status for men and women in occupational pension schemes in 1975. (The Social Security Pensions Act 1975 requires that men and women have equal access to membership of such schemes.) They reported in 1976 and concluded that 'equal status must mean equal pension ages. Any other arrangement can be based only on the assumed requirements of each sex, an approach which we consider to be incompatible with equal status'. They recognised that 'as long as the State Scheme has different ages, we do not see how occupational schemes can be obliged to have the same ages for men and women' (Occupational Pensions Board, 1976, p. 52). In 1975, one-third of the total number of members covered by occupational pension schemes were in schemes which had equal pension ages and they hoped that even without legislation this number would be increased by negotiation and voluntary agreement. However, they stressed that the problem of different pension ages must ultimately be tackled, and this means changes in the state scheme.

Successive governments, however, have made it clear that any alteration of the state pension ages is unlikely. As the Minister for Social Security said in 1976:

a reduction in men's pensionable age is ruled out for the foreseeable future on grounds of cost . . . on the other hand, the government believes that raising the pensionable age for women would be unfair to women who have contributed over the years in the expectation of a pension at 60. (DHSS, 1976c, p. 18)

In 1976 the Department of Health and Social Security estimated that the total cost to central and local government funds of an equal pension age of 60 would exceed £2,000 million a year, or about £100 a worker. (This compares with expenditure on retirement pensions of £4,800 million pounds in 1975/6.) The labour supply would have been reduced by about 5 per cent and the reduction in potential output was estimated to be some 3–4 per cent of the gross national product. At the time unemployment was only half what it is today, six years later. Thus, assuming two-thirds of those retiring were replaced in work by unemployment beneficiaries, the financial costs could have been halved. However, the prevailing view seems to be that it is preferable for women to withdraw from the labour market rather than for men to have to retire five years earlier. As a result, what *The Times* called 'the main stumbling block' (The Times, 19 September 1976) against full equal rights for men and women in the state and occupational pension schemes remains for the foreseeable future.

The second characteristic of the post-war national insurance scheme, which will perpetuate the treatment of women as dependants on their husbands for some time to come, is the married woman's option. Until May 1978, all married women and widows had the right to rely on their husbands' contributions and forgo claims to short-term benefits (sickness, unemployment and maternity) as well as claims to pensions in their own right. Only when their husbands retire can they receive pensions as dependants (Dependants' benefits equal 60 per cent of a single person's basic pension.) In the early 1970s, three-quarters of married women chose to opt out of the national insurance scheme. This is not surprising as there was much to encourage them to do so. For example, married women who contributed fully in order to claim a retirement pension had to satisfy additional tests (Land, 1976). This inequality was removed under the 1975 legislation.

Under the Social Security Pensions Act 1975, only married women and widows already exercising their option to rely on their husbands' contribution could continue to do so, provided they did not leave the labour market for two or more years. The Government Actuary in 1975 estimated that only 15 per cent of those who would have exercised the contribution option would choose to be full contributors when the new scheme took effect. He therefore concluded that:

> It will be well beyond 30 years before the majority of married women and widowed retirement pensioners come to consist of persons who have paid full contributions throughout their periods of employment. (DHSS, 1975, p.18)

The effect of Beveridge's view of marriage being a relationship which created economic dependency in the wife is therefore one which will remain in practice until well after the end of the century.

The gradual phasing out of the married woman's option has been accompanied by the introduction of credits towards the basic state pension for those who are out of the labour market because of home responsibilities. Home responsibilities include the care of children until the age of 16 as well as the care of the sick or disabled. Married women who were not full contributors prior to leaving the labour market are not credited. Being 'out of the labour market' is defined as earning less than a quarter of the average male industrial earnings – £29.50 per week in 1982. Recently, home responsibility was extended to include the care of elderly relatives not living in the same household. This was important, because a national study in 1965 showed that one-fifth of women who were working part-time did so because they were caring for a sick or elderly person. In addition, it was shown that women living in the same household as the person for whom they were caring were more likely to be either working full-time or not at all; part-time employment was taken when the sick or elderly person lived elsewhere.

In order to qualify for the basic pension, men and women must either be full contributors or be credited with contributions for all of their working lives subject to a minimum of full contributions paid for twenty years. The additional earnings-related components of the state pension is based on the *best* twenty years' earnings, so those who are out of the labour market for substantial periods (mainly women) have little choice of which periods of earnings to take. In addition, women's earnings on average are far lower than men's so almost certainly women will earn a lower earnings-related component than men.

Under the Act the principle of earnings-related pensions in

return for earnings-related benefits was firmly established. It is important to note, however, that contributions are not levied over the entire earnings range. This means that nearly all female workers and male manual workers pay a completely earnings-related contribution. However, about 25 per cent of male non-manual workers have earnings above the contribution ceiling: they therefore pay proportionately less than anyone else. Moreover, they are more likely to be members of an occupational pension scheme and those contributions attract tax relief, whereas contributions to the state scheme do not. (Under the scheme, those who belong to an occupational scheme which provides a pension at least as good as the state can partially contract out of the state scheme and pay a lower contribution.)

Survivors' pensions, too, will be based on the earnings-related component of *both* spouses. Moreover, a married woman can use her husband's contribution record to make up her basic pension to the level she would have got as his dependant. Only a widower who was retired or chronically sick or disabled when his wife died can use his former wife's contribution record. There are no age or health conditions for widows, for by definition a woman must have been dependent on her husband. This is the closest the British pension system has got to earnings sharing between spouses, and it does not apply to men and women whose marriages end in divorce. A divorced woman can only use her former husband's contribution record to establish her right to the basic pension and only provided she contributes in her own right as soon as the marriage ends and she does not remarry (unless she is divorced over the age of 60). Her claims are not affected by his remarriage. The same holds for divorced men. Widows also loose rights to pensions based on their former husbands' contribution records, if they cohabit or remarry.

Instead of taking account of and sharing variations in earnings and living standards between spouses, whatever the number of marriages, and then treating them as individuals, the British system as described above has preferred to recognise the work of caring for the young, the sick and the old by giving credits which maintain the care-taker's entitlement to the basic state pension. This is a more selective version of Beveridge's married woman's option, which in effect entitled every woman by virtue of being a wife to a pension (worth 60 per cent of the basic pension) on the basis of her

husband's contributions record. Because of this all men paid a
higher contribution than women. Now women pay contributions on
the same basis as men. Broadly speaking, the introduction of the
home-responsibilities credit is a subsidy to those (mainly, but not
exclusively, women) who care for the young, the sick or the old on a
nearly full-time basis. Women who combine their responsibilities in
the home with a greater degree of participation in the labour
market, together with men and women without those responsibilities will be subsidising them. In other words, the traditional
division of unpaid labour in the home is being upheld rather than
changed by the new scheme. One of the more radical features of the
Social Security Pensions Act was, for the first time in the history of
the British social security system, the recognition of voluntary role
reversal. It was always intended that single men would have their
pension rights protected while at home looking after children or
dependent relatives, but it was not until the regulations were
published in January 1978 that it was clear that married men would
be included.

The tentative nature of this small recognition of husbands as
carers (rather than recognition of wives as breadwinners) is underlined by the limited changes in the Social Security Act 1975. Under
this legislation, for the first time a married woman who paid full
contributions became entitled to unemployment and sickness benefits at the same rate as her single sister.[1] However, currently,
unlike her husband she has no automatic rights to additional
dependency benefits for her children and, unless her husband is
incapable of paid employment, she gets no extra benefit for him
either. As a result of the EEC directive requiring equal treatment
for men and women in member countries' social security schemes,
the British system has had to be further modified. Dependants'
benefits will disappear as they are being held down until the
universal child benefit catches up with them. From January 1983,
married women will have the right to apply for Family Income
Supplement (a means-tested supplement for low wage-earners with
children which currently specifies that only the husband in a married couple may apply) and, provided the couple agree that she has
been and is the main breadwinner, a married woman may then
apply for means-tested supplementary benefit.

Under the EEC directive further changes will eventually have to be made in two new non-contributory benefits introduced in legislation passed in 1975. One, the non-contributory invalidity pension, is paid for those who are incapable of work and do not qualify for a contributory pension. Work is taken to be paid employment if the claimant is a man or single woman, but if she is a married or cohabiting woman then eligibility is based on her capacity to perform 'normal household duties'.[2] The other change is the invalid-care allowance which is paid to men and women who give up paid employment in order to care for a sick or elderly person, not necessarily a relative. However, married or cohabiting women are not eligible in any circumstances, although all the evidence shows that they provide substantial care for the sick and elderly and that their opportunities for paid employment are thereby reduced or removed altogether. These benefits, which were introduced in legislation passed in the year of the British Sex Discrimination Act, are perhaps two of the most blatant examples of the way in which married women are seen first and foremost as housewives and thus responsible for all the domestic work within the home.

Altogether none of these changes really recognise that the majority of families depend on the earnings of *both* husband and wife, even if the wife's contribution in most instances is smaller. (In 1980 it averaged 28 per cent of family income.) Families are still perceived as consisting of one breadwinner who only exceptionally is a woman, and one dependent spouse whose primary responsibilities lie in the home. These families are, in fact, a minority. The General Household Survey in 1979 found that only 20 per cent of economically active married men supported a dependent wife and children. There is even less recognition of the needs of women who combine paid employment *and* care for their families, especially if their employment is part-time.

There are other processes which are undermining women's access to the social insurance system. Although married women have won rights to benefit which are not affected by their marital status as directly as in the recent past, more women are being pushed beyond the reaches of the scheme altogether. In 1977, 22 per cent of female part-time employees were earning less than £15 a week, which at the time defined the boundary of non-employed for social insurance purposes (that is, neither they nor their employers have to pay national insurance contributions). By 1979 this had more than doubled (Social Survey Division, OPCS, 1981). National insurance contributions now constitute 9 per cent of labour costs compared with 6 per cent in the mid-1970s, so these workers are very attractive to employers. If their hours of work can also be limited to less than 16 hours a week, then these workers will also fall outside the employment protection legislation, which means they can be used even more flexibly and cheaply as they then forgo rights to certain occupational benefits (which now comprise a further 9 per cent of labour costs). In other words, the boundaries of the formal labour market are being more tightly drawn, a process associated now as in the past with high rates of male unemployment, and it is largely women, with responsibilities for caring, who are being pushed out. The lack of provision of income maintenance for those with part-time earnings stems from a failure to recognise that most women work part-time not from choice, nor because their earnings are inessential, but because their employment opportunities are severely constrained by their family commitments.

Even those within the scheme are finding their rights to benefit in practice are limited not by the fact of marriage *per se* (as in the 1930s), but by their caring responsibilities. For example, part-time workers who earn enough to pay contributions may not qualify for unemployment benefit unless they can produce evidence that they have a 'reasonable chance' of getting part-time employment in the locality. In addition, as the responsibility for the registration of unemployment benefit is changing from job centres to unemployment benefit offices, pilot studies are being conducted in twenty of the latter to test new administrative procedures for establishing 'availability for work'. Women are being asked detailed questions about their child-care arrangements, and failure to produce satisfactory answers may disqualify them from benefit. In other words, women's caring responsibilities are being used as a ground for *excluding* them from benefits.

Barbara Castle's attempts to make women full citizens of the social insurance scheme, irrespective of their marital status, have had only limited success. Moreover, even full citizenship is being devalued as the earnings-related supplements to short-term benefits disappeared in January 1982, and the present administration is attempting, in the face of considerable opposition, to dismantle the sickness benefit scheme and pass responsibility for short periods of sickness on to employers. (Perhaps there are analogies here with occupations which open up membership to women and subsequently decline in status and pay.) Certainly greater reliance on occupational benefits will disadvantage women until they have better pay and opportunities within the labour market.


## Notes

1. Prior to the enactment of the 1975 legislation they received unemployment and sickness benefit at two-thirds the rate for men and single women.
2. 'Normal household duties' include shopping, planning meals, cooking, cleaning, ironing, etc.

# The Cohabitation Rule – Why It Makes Sense

## ZOË FAIRBAIRNS

Where a husband and wife are members of the same household their requirements and resources shall be aggregated and shall be treated as the husband's, and similarly, unless there are exceptional circumstances, as regards two persons cohabiting as man and wife. (Supplementary Benefits Act 1966, para. 3 (1), Schedule 2).

This is the official language of the 'cohabitation rule'. What it means in practice is that just as a wife has no entitlement to supplementary benefit (SB)[1] in her own right – her husband must claim for her as his 'dependant' – so a single woman living with a male lover may be denied SB and required to look to him for support.

Sexism rarely manifests itself so grotesquely as in the cohabitation rule, and hostility to it among feminists is virtually unanimous. Arguments against it are many and convincing: it is wrong to require a woman to depend on a man, particularly when he has no legal or moral obligation to maintain her. It makes a prostitute of any woman SB claimant who wants a male lover. It singles out one form of non-marital living arrangement and penalises it (if the woman sets up house with her sister, her father, her adult children or her lesbian lover she would still have some entitlement to SB). It invades privacy, with investigators spying on claimants' homes and questioning their children (Lister, 1973). It perpetuates the loneli-

*Source:* slightly abridged from Zoë Fairbairns, 'The Cohabitation Rule – Why It Makes Sense', Women's Studies International Quarterly, Vol. 2, 1979, pp. 319–27.

ness of the single mother, since both she and a male friend will be
cautious of continuing a relationship that can be turned into a
financial arrangement on the whim of a civil servant. It carries the
smack of moral judgement, penalising 'fallen women' (single
mothers) for wanting sex outside marriage. And so on. It would be
hard to find any feminist with anything good to say about the
cohabitation rule.

It is thus with some trepidation that I say the cohabitation rule
makes sense. But it does make perfect sense in context. It is an
entirely logical, equitable and indeed unavoidable consequence of
British social policy with regard to women, marriage and motherhood; and its abolition, demanded by many feminists, would be
utterly subversive of that policy. Needless to say, this is no reason
why feminists should cease their demands (quite the reverse), but it
is a reason why the demand for abolition will never be met in
isolation; and even if it were it would be pointless overall, since
further anomalies would be created and the burden of injustice
simply shifted to other women.

### 'Living together as husband and wife'

In 1976, following several years of lobbying by feminists, poverty
pressure groups, etc., the Supplementary Benefits Commission of
the Department of Health and Social Security produced its defence
of the cohabitation rule, a paper entitled *Living Together as Husband and Wife*. The argument of this paper is roughly this: there is
room for improvement in the way this rather delicate rule is
administered, but as a matter of principle it must stand. And the
logic is convincing. It goes in stages, as follows:

> It cannot be right to treat unmarried women who have the
> support of a partner both as if they had no such support and better
> than if they were married. (DHSS/SBC, 1976a, p. 6)

Fair enough, you may think, particularly remembering that SB is
only for people whose 'resources are insufficient to meet their
requirements'. Unfortunately it does not follow that just because a
woman is living with a man she necessarily has (or wants) his
'support'. The Supplementary Benefits Commission recognises the
dilemma:

The suggestion is often made that a couple should not be treated as if they were living as husband and wife unless the man is actually giving the woman financial support. We cannot accept this as a reasonable test. Apart from the very great difficulty of establishing how a couple manage their finances (in effect one would have to take their word for it) and the strong incentive they would have to arrange their affairs so as to safeguard the woman's claim to benefit, the fact that she is receiving benefit may itself make it unnecessary for the man to give her more than is required for his own keep. The suggestion that he is not supporting her while she is receiving benefit cannot therefore be taken as positive evidence that their relationship is not comparable to that of husband and wife. (DHSS/SBC, 1976a, p. 16)

They admit that to withdraw benefit from the woman when the man is not giving her money may cause 'distress and hardship' but 'to continue to pay it would be unfair to the majority' (DHSS/SBC, 1976a, p. 7) – 'the majority' meaning in this case married couples and those cohabiting males who do accept their 'responsibility' to give money to the women they sleep with.

This theme – the need to be fair to 'the majority' – emerges again and again in this document's defence of the rule, and bolsters up the most tenuous arguments. For example, even if one accepts that a man ought to pay his mistress, to require him to support her children, even if he is not their father, seems outrageous. The SBC again acknowledges a dilemma, but

we do not think that this is a question which can be left to the Commission to solve, solely within the Supplementary Benefits scheme. Any question of providing long-term support for children in the family of a man who is not their father should be considered in the wider context of financial provision for families generally. Our own powers certainly do not extend to making permanent allowances for children in families not otherwise entitled to supplementary benefit. (DHSS/SBC, 1976a, p. 20)

In other words, fairness to 'the majority' requires that no payment be made in these circumstances.

Again, the suggestion has been made that in cases where a woman's SB is withdrawn because she is found/thought to be cohabiting, a 'tiding over' allowance should be made to ease the adjustment. Although such a payment is made in a very limited number of cases, this booklet's authors are dead against it being made automatic; after all

> No such allowance is paid to a claimant who marries, whatever the circumstances. (DHSS/SBC, 1976a, p. 20).

All this is very convincing. There is no good reason – feminist or other – why cohabiting couples should be treated *better* than married ones. (The fact that some people move from this argument to suggesting that they ought to be treated *worse* does not obscure the fairness of the principle.) Why, though, is it necessary to treat a couple (married or not) as a unit? Why can't the woman be assessed as an individual, and benefit paid in so far as her resources are insufficient to meet her requirements?
They've thought of this:

> Some people would even question whether it is any longer right for a married woman to be expected to depend on her husband and to be unable to claim SB in her own right. The trend towards equality between the sexes and the sharing and even exchange of roles in the marriage partnership have already, to some extent, changed the traditional role of husband as sole breadwinner. But if the resources of husband and wife were not to be aggregated, and each had a right to claim benefit independently, the Commission *would be paying allowances to almost all wives who are unable to work or have the care of children regardless of the husband's income.* (DHSS/SBC, 1976a, pp. 5–6, my emphasis)

There, then, is the nub of the matter. Abolish the cohabitation rule and you establish the right of a mistress to draw SB in her own right. Establish that, and you cannot in fairness deny the same right to wives at home with children, be their husbands company directors or on the dole themselves. It is social policy's version of the domino theory: the cohabitation rule is logic's last bulwark against the spectre of wages for housework.

### Wages for housework and the women's liberation movement

The reason that such a sequence of events might horrify a patriarchal-capitalist state are obvious – but the women's liberation movement is also ambivalent about paying housewives. On the one hand the Wages for Housework campaign declares:

Our housework goes on behind the scenes, unnoticed, uncounted, uncharted as long as it is unpaid. But if we demand to be paid for it, if we demand Wages for Housework from the State, we are saying first of all that housework is work ... we are saying that we women need money of our own – if we weren't forced to depend on men for money, we wouldn't have to put their needs before ours, to service them sexually, physically, emotionally ... we say TO BRING UP CHILDREN IS WORK and we want a WAGE for all the work we do – whether cleaning offices OR homes, producing electrical parts OR babies. (Edmonds and Fleming, 1975, pp. 7 and 94)

On the other hand, Angela Phillips and Ruth Wallsgrove (writing as individuals but expressing views many feminists share) reply:

(wages for housework) would take us further away from a society in which childcare was integrated with the rest of life, and in which women are not automatically banished from all decision making about how our lives are run ... The answer ... is not to resign ourselves to our women's role – in a woman's place – and demand payment for staying put, but to collectivise childcare, to share the responsibility for bringing up children within the community. (Phillips and Wallsgrove, 1978, p. 34)

There are also areas of confusion: it is not uncommon to meet feminists who disagree with Wages for Housework (on grounds similar to those quoted above) yet would support increases in child benefit or the right of wives and cohabiting women to claim SB for themselves. On the other hand, some feminists' objections to the principle of Wages for Housework lead them to oppose any proposal that might, in their view, 'look like' or 'lead to' it. *Spare Rib*, May 1977, reported that at the national Women's Liberation conference, the Fifth Demand group (for Financial and Legal Independence) opposed the demand that 'every individual person, whether in or out of employment, should receive a Guaranteed Minimum Income as of right' on the grounds that 'it would amount to implicit support for the Wages for Housework Campaign' (p. 11). I have also had it explained to me by other feminists campaigning for equality of treatment of wives under social security laws, that their concern was only with the wives *of claimants*, not of company directors – thus accepting the DHSS principle that wives should be means tested on their husbands' resources, regardless of the extent of their access to them.

Some, at least, of this confusion and inconsistency arise out of misunderstanding as to what is meant by Wages for Housework, so before proceeding any further I propose to change the term in order to indicate (a) that I am not spokeswoman for, nor even in complete agreement with, the campaign of that name; (b) that I do not propose to be sidetracked into an interesting discussion of the precise scientific definition of 'wage'; what I am talking about is cash, money, pound notes, that to which a housewife is not entitled, that to which she should be; and (c) that there is housework and housework.

Let's call it Pay for Childcare. Even this is inadequate, but I want to forestall the objections (because I agree with them) of those who say that Wages for Housework simply means providing married men with state-paid servants ... an argument which the Wages for Housework campaign does little to dispel, since their line makes no distinction between the 'housework' of skivvying for a demanding but fit husband, and the 'housework' of caring for a dependent baby. I think there is a very important distinction to be drawn between the first, which is unnecessary and demeaning, and the second, which is necessary and useful. Thus when I favour pay for 'childcare' I mean the day-to-day domestic care of people who *need* it (obviously I would include adults too infirm to care for themselves).

### Social policy and the housewife

But even thus narrowly defining 'housework', the women's movement is ambivalent (to say the least) about the notion of paying women to do it. And it is not just the movement that is confused; the financial status of the housewife is as much of a poser for those who would confirm women's traditional role as for those who would change it. Social policy planners in particular are perplexed and tie themselves in appalling knots trying to work out equitable ways of dealing with this anomalous creature. The housewife, who:

– is an adult but must for bureaucratic reasons be treated as a child;

– works full-time but is 'not economically active';

– ought really to be one parent in a two-parent family but must not actually be permitted to starve if she falls short of this ideal;

– makes a vital contribution to the nation's economy, but must remain an exception to the general principle that the way to keep key workers at their posts is by reward and incentive.

The problems thus posed are seen clearly in the early history of the British welfare state. The Beveridge Report was revealing on this. It made clear that married women were expected to be housewives first and foremost; and that since this did not involve any independent income, wives were to be covered by, and dependent on, their husbands' insurance:

All women by marriage acquire a new economic and social status with rights and risks different from those of the unmarried. On marriage a woman gains a legal right to maintenance by her husband as a first line of defence against the risks which fall directly on the solitary woman, she undertakes at the same time to perform vital unpaid service and becomes exposed to new risks, including the risk that her married life may be ended prematurely by widowhood or separation. (Beveridge, 1942, p. 49)

This was entirely logical, given that married women would spend most of their lives in unpaid domestic work, and Beveridge was nothing if not logical. Confusingly for him he saw where his logic was taking him.

Of the two 'new risks' which Beveridge saw women taking on at marriage, only one – widowhood – was beyond the control of the insured couple. Widowhood was thus duly recognised as an insurable risk – like unemployment or sickness – and widows' benefit was introduced. Separation, though, was different. Separation might be the 'fault' of husband, wife or both. It is bad actuarial practice to insure against something that can only happen with the consent of the insured person – you cannot, for example, 'insure' yourself against committing suicide. By the same token, Beveridge realised that if the man was paying the insurance contributions, cover could not be provided against the possibility of him leaving his wife. Yet on Beveridge's own admission, loss of support due to marriage breakdown was a serious risk to a dependent wife, equivalent to an

70    *Women and Social Security*

employed person's loss of income due to unemployment. Beveridge made proposals for a separation benefit, to be paid only in cases of formal separation not caused by the wife.

This proposal was widely criticised. Women's organisations pointed out that it was impractical (who was to say who 'caused' a separation?) and urged that there should be independent insurance for married women. The Cabinet also felt it was impractical, expensive and open to abuse, and the proposal was dropped. Separated women – like single mothers and other persons unable to take paid work but uncovered by insurance – were to rely on National Assistance, the meagre 'safety net' that was the precursor of today's Supplementary Benefit. So much for Beveridge's 'new risks'.

This controversy, usefully outlined in the *Report of the Committee on One-Parent Families* (Finer, 1974, Vol. 2, pp. 136–47) crystallises the state's dilemma of how to deal with women who, by 'failing' to play the part expected of them (i.e. by ending their marriages or by having a child without ever having been married) find themselves without the support of a man. On the one hand the state is reluctant to make them better off than the 'good' housewife, married and 'supported' by her husband (the exact amount of 'support' decided by him alone); on the other hand, of course, the status of the married housewife is so low that virtually anything going to the single mother makes her better off. *Living Together as Husband and Wife* is very concerned about being 'fair' to the married couple, but the only way they could truly be 'fair' to the married housewife would be to entitle the single housewife to less SB than she gets . . . and you cannot entitle even a single housewife to less than nothing.

And the point is that all this is good, fair and equitable if you start from the conventional wisdom that: housewives don't need money of their own because they are supported by their husbands; they are supported by their husbands because they are dependants; and they are dependants because they 'don't work'. Dependency is the key to women's oppression. And childcare is the key to dependency, for the very simple reason that it takes a lot of time and is unpaid. In a money-based society, the unpaid worker is doubly oppressed.

**Feminists vs housewives?**

Many feminists will come this far with me but still shy away from the idea of pay for childcare, even when we've clarified that it's not the

same demand as Wages for Housework. It is suggested that pay
would in some way 'institutionalise' the oppression of the housewife, yet many people who point out this danger are happy to accept
pay for *their* work, even though this also presumably 'institutional-
ises' whatever forms of oppression they suffer in their jobs. Are they
saying that housewives are less able to understand and resist the
dangers than other workers, or that all oppressed workers should
renounce pay as the way to liberation? Of course paying for
childcare could be used against women – the most obvious danger
being that it could be made selective (on class or race lines) or
conditional upon certain standards of maternal behaviour[2] – but
there are risks in any advance. We do not demand a ban on all
sterilisation just because some women are forced to be sterilised, we
do not even attack the whole concept of a welfare state just because
of abuses like the cohabitation rule, so why oppose pay for childcare
solely because it might be abused? (Incidentally, I suspect the risks
of abuse would be considerably less if the 'pay' were fought for and
won by a united feminist campaign on the grounds that housewives
*work* and deserve money *for that reason*, than if it were graciously
granted by government in a mood of pronatalist, pro-family,
antifeminist zeal to cut the costs of the social services.)

Demanding pay for childcare does not necessarily imply that only
women at home would receive it. It could work in the same way as
the present 'attendance allowance', a payment made to severely
disabled people which they can then choose how to spend on their
care. There is no reason why a similar notional sum should not
attach to any dependent person, including children, enabling payments to be made to whoever looks after them, whether at home or
in some privately or publicly organised communal arrangement. As
to the question of where the resources should come from, avoiding
the easy (albeit probably correct) let-out of 'abolish capitalism', I
would say simply that the transfer of money to unpaid workers
ought to be the next stage in the redistribution of wealth, taking
precedence over "breadwinners'" pay claims, tax-cuts or 'family'
benefit increases. After all, if it is true that husbands and wives
invariably pool their money and share it fairly, it doesn't matter who
earns what, does it? Whereas if it isn't true . . .

The demands of the women's movement in Britain seem overwhelmingly concerned with women who want to avoid having or
caring for children, either full-time or at all (e.g. abortion and
contraception, day-care centres, rights in paid employment). Such

women (I include myself) are probably a majority in the movement (it was the sort of feeling that brought us into it in the first place, and anyway we have more time than mothers) but not among women as a whole, most of whom appear to want to spend at least part of their lives having and raising children. To argue that this is always and necessarily a result of 'conditioning' sounds like a feminist version of 'I don't know what you housewives do all day'. Besides, even those who argue that the answer to women's dependency/oppression in the home is for them to take outside jobs (as if the sort of jobs open to most women were in any way more congenial and less exploitative than housework, except in so far as they are paid) and put their children into publicly funded day-care centres, must surely allow that some women (as well as men, of course) would choose freely to look after children, otherwise how are the centres to be staffed? Conscription? To argue as some opponents of Wages for Housework do (Phillips and Wallsgrove, 1978) that there should be 'adequate payment for everyone who wants to work in these collective childcare facilities' while opposing any payment for mothers looking after their own children at home is astonishing. I accept the need to counter the myth that only a biological mother can adequately care for a child, but to say that in the interests of women's liberation we will pay anyone *except* the child's mother to look after it seems to be going a little far in the opposite direction!

### I don't know what you do all day, dear

It is a view that has its reflection (though doubtless for different reasons) in social policy and the social security system. The state's version of 'I don't know what you do all day, dear' is to ignore what women do all day until they don't; then the state puts up some money. As we have seen, the securely married mother playing the role and staying at home has no social security entitlement; let her 'break the rules' and leave her husband and she can draw £14 a week *for herself*, besides allowances for rent and for the children. (The fact that this pittance is a step up says more about the depressed position of the housewife than about the wonderful privileges of the separated.) It costs £700 a year to keep a child in a council day-nursery, and only children in real need – i.e. those whose mothers cannot or will not care for them adequately at home – will get a place. Where is that £700 a year when the mother *is* coping? Foster parents can often claim fostering allowances of 2–3 times the Supplementary Benefit that the natural parent would have received for looking after the same child . . . which is peculiarly ironic when one considers that some children might not be in foster-care at all if their parents had adequate incomes in the first place (Fiarbairns, 1976). It does seem that the only way a housewife can get any recognition of the value of her work is to refuse or fail to do it. Thus, for example, the disabled wife (or cohabitee) can only draw the Non-contributory Invalidity Pension if she is unable to perform normal (as defined by the DHSS) household duties, regardless of whether housework is her normal profession, regardless of the fact that men and single women only have to prove inability to do *paid* work to qualify for the pension; and conversely, the Invalid Care Allowance, for people who lose their incomes because they must stay at home and care for a sick relative, is not payable to wives (or cohabitees) because it is assumed that they would be at home in any case! The normal principle – that people get paid for doing their jobs and not for not doing them – is reversed in the case of housewives.

The point of all this is not that the entire women's liberation movement should support the Wages for Housework demand (as at present formulated) – a pretty remote possibility – but that it should recognise – as WfH does – the importance of feminism's attitude to housewives. Remembering that I am not defining housewife as a woman dancing attendance on a healthy but indolent male but as a person looking after babies and others who need looking after, *what do feminists think the housewife should live on*? Should she depend on her husband? Then we must accept all the DHSS's arguments in favour of the cohabitation rule, along with all forms of discrimination and oppression rooted in the assumption that women are men's dependants, for the simple reason that the assumption is correct. Is she to give up being a housewife, put the children in a day-care centre and take paid work? Well, of course this option must be open, but the needs of the women who choose to stay at home, if only for a short time, cannot be ignored.

To present the issue as *either* pay for mothers *or* better state facilities is an unnecessary conflict. The one implies the other. If mothers had money of their own earmarked for childcare, they could choose whether to use it to 'pay' themselves or pay someone else – workers in day-care centres, for instance.

The point is choice. The point is also that the raising of children is work. It is worth money and it costs money. If society as a whole does not pay, women pay – by being penniless dependants while working full time. But if it's all right for wives to have this status, then it's all right for cohabitees too. On the other hand if we demand the right of cohabitees to an income regardless of their man's resources (i.e. abolition of the cohabitation rule), how can we deny the same right to wives?

*Living Together as Husband and Wife* shows that the state clearly recognises the importance of maintaining housewives as dependants since the alternative – redistributing wealth not just within the state but within the family – is too expensive and subversive to contemplate. It is time that feminists did too.

Meanwhile, the cohabitation rule is fair, equitable and makes perfect sense.

## Notes

1. Supplementary Benefit in Britain is a state payment to people over 16 'whose resources are insufficient to meet their requirements' (Supplementary Benefits Act 1976, Section 71). It differs from other state benefits such as unemployment pay or pensions in that it has not been 'earned' by National Insurance contributions; it is a safety net, a last line of defence against starvation for those with no right to money from any other source. As such it is small, means-tested and hedged about with restrictions.

2. My novel *Benefits* (Virago, September 1979) envisages a future Britain in which just this sort of thing happens – not simply because mothers are paid, but because a divided and inadequate feminist response allows the state to believe it has bought the right to control women's fertility.

# The Cohabitation Rule

## DAVID DONNISON

We also had to deal with the old issues too. 'Cohabitation' was one of them. Even to explain exactly what it meant was difficult.

In a working-class suburb of Birmingham a woman, separated long ago from her husband, lived with her mentally handicapped son. They had nothing but the meagre income provided by supplementary benefit. Down the road a man in his fifties – a window cleaner – lost his wife who died after a long and harrowing illness. Stricken by grief, he was unable to look after himself properly. So the woman took him in and cared for him. He managed to keep working, paid for his board and lodging, helped her to look after the handicapped boy and did a few jobs around the house. But a neighbour wrote an anonymous letter about them to the DHSS and before long an official was knocking at their door. He asked a lot of questions. What rent did the man pay? Who did the shopping? How much help did he give in the house? Where did they sleep? What did they call each other? Did he take the boy fishing with him? Later the woman's benefit was cut off on the grounds that she and her lodger were living together as husband and wife, and he must therefore maintain her. Since he could not afford to keep her and the boy out of his meagre earnings he drifted away, leaving her to claim supplementary benefit again a few weeks later. Both insisted that they had never thought of themselves as husband and wife, and there was no reason why anyone else should do so.

*Source*: David Donnison, *The Politics of Poverty* (Martin Robertson, 1983).*
**Editor's note*: this book describes David Donnison's experience as Chairman of the Supplementary Benefits Commission, 1975–80.

A graduate student in Oxford claimed supplementary benefit. His grant had run out before his thesis was completed. The visiting officer found him living in one room which was almost entirely filled by a double bed. The garments and cosmetics scattered about made it clear that the room was shared – by a girl working as a secretary, he explained. But they were not living as husband and wife. They were only together for this term: after that – who knows? The DHSS did not cut off his benefit, deciding that this was not what most people meant by a husband-and-wife relationship. Not in Oxford, anyway. 'And besides', said the visiting officer, 'how do you argue with a man who's studying to be a doctor of philosophy?'

When I first came to the Commission, cases like these caused more anxiety and provoked more anger and complaint than any others we dealt with. Benefit was refused or withdrawn on grounds of 'cohabitation' (as it was then called) in about 8000 cases a year. The claimants were nearly always women, and three out of four of them had dependent children. These cases brought the state into the most private areas of people's lives. They compelled officials to investigate matters they would much prefer to keep out of: all for the administration of a basically unworkable rule.

Decisions about people's claims for benefits should be based on clearly defined principles and ascertainable facts. But what does 'living together as husband and wife' mean? Could *any* definition of this relationship be devised which would fit equally well the circumstances of middle-aged working-class mothers and young male students, remote Highland villages and the anonymous, teeming metropolis? Parliament, which compelled us to apply the rule, had never tried to define it. And when in 1973 the Lord Chief Justice was asked to 'give some guidance upon the phrase "cohabiting as man and wife"' he swiftly handed back the poisoned cup, saying that the phrase was 'so well known that nothing I could say about it could possibly assist in its interpretation hereafter'. How on earth did the state get into all this?

In most countries people compelled by poverty to ask for social assistance have to show that their families, wherever they may be living, cannot support them. In Germany they have to pass a three-generation means test, calling for information about the incomes of the claimant, his parents and his children. But in Britain, even in the days of the local poor law, questions were only asked about relatives of the claimant who were living with him. It was a household means test, not a family means test. And it was hated. That's why it was abolished at the insistence of Labour Ministers who served in the coalition government during the war. Henceforth the 'unit of assessment' became the individual or a married couple, and any dependent children living with them. No special arrangements were made in the law for people 'cohabiting', but the Assistance Board and their successors were expected to use their discretionary powers to ensure that such people were treated just the same as married couples. That meant that a man living with a woman could claim money for her and her children whether they were married or not. But it also prevented her from claiming in her own right. And if he had a full-time job he was expected to support her and her children. There were very few lone parents on the books at that time: so few that no separate statistics were kept of their numbers. Since then the numbers of divorced, separated and unmarried parents have grown steadily all across Europe. And in Britain the proportions of them who depend on social assistance seem to be higher than anywhere else. That is due partly to quite creditable reasons: mothers on their own have more assured rights to benefits and to housing than they have in many other countries; they are not compelled to go to work; and their benefits are more generous in comparison with wages. But it is also due partly to less creditable reasons: women's wages and the benefits they can draw for their children when they are at work are generally lower here; and day care for children is scarcer and poorer than in many other countries.

Whatever the reasons, constantly growing numbers of lone parents live on supplementary benefit. There were 320 000 of them in 1979 – 11 per cent of all our claimants, caring for nearly 600 000 children between them. A count made in 1971 showed that one-parent families on supplementary benefit amounted to two-thirds of all the unmarried mothers, more than half the separated mothers, one-third of the divorced and one-fifth of the widows in this country. Meanwhile sexual relationships and other patterns of behaviour have been changing. In the early 1970s more and more allegations of cohabitation were being investigated, and more women were being deprived of benefit on these grounds. But they were less inclined to tolerate this kind of thing than they used to be. More and more of them were appealing to the tribunals and to their MPS. What should be done?

There are similar cohabitation rules all over the place. They are supposed to apply to widows' pensions, war pensions, civil service pensions, family income supplement, child benefit – indeed, to every scheme which makes any special provision for widows and other people left on their own, or for people caring for children single-handed. But other schemes are less contentious: partly because the extra money gained from child benefits and other payments which favour lone parents is less than the extra money lone parents gain when the whole household is living on supplementary benefit; and partly because the public tolerates laxer or more generous administration in other schemes than it is prepared to tolerate when it comes to means-tested benefits for the poor. They are less likely to write anonymous letters to the DHSS about widows and war pensioners: 'After all' they say, 'how she lives is her own business: she (or her husband) *earned* her benefit'.

Over the years the SBC, perturbed about this part of their work, made successive studies of the question. The latest and most thorough had been completed just before I took over the chairmanship. We found that although most cases were well handled, things went wrong much too often. A lot of the women whose benefit was cut off were back on our books again a few weeks later – which suggested either that their relationships had not really been like that of husband and wife, or that our intrusion had broken up what might have become a more lasting union. So we went back to the basics to see whether we could ask the Government to abolish the 'cohab rule' altogether. But nothing we could do would reverse fundamental social trends which were producing more and more lone parents. Like other fair-minded people, we wanted to see more help given to these parents and their children; and it was plain that over the next ten years or so Parliament would be doing that, and our scheme would be one of the instruments used for that purpose. But you cannot expect the taxpayers to provide extra help for one-parent families unless someone tries to ensure that the money only goes to families which really do have only one parent in them. Whatever the pressure groups might say, Parliament was not interested in abolishing the rule and neither was the electorate.

Since we could not get rid of the rule, there was nothing we could do but try to operate it more sensibly. So we resolved to lay out much more clearly what we meant by 'living together', and to give every claimant involved in the procedure a printed explanation of the rule and our principles for administering it. Henceforth *no* questions should be asked about sleeping arrangements or sexual behaviour. We resolved to give claimants more time, if they seemed to need it, before deciding whether or not they were 'living together'. And when benefit had to be cut off we resolved to be more generous in tapering off payments in cases where hardship would otherwise result. Indeed, we would go on paying indefinitely if low wages and the presence of children from an earlier partnership would otherwise have driven the family's income below the supplementary benefit level. We called for better-trained staff who would specialise in dealing with these cases. They should consult their supervisors more carefully before taking drastic decisions, and collaborate more closely with other services whose help might be needed. Finally we asked for a change in the wording of supplementary benefit law which would abolish the term 'cohabitation', with its sexual connotations, and substitute what seemed the more decent and objective phrase, 'living together as husband and wife'. We published our report *Living Together as Husband and Wife*, on 4 March 1976. The press conference was a shambles. The BMA called a press conference on the emigration of doctors an hour beforehand, half the journalists went off to that, and the fierce women sent along by the pressure groups whom I had invited to liven up the occasion terrorised the few press men who remained into almost complete silence.

But of all the leader writers, only one – in *The Morning Star* – failed to approve our main conclusions. An MP wrote to me, saying it was high time the Commission dropped all this 'Victorian nonsense' and abandoned such rules. An emollient reply was drafted for me to send back. But I threw it away and wrote instead to tell him that the Victorian nonsense was his, not ours, since the rule was imposed on us by Parliament. Any time he could get a majority of his colleagues in the House to repeal it I would be delighted. Till then, we had to administer the present law. (He saw the joke and wrote a friendly reply.)

Our proposals were the best choice of evils. But the whole experience left me ruefully feeling that it had perhaps been a mistake to publish a report about them. (An unavoidable mistake, for the public were entitled to know where we stood.) I tried repeatedly to explain at public meetings that we were not sex police and not in the least concerned with people's morals. 'You don't have to do a lot of snooping to find out who my wife is. We use the same name. We live together in the same house and have no other home. We have children, eat together, go shopping together, go on holiday together, share the same overdraft, quarrel about who uses the car .... Unless *some* of these things are to be found in it, the relationship is unlikely to be that of husband and wife.' But it was no good. Whatever I said, any public discussion left people (including, I feared, our own staff) with a confused idea that it was really all a matter of who slept with whom. Meanwhile, we still had to get something done about our new procedures. This would call for fresh instructions to staff, training, and endless negotiations with the civil service trade unions who opposed the creation of new specialists. These, they argued, tended to make other people's work less interesting and responsible (which also weakened their case for higher pay).

What, in the longer run, should be done about this rule, in a world where there are going to be more separated and divorced couples, and more lone parents? (A world, too, in which the Finer Committee's expensive proposal for a guaranteed maintenance allowance, paid by the state to all lone parents, is dead.) For lone parents who want to earn their own living there should be more opportunities to work, full time or part time; better wages for women; and better child care arrangements. Until we can organise our economy properly and bring the general level of unemployment down, progress in those directions is bound to be slow. Mothers or fathers on their own who cannot earn their own living, or who decide (as they are fully entitled to) that they would prefer to care for their children instead, must get paid for the important work they do. If the Social Services had to do the job instead it would cost far more. The payment can be based on any one of three different principles.

1. We can treat lone parents as poor people, needing means-tested social assistance of some sort – as we do now. That is the cheapest solution. It gets help to those who need it most. But it fastens some sort of cohabitation rule upon them.
2. Or we can treat them as victims of an insurable risk. We already do that for widows, most of whom get enough in benefits – paid regardless of their incomes – to lift them well above supplementary benefit levels. They are a popular group, and the fiercest lobby in the business: no one asks of widows – as they do of unmarried mothers or the divorced – whether they were responsible for their

own plight. In future we could extend their kind of insurance benefit to people who are divorced, separated or unmarried and looking after children. Insurance benefits, being linked through contributions to the level of wages, have until recently kept pace with inflation better than other benefits. A new contributory scheme of this kind would be expensive because it must be generous enough to lift people off means-tested supplementary benefit; and it would still leave them entangled in a cohabitation rule of some sort. If the extension of such benefits to new groups of lone parents took shape piecemeal, it might divide the 'family lobby' rather than unite them. Moreover this device would not really be aimed at the crucial needs involved.

3. The crucial needs arise from an unavoidable responsibility for caring for someone who depends on you. That could be recognised in a scheme for supporting lone parents, along with many others who care single-handed for particularly frail or handicapped people. The scheme for parents would have to start with a really adequate level of child benefits. Likewise, for those caring for an adult the scheme would have to be built on an adequate system of disability benefits. Then, as with child benefits today, a premium could be added to both schemes for those who have to do the job single-handed. That premium should not grow too large lest it bring increasingly intolerable cohabitation rules with it – which is why the basic level of child benefit should be raised first. Being addressed to family responsibilities, this proposal should help to unify rather than divide the pressure groups which together constitute the family lobby. But such benefits have not in the past kept pace with inflation. And, even if in future they were taxed, they would be expensive. Yet they would be a much better way of spending money than the present married man's tax allowance which reduces income tax for all married men, rich or poor, whether or not they have dependants in their households.

None of these solutions would altogether solve the problem. But the third would be best because it deals with the essential needs involved. These arise from a household's obligation to devote many unpaid hours of work to caring for its dependent members, and from the fact that some households have only one fit person of working age who has to choose between doing this, or going out to earn a living, or driving themselves to exhaustion trying to do both.

# II

# Women and Housing Policy

# Introduction

In 1980, over three-quarters of all British households lived in houses with gardens (Social Survey Division, OPCS, 1982). Moreover, despite popular views to the contrary, the majority (65 per cent) of households in publicly owned council housing also lived in houses with gardens. Indeed, British council housing, compared to public housing in other developed nations of the world, is unusual in just this respect (Stretton, 1975) and, as a result, often singled out for special praise. Rather than develop a peculiarly urban form of housing, housing authorities in this country have preferred on the whole to continue a century-long tradition of *sub*urban housing form. Only during a relatively brief period in the 1950s and 1960s did another form – the high-rise block of flats – become almost as dominant in new local authority construction as the house with the garden, and then generally in the more densely populated urban areas (Dunleavy, 1981). (Enough was built, though, to ensure that outside Scotland, most high-rise dwellings in this country are publicly owned.) However, as Austerberry and Watson point out, *both* high-rise living *and* suburban living have severe disadvantages for women. In the former, women who are housewives and mothers often have to struggle with inadequate and unsupervisable playspace for their children, bleak and frequently vandalised communal facilities, and the unlit terrors of urban pathways at night. (For a further and graphic description of the lives women lead in this kind of environment, see Campbell, 1984.) In the suburbs, in houses with gardens, women like Myra, the fictional heroine of *The Women's Room*, lead lonely and often depressed lives, and discover that the additional space that goes with 'higher' housing standards daily threatens to whirl out of control unless they invent – as Myra does – controls which themselves threaten to take over their entire lives.

Moreover, at an ideological level, despite being so different in housing form, both these dwelling types have one other thing in common: they embody a view of appropriate domestic behaviour and the place of women within domestic life. Suburban style housing is intended to do so; high-rise housing does this *in spite of* some original radical intentions and has now become, in practice, an important part of the apparatus of reinforcement of traditional domestic norms. In the case of suburban-type housing, the view of domestic life it ultimately reflects is a strongly traditional one that has its origins in the early development of industrial capitalism and the ensuing ideological split between 'public' and 'private' life developed by the Victorian bourgeoisie. In this view, women's place is firmly in the home, providing a 'haven in a heartless world', servicing the needs of their men – who spend most of their time in the 'public' world of work – and socialising their daughters and unmarried female servants into the ways of domesticity and sexual chastity (Davidoff *et al.*, 1976). While many of these *ideas* have lost some of their tenacity, the length of life of the housing stock and the sluggishness of change in urban structure means that it is particularly difficult to change house design to conform to changes in the position of women in society in general and the family in particular. While it is true that many large Victorian family houses have been successfully converted into small flats, the smaller suburban-style houses built in the 1920s and 1930s and copied in the 'garden cities' and new towns of the 1940s are less amenable to conversion and are often located in such a way within the city that they will have an effect on the life-style and employment opportunities of men and women for generations to come (McDowell, 1983).

In contrast, high-rise housing was originally intended in part to undermine this definition of the domestic ideal; by using a quite different urban built form and providing communal facilities such as creches and canteens, it was thought that women would be liberated both from the ideology of domesticity and its actuality. Examples of such housing were built in Europe in the 1940s, but when it came to the public sector imitations in this country, narrowness of conception and meanness in execution translated the idea into the publicly owned slabs and boxes that have become a feature of the landscape in our major cities (McDowell, 1983). Mothers with small children particularly hated them and longed for a house with a garden (Gittus, 1976). Those that could moved away, and those that were confident that the local authority would offer them something better refused to accept them. Increasingly such flats have come to be part of a system of 'less eligibility' for those households whose actual behaviour is judged not to conform to the domestic ideal: women single parents dependent on state benefits, families with housewives who are defined as 'poor' housekeepers by other women employed by the local authority to make such judgements (Ungerson, 1971), families headed by men who have been unemployed for years, and single women (Austerberry and Watson, 1983). The fact that flat-dwelling in the public sector has become a relatively stigmatised form of housing in this country means that women dependent on public sector housing are caught in a design 'Catch 22': deviance is punished with badly designed and poorly maintained housing; conformity is rewarded with better standard living conditions that nevertheless tend to reproduce patriarchal power relations.

Despite these dilemmas and contradictions, there have been feminist movements in the past that have had clear views about the kind of housing that women want. These movements have occurred chiefly in the United States and have generally been anti-suburban in tenor. Dolores Hayden has brilliantly documented these campaigns (amongst other things, for kitchenless houses) and described the seemingly bizarre utopias that an earlier group of American feminists – less blinded than we are by shiny domestic technology – designed at the turn of this century (Hayden, 1981). Anti-suburbanism continues to be a strand in American feminist thinking; in *Women and the American City*, Susan Saegert suggests that suburbs are bad for women and good for men (Saegert, 1981) while Betty Friedan's classic of the second wave of feminism *The Feminine Mystique* (Friedan, 1963) and its fictionalised version in Marilyn French's *The Women's Room* (French, 1978) have popularised the American feminist revolt against suburban life.

In this country and in others with a British-type tradition, anti-urbanism still holds relative sway although, perhaps significantly, the chief advocates of suburban design are men. In particular, an Australian, Hugh Stretton, has put together popular revulsion against high-rise living with feminist ideas about the productivity of housework, and come to the conclusion that, if housework had a place in national accounting systems, then governments would be easily persuaded on economic grounds alone to invest more in housing with generous space standards and of a suburban style (Stretton, 1974). Moreover, far from generating isolation and introversion, he suggests that suburban living generates neighbour-liness, co-operation and collective action:

> People who work urban land of their own take more knowledge-able interest in public gardens and parks, and they go (more often than people without land of their own) to enjoy any accessible wilderness. Community workshops and trades and crafts get used where people have space to practise the crafts at home; people practise the crafts at home, where there are community work-shops to attract them to meet, learn, use common equipment, and compare work. (Stretton, 1975, p. 789)

Such an analysis suggests that house design is the fundamental determinant of social life; while this, in itself, is a very difficult position to maintain, the argument is also fundamentally flawed on its own grounds since it fails to take account of who in the household actually does the work generated by the 'hobbies'. As Lee Davidoff reminds us:

> When the rosy spectacles are laid aside, it is clear that what to the husband and children can be a refreshing hobby – after all they are more often than not the consumers, not the producers, of the home-made jam – to the wife can be another variant of the natural mother image and in everyday terms can mean longer than ever hours at the chopping board. (Davidoff *et al.*, 1976, p. 173)

At the root of these problems of selecting dwelling designs and planning goals that optimise the interests of women is the truism that housing generates housework. Whether it is the kind of high quality housing that Myra lives in, or the rotten housing that the people studied by Coates and Silburn in the Nottingham slum of St Ann's once lived in, and which people in leaking tower blocks continue to live in (Campbell, 1984), the end product is *work*. That work can be modified by raising the standards of damp insulation, changing the size of the garden or abandoning it altogether, and introducing running hot water and central heating, but it will remain repetitive, and almost always compulsory rather than voluntary. Someone has to do it, and given the sexual division of labour which itself is reinforced by urban planning (Harman, 1983), it will usually be left to the women. The problem for social policy-makers and for feminist commentators on social policy is whether to take that sexual division of labour for granted and plan neighbourhood services and housing design such that it is taken into account.

However, and perhaps more importantly, it must be remembered that housing is more than simply a place to live in. It is also an extremely important form of property, and rights of access to it are governed by legislation and custom. Over the past hundred years, various pieces of legislation, from the 1882 Married Woman's Property Act, which gave married women the right to hold their own property, to the 1980 Housing Act, which makes it mandatory for local authorities to give married couples joint tenancies, the property rights of women both in the public and private housing sectors have been gradually extended (Brion and Tinker, 1980). But social legislation that directly relates to women's property rights is not the only way in which social policy regulates women's lives. The fact that the housing market is divided into different tenure categories which are governed by different laws and customs means that, when changes in the structure of the housing market occur, and particular tenure categories expand and contract, so the number of people affected by the rules and regulations governing access to and maintenance of rights in particular tenure categories will also expand and contract. Thus, as Austerberry and Watson point out, government's efforts to increase the proportion of owner occupied housing in this country has the unintended consequence of profoundly affecting the property rights of women, particularly when marriage ends.

As part of this policy of expanding owner occupation, council tenants now have the right to buy the council housing they occupy. As a result the local authority sector will increasingly contain the least popular form of council dwelling: the council flat on the 'sink' estate. For women on their own, with and without children, disadvantaged as they are in the labour market, such council housing will increasingly be their only source of shelter. However, given the previous discussion of the patriarchal roots of the ideology of suburbia, does it matter that poor women without husbands and with children will find themselves increasingly dependent on flats in decaying inner-city areas rather than houses in the leafy suburbs? If it does matter, as I think it does, then what is to be done?


**Additional reading**

Apart from the works cited in this introduction, some of which refer to the American and Australian literature, there are now two books specifically directed to the analysis of many of these issues within a British context. The first is *Geography and Gender: an introduction to feminist geography* (Women and Geography Study Group, 1984). Readers interested in social policy should not be put off by the disciplinary context of geography: in many respects present-day geography is the next-door neighbour of social policy studies. The second is *Making Space: Women and the man-made environment* (Matrix, 1984), a collection of essays by feminist architects who live and work in Britain.

# A Woman's Place: a Feminist Approach to Housing in Britain

**HELEN AUSTERBERRY and SOPHIE WATSON**

An exciting development in the women's movement over the last few years has been an attempt by feminists to organise together around housing issues and to develop a feminist analysis of how the organisation of housing in Britain specifically affects women. This is not to say that women have not played an important and active role in numerous tenant struggles. In the famous rent strike on the Clyde in 1915, which resulted in legislation to control the level of rents, women demonstrated in their thousands, filled the court-rooms when tenants faced eviction and were the organisers of the struggle. More recently accounts of women confronting the rent collectors in Northern Ireland with the din of beating pots and pans are typical of women's involvement in housing campaigns before and since (Cowley, 1980).

However, it is only comparatively recently that feminists have begun to raise the issue more generally within the women's liberation movement. The exception to this has been the work of Women's Aid groups and the National Women's Aid Federation, who have consistently and successfully fought for battered women's rights to housing in cases of domestic violence. But in the last few years feminists have begun to organise together as architects, housing workers, builders, designers etc, to question seriously assumptions around housing policy and structure; assumptions held not only by politicians, housing officials and housing workers, but

*Source*: slightly abridged from Helen Austerberry and Sophie Watson, 'A Woman's Place: a Feminist Approach to Housing in Britain', *Feminist Review*, No. 8, Summer 1981.

also by socialist housing activists. A national conference in March 1980, organised by the Women and Housing Group, attracted 200 women, and a women-only housing co-operative has started in the last couple of years to house its members. Inevitably, political differences in priorities and analyses exist, some women emphasising the need to work for changes within the present housing system, while the priority of others is to construct alternative housing situations for women.

Through their involvement in housing work as employees of statutory and voluntary housing organisations and as activists, women have become increasingly aware of the need for a feminist perspective on housing. Housing is located within the domestic sphere, the traditionally privatised area of life, but its role in moulding and reinforcing the patriarchal and capitalist structure of the family has been largely ignored. We believe that this weakness is one of the reasons which explains the failure of left parties and the trade unions to develop coherent socialist housing policies. They have concentrated almost exclusively on public housing and have never really challenged owner-occupation as a form of tenure, or the quality of housing and its organisation and control.

Although socialists are now beginning to take up these questions, a feminist perspective highlights these as central issues. We are still, however, a long way from a socialist feminist policy on housing, and much more work needs to be done at the theoretical and political level. This article only sets out what we consider to be some of the major problems which any socialist feminist analysis of housing must confront, and raises more questions than answers.

Why has housing never been a central issue for the women's liberation movement in Britain, despite the crucial place that it occupies in all our lives? And why is it that not one of the seven demands of the women's movement specifically addresses questions of housing? A tentative reply to these questions we think would be that an attempt to construct a purely feminist demand around housing presents major problems, in the way that demands around financial independence, sexuality, childcare and so on, do not. As socialists we would demand decent and secure housing for everyone at a reasonable cost, but the difficulty arises when we consider what we can demand specifically as women without simply constructing an alternative women's culture or further reinforcing women's place in the home. For example, recognising women's present housing needs as wife and mother, we might fight for such things as a roomy efficient kitchen to make women's work at home less burdensome. Yet such a demand must be clearly formulated so that it challenges the stereotypes of women's role. There are many contradictions therefore in the relationship of women to housing, and in the demands that we might want to make.

We begin by looking at some of the fundamental assumptions on which housing policy is based, present government housing policy, the various forms of housing tenure in Britain, and the particular problems for women that these forms of tenure raise. We then consider the way in which housing structure and design affect women's lives.

## The household

All present housing policy is based on the notion of the household. Despite the fact that single-parent families, people on their own, or unrelated people living together constitute 32 per cent of all households (Central Statistical Office, 1979, p. 44), the household is generally assumed to be the nuclear family. All other housing, apart from nuclear family accommodation, is defined as 'special need' housing. There has been scanty analysis of either the individual members of the household's different structural relationship to housing, or of households that do not comply with the nuclear family model. In addition to this, the head of the household is almost always assumed to be the man in the household, even if the wife is working. A classic example of this can be found in the Interviewers Manual (Social and Community Planning Research, 1977) in the section defining the head of the household as the man who owns or rents the property, or is in tied accommodation because of his job:

> there is only one exception: if a wife owns the property or has her name on the rent book or has the property because of her job, *her husband is regarded as the head of household*, provided that he is resident (our italics). (SCPR, 1977, p. 54)

### Financial dependence

A prevailing assumption of this society, which has profound consequences for women's access to housing, is that a woman and her children will be supported financially by her husband. A major part of this support will be the cost of the family's housing, be it in the form of mortgage repayments or rent. According to the Family Expenditure Survey, average personal expenditure on housing rose from 9 per cent of total consumer spending in 1953 to 14 per cent in 1973. Moreover, lower income groups tend to spend more proportionally on their housing than higher income groups (Ginsburg, 1979, p. 5). Of course, not everyone lives in a nuclear family, and there are families where the costs are shared equally or nearly so, or where the housing tenure is held jointly by both partners, but they are not the norm. As a rule the man's salary or wage is the primary source of income within the family, while the woman's income, if she has one, is seen as a supplement to this.

*Division of labour*

The corollary of this is that it is women who are expected to undertake the reproduction of labour-power within the family, whether they also have waged jobs or not. Despite some changing patterns in this respect, woman's role is still seen to be primarily in the home. She is the housewife, bearing, raising and socialising children, and succouring her husband's and children's emotional and physical needs (Oakley, 1974). The women's movement has presented a major challenge to these assumptions, but the law, the media, the social services, education and many other facets of the state continue to reinforce this pervasive ideology. As we shall argue below, society's expectation and acceptance of the male head of the household as the chief breadwinner, with the woman as an economically dependent housewife and mother, has important and specific repercussions in relation to housing policy and tenure.

## Government housing policy

A brief examination of government housing policy is necessary before the relative importance of different forms of tenure can be fully understood. The Housing Act 1980 contains three major sections which affect access to housing in the public and private sectors. The first and major thrust of the Act is the clause enabling council tenants to purchase their dwelling at a huge discount – not a new trend of either Labour or Conservative housing policy, but certainly it represents a greater encouragement to owner-occupation than ever before.

Secondly, under the new Act, tenants in council property are granted security of tenure, whereas previously they did not have this protection. Socialists have long fought for security of tenure for council tenants, so this represents a major gain in the housing struggle. But feminists saw the serious implications for women in this clause, since problems in the rehousing of the other partner in cases of marital breakdown were bound to result, and campaigned, unfortunately with no success, against this clause.

Thirdly, the Act has created a system of 'shorthold' tenancies – an attempt to open up the ailing private rented sector. Socialists and feminists oppose this move, not only because it enables landlords to evict tenants easily and raise rents, but because they recognise that the demise of this sector is, broadly speaking, a result of the decreasing profitability of investment in this sector (Merrett, 1979, p. 281), not of legislation concerning rent control and tenants' rights.

Finally, the major overall result of the government's monetarist economic policy has been a severe reduction in public expenditure, particularly in housing expenditure, which will inevitably lead to poorer quality public housing, with less possibility for transfers within this sector.

## Housing tenure

The two major forms of housing tenure in Britain are owner-occupation, which accounts for 51.5 per cent of the population, and local authority (or council) housing, which accounts for 33.4 per cent of the population, with housing associations, co-operatives and the private rented sector making up the remaining 15 per cent (CSO, 1979, p. 146).

As can be seen in Table 1, throughout this century there has been a large decline in private renting, and a corresponding increase in owner-occupation and council housing, which began to get under way after the First World War. Predictably, the middle classes have tended to move into owner-occupation, while council tenants tend to be the lower-paid and lower-status workers (Ginsburg, 1979,

**Table 1**    *Housing tenure, England and Wales (millions of houses and percentage of stock)*

| Year | Owner occupied number | % | Local authority and new towns number | % | Private rented and miscellaneous number | % | Total number |
|------|------|------|------|------|------|------|------|
| 1914 | .8 | 10 | 0.02 | 0.2 | 7.1 | 89.8 | 7.9 |
| 1938 | 3.7 | 32 | 1.1 | 10 | 6.6 | 58 | 11.4 |
| 1951 | 3.9 | 31 | 2.2 | 17 | 6.4 | 52 | 12.5 |
| 1960 | 6.4 | 44 | 3.6 | 25 | 4.6 | 31 | 14.6 |
| 1966 | 7.8 | 49 | 4.3 | 27 | 3.9 | 24 | 16.0 |
| 1971 | 8.9 | 52 | 4.9 | 29 | 3.3 | 19 | 17.1 |
| 1976 | 10.1 | 56 | 5.3 | 29 | 2.8 | 15 | 18.2 |

*Source:* Ginsburg, *Class, Capital and Social Policy*, London, Macmillan, 1979.

p. 138). Private renting tends to be a residual tenure for all the social classes. We shall therefore concentrate predominantly on the two major forms of tenure, and go on to look at their significance for women.

**The owner-occupied sector**

As was stated above, 51.5 per cent of the population at the present time have purchased their own housing, 28.5 per cent with mortgages (CSO, 1979). It is in this sector that women's inferior economic position is of particular relevance, although it has specific repercussions in relation to council housing, too, as we discuss below. Women tend to earn less than their male counterparts (women's wages were 73.5 per cent of men's in 1979), and to be in less stable areas of employment and more frequently in part-time work than men (Bruegel, 1980). Consequently, women have far less purchasing power than men, a situation which inevitably will be exacerbated in the current economic crisis. Traditionally, therefore, building societies have been extremely reluctant to grant women mortgages on their own, since they are generally regarded as a bad risk on the grounds of their present or future income. Secondly, the attitude that women are on their own only until they find a man to support them is a prevalent one. A study of building societies in Huddersfield found:

there was not only a preference for apparently conformist middle class couples, but also the dislike of deviators from this norm, such as is represented by marital breakdown or career oriented women. (Duncan, 1976, p. 6)

Even in the case of married applicants for joint mortgages, the Equal Opportunities Commission (EOC) found that 36 per cent of building societies in their study discriminated in some way against a couple with a higher earning wife (EOC, 1978). Women's freedom to purchase their own housing, should this be their desire, is thus severely limited. Surveys of ownership of property provide further evidence of this. A survey of married owner-occupier couples in 1971 found that 42 per cent had the home in the husband's name, and only 5 per cent in the wife's name, the remainder being joint mortgages (Todd and Jones, 1972). Clearly, then, women's access to home ownership is often through association with a male bread-winner, a fact which further reinforces women's economic dependence on a male partner.

However, it is on marital breakdown that the crucial implications of this situation are particularly illuminated. On divorce a married woman may now apply for a property transfer order, and this can be made even if she has made no direct financial contribution to the purchase or improvement of the matrimonial home. However, numerous problems still arise. The starting point the courts use in making financial orders is the one-third rule: that a woman is entitled to one-third of her husband's joint income and capital. In practice this means that if an order is made transferring the home, the wife's maintenance will be consequently reduced. Where there is an order for sale the division of the proceeds of sale rarely gives the woman enough capital to purchase a new home. Orders which allow a wife to remain in occupation of the marital home until her youngest child leaves, in effect, put off her housing problems until middle age, when she is often without an income or sufficient capital to make continued owner-occupation a realistic alternative.

Even when an outright transfer is made, problems can also arise, as women on their own find it difficult to meet the mortgage repayments. In this situation a woman has two options. One is to depend on supplementary benefit, which will generally include money for the payment of the interest on an existing mortgage. The other is to find well-paid employment which will provide her with an adequate income to afford the repayments. In the first case, therefore, the woman has had to shift her economic dependence from her husband to the state. In the second, we are talking about the likelihood of a woman finding adequate childcare facilities for her children and entering the labour market, at a fairly high income level, possibly after many years' absence from paid employment. In the current situation of economic recession, and cuts in the few nursery facilities that do exist, this option does not appear to be a very feasible one. An additional financial burden for a woman in situations such as these may be that of arrears which have accrued, of which she may have been previously unaware (Ginsburg, 1979, p. 128). There is also the problem of repairs and maintenance of the property, which a woman may well not be able to afford, or be able to do herself through lack of experience or time.

Why, then, have socialists, and the major parties on the left, tended to maintain an equivocal attitude towards owner-occupation, and why has the whole question of land and property nationalisation never been confronted head-on? In part it would appear that this has arisen from a tendency to see questions of housing and home life as matters of individual and privatised choice, to be set aside from the mainstream of political life where employment is the crucial issue. Also, there is the recognition by these parties that many members of the working class, and many of their voters, do want to own their own property. Indeed a similar equivocal attitude exists towards the issue of council-house sales, some women (like some socialists) even appearing to endorse the 'right to buy' clause in the new Act, presumably on the basis that it represents an avenue for women to enter into the private market (Brion and Tinker, 1980, p. 43). We would argue that as socialist feminists it is important to challenge owner-occupation as a form of tenure. Bearing in mind women's income levels, it is too expensive not only in terms of the initial and ongoing payments, but also in terms of the ongoing costs of upkeep. The common argument that owner-occupation offers greater mobility does not generally hold true for women, as was clear in our discussion of what happens on marital breakdown. Likewise, the myth that owner-occupation offers greater control over one's housing is one that feminists must challenge, for which member of the household is frequently the one to exercise this control?

To conclude, then, women's economic dependence on men within the family, and their primary role as wife and mother, is ultimately reinforced in the private housing market. Furthermore, because of the importance of women's unpaid domestic labour, particularly as a child rearer, the state, albeit reluctantly, provides some financial support, with social security payments for example, once the marital relationship breaks down. So women have to challenge owner-occupation and, in particular, council-house sales and cuts in public expenditure in housing, since it is they as housewives, mothers and single parents who inevitably bear the brunt of reduced decent public housing, and the increased push towards owner-occupation.

## Council housing

It is often said that women have greater access to housing in the public sector than men, or that housing officials tend to be more sympathetic to women. Under the Housing (Homeless Persons) Act 1977 housing departments have a duty to provide housing to anyone 'unintentionally homeless' and in 'priority need' of housing. This category includes: those with dependent children normally living with them, pregnant women, and those vulnerable as a result of old age, mental illness or handicap or physical disability or other special reason. In fact the wording of the Act makes it clear that it is only as mothers that women are given priority in the public sector. The state provides housing for children, and hence for whoever is caring for them. The only other specific category where women outnumber men in council accommodation is the elderly, simply by virtue of the fact that they live longer.

### Single women with children

An examination of the treatment of single women with children in council housing demonstrates that, far from being favourably regarded by local authorities, they are often penalised. Principally, single-parent families are allocated council housing under the 1977 Housing (Homeless Persons) Act, or from the housing waiting-list. Typically women become eligible for housing under the Act in situations of marital breakdown, but rehousing is not automatic, and neither is being homeless an open door to decent housing. Women often have to prove to housing officials that they have not made themselves 'intentionally' homeless. In these circumstances, they tend to be in desperate need and thus have little power, so are frequently offered the worst properties with little possibility of being offered a better property on refusal.

The other basis of housing allocation to single-parent families is the housing waiting-lists. Formerly the largest group of people to be housed by local authorities (64 per cent in 1975) came from these lists; some of these people were council tenants hoping to move to better property. With the current cuts in housing expenditure, however, very few tenants are likely to be rehoused from the lists at the present time. Local authorities house people from the waiting-list on the basis of a points system, which varies between different local authorities, points being gained according to such criteria as length of time on the waiting-list, current housing situation, numbers of children, and so on. The Finer Report (1974) on one-parent families found that the system discriminated against such families because they gained points for only one adult, not two. Moreover, the report found that single parents were often expected to share a bedroom with a child, where two parents were not, and were seldom offered houses with gardens because it was thought that they could not look after them. Overall, these families frequently tend to be placed in the worst housing or on the worst estates, partly perhaps because of their inability to pay higher rents, and partly because local authorities have always been inclined to allocate poor people and slum dwellers to particular estates (Gray, 1979). Likewise, there has been a policy for people who are seen as 'problem families' (which often includes single-parent families) and 'unsatisfactory' tenants to be selected for these estates (Gray, 1979). The estates then come to be seen as 'ghetto', 'sink' or 'residual' estates, where no one wants to live, where the repairs are not done, and only people who have no chance of being offered anywhere better are forced to live. However, some councils have had to modify their policies in this respect in view of the management problems on these estates. Families who are desperate for housing are forced to accept bad housing offers simply because they have no other choice. Once someone has accepted an offer and become a council tenant, local authority management policies come to be an important aspect of their lives.

## Housing management

Fundamentally, the system of local authority housing management has its roots in the early work of Octavia Hill. She was a pioneer in the development of working-class housing in the second half of the nineteenth century. Her attitudes were extremely paternalistic and authoritarian, and based on the idea that poor people needed to be trained in household management, so that they would be able to pay their rent more regularly. In many ways these attitudes remain today. A study of several local authorities in the 1960s revealed:

> Councils for the most part are preoccupied with behaving as efficient landlords – balancing the account, furbishing the properties, gathering arrears. They prize above all a good, i.e. solvent tractable clean and quiet tenant and tend to favour him [sic], as any private landlord would. Because he is deemed likely to treat it carefully, he is generally given one of the newest and best homes. This is what is meant by sound management. (Tucker, 1966, p. 11)

Despite the tenant being referred to as 'him', it is generally the woman of the household who bears the brunt of housing management principles. An extreme example of this was discovered by community workers in Paisley:

> where a special area in one housing estate has been set aside for problem families, where they are given daily supervision combined with training and instruction designed to teach them the elements of home craft and mothercraft so that in due course, when they have proved they can manage their affairs, domestic, financial or otherwise, they can return to a better house in a more desirable neighbourhood. (Community Development Project, 1976, p. 82)

The connection between these attitudes of housing management and allocations policy is raised by this example. As F. Gray points out, 'selection and allocation may reflect, in part at least, the desire of the local authority to minimise management tasks' (Merrett, 1979, p. 207). New tenants, particularly from non-conforming households such as single parents, tend to be given the poorer standard housing and are expected to prove their ability to look after and improve their home before being transferred to a better property. Likewise, 'moral rectitude, social conformity, clean living, and a clean rent book on occasion seem to be essential for eligibility for at least a new house' (Central Housing Advisory

Committee, 1969, p. 32) – qualifications that a woman left on her own with dependants on a low income or social security benefit may well find hard to fulfil.

What conclusions should we draw as feminists concerning housing policy in the public sector, and what demands should we make? Clearly, then, housing policy operates at present to reinforce the nuclear family. The majority of housing is provided for this group – housing schemes for single people being rare, and the few that exist being blatantly restricted and cut at the present time. So public housing fails to provide for personal mobility in changing relationships, or for different needs that people may have. As the better council housing is sold off, those that are dependent on the public sector for their housing will be increasingly relegated to the worst estates.

It is important, therefore, that feminists challenge the current definitions of housing need, and campaign against the public sector becoming a residual category for those who cannot afford their own housing. Secondly, we need to demand tenants' control over their housing in order that decisions can be made democratically by the people who occupy the council property and not others. Finally, it is important to keep abreast with housing legislation, and analyse its implications, campaigning for changes where they are needed.

### Private renting, housing associations and housing co-operatives

Some mention of other forms of housing tenure is necessary. The private rented sector has declined considerably throughout the century. It is now so scarce and expensive that luck and money are needed to find a half-way decent flat to rent, particularly in big cities. Women's inferior economic position must affect their access to the better places, but no work has been done to substantiate this point. However, with their habitual thrust towards the private market, the Tory Housing Act, by incorporating provision for shorthold tenure, and permission to council tenants to sublet and take lodgers, is designed to open up the private rented sector. It is difficult to assess at this stage what the repercussions of these provisions on this sector will be, but it is important to oppose yet another Tory move to minimise statutory responsibility to provide housing for people without homes. These new provisions legitimate in particular the common claim that single people's housing needs can be met by the private rented sector.

Housing associations are non-statutory organisations set up by groups of individuals. Since the 1974 Housing Act many have been publicly funded. They are essentially of two kinds: 'fair rent', a system by which tenants pay a rent determined by a rent officer, and 'co-ownership', where part of the tenant's rent goes towards partial ownership of the dwelling. Co-operatives are broadly speaking self-run, as opposed to management committee-run, housing associations; hence their attractiveness to autonomous groups. Until very recently housing associations have been able to have their own policies as to whom they can house, as well as housing a certain proportion of people from the housing waiting-list as part of their financial agreement with the local authority. Likewise, co-ops decide who their own members can be. For this reason housing associations, as well as housing families, have tended to house people who are considered to have 'special needs', in particular those who cannot be housed in the traditional nuclear family unit. Inevitably single women with children and elderly women form an important part of this group, and indeed, housing associations and co-ops have been important in providing groups with an opportunity to live collectively as a positive alternative to the nuclear family. Now, in 1980, having largely escaped the first round of cuts by the Tory government, the Housing Corporation, which is a major source of funding to housing associations and co-ops, has been cut too, leading to an ever worsening situation for those ineligible for council housing or unable to buy into the private market.

**Housing structure and design**

The weak position of women in the labour market, and their responsibilities within the home as domestic workers and child rearers, affect not only women's access to housing, but its structure and design. This is an area which has received considerable attention from feminists in recent years, particularly feminist architects and builders in groups such as Matrix, The Women and Built Environment Group and the Feminist Design Co-op, who have begun to challenge traditional attitudes and assumptions held within the architecture profession.

*Working conditions in the home*

Because the home is a workplace for women, they tend to spend more time there than men or children. Clearly there are vast differences in this respect between married and unmarried women, mothers and non-mothers and those who do paid work as well as housework. However, it is generally the case that women do more housework than men. We would therefore argue that housing conditions are more important to them and their needs broader. Yet the home is regarded as a private sanctuary and conditions in the home are largely outside the law. Housewives are isolated, without the protection of their rights corresponding to those won by waged workers through trade union organisation and solidarity. There is no counterpart to the health and safety legislation of waged employment. Pre-school child care, for example, when socialised and undertaken by registered childminders or in nurseries and creches, is subject to stringent regulations. It is hardly surprising that the highest number of accidents occur in the home.

*Design*

Despite this relationship of women to the home, they have little control over the nature of their housing. Architects and planners are usually men and, in the case of local authority housing estates, not of the class of those who actually spend most of their time in the flats and houses they design. It is women who bear the brunt of high-rise flats, estates with no open play spaces, inadequate laundry facilities, noise, vandalism and bad access to shops and transport. Cramped kitchens, damp, thin walls, broken lifts, dark and dangerous stairways and the numerous other consequences of low cost building, make taking care of the home and rearing young children doubly difficult and time-consuming. The current cuts in public expenditure will inevitably exacerbate this situation. The government also intends to reduce the Parker Morris standards. These are the recommended minimum space and heating standards proposed by the Parker Morris Committee in 1961, which were required to be incorporated in public housing design from January 1969 – yet another gain made in the early 1960s to be whittled away under the current government. Repairs and redecoration will be relegated by councils to the unforseeable future, leading to further deterioration of the housing stock.

Moreover, as is well known, bad housing can lead to illness and injuries, which women have to deal with. A recent study of women living in Camberwell, South London, found that living in the isolation of the family with small children, in poor and overcrowded housing conditions, was a major cause of depression (Brown and Harris, 1970). It is the poor who fare worst in relation to housing facilities, heating and indoor playspace for their children, and it is often single-parent families that are particularly hard hit in this respect (Townsend, 1979, Chapter 13). For these reasons, it is often women who provide the impetus for, and who are extremely active in, campaigns against dampness, for central heating, for improved playspaces and other necessary facilities.

### The isolated nature of housing structure and its links with domestic labour and consumption

However, to demand better working conditions in the home is in a sense contradictory in that this reinforces the social and spatial oppression of women within their domestic roles. For the more ideal and self-contained the housing conditions, the more self-sufficient the housewife becomes and the more pressure there is on her to maintain a perfect home. The present nature of housing cannot be fully understood without relating it to the nature of domestic labour. Thus demands for change in the two spheres must interlink.

Housework and childcare have remained largely privatised, neither integrated into socialised commodity production, nor taken over by the state, unlike education and the health service. Individual tasks are repeated by each separate woman in the home in a way that, with the possible exception of pre-school child care and socialisation which is highly labour-intensive work, would be more efficient if socialised. Housing mirrors the isolated and privatised nature of domestic labour and reinforces each self-contained family unit. As we said earlier, family housing is regarded as normal, and other housing is defined as 'special'. Hence sharing facilities, such as for cooking or washing, between families is regarded as a sign of poverty and housing stress (Townsend, 1979, p. 480). Instead, similar facilities are duplicated in row upon row of separate homes. However, a large proportion of married women do work outside the home, particularly in part-time work. But the addition of paid work to the housewife's activities does not mean that she is no longer a housewife. The definition of housewifery is cast in terms of responsibility for the running of the home (Oakley, 1974, p. 38). According to the findings of a national survey described by Audrey Hunt about 85 per cent of all adult British women are housewives (Oakley, 1974, p. 29). So, for women in waged jobs, the reduced time available in which to perform domestic labour acts as a pressure to heighten labour productivity in the home, and contributes to the successful penetration of capitalism into this still privatised sector, by the creation of a market for domestic mechanisation. The purchase and use of washing-machines, dishwashers, vacuum-cleaners, cookers, micro-wave ovens, freezers and other such goods, is an act which, while not changing the relations of production and the mode of production, does alter the productive forces in this sector of the economy. Furthermore, it is probable that more labour-saving commodities do not necessarily replace domestic labour, but simply serve to make more domestic labour possible (Molyneux, 1979).

However, as feminists have consistently argued, potentially housework could be organised in a different way. For example, washing-machines enable individual households to have their washing done more quickly, but they are used inefficiently. At present domestic labour is organisationally inefficient because it is not socialised like the industrial sphere, which counterbalances increased productivity through mechanisation. These factors appear contradictory, but in fact both individualist and mechanised lifestyles serve capitalism by increasing demand and facilitating the circulation of commodities produced. The more efficient and mechanised housework becomes, the more the housewife's standards can rise. Therefore she tends to become more competitive and her commodity consumption tends to increase. For to compensate for any increased leisure time which the acquisition of machinery could bring, women are encouraged to be generally more house-proud. It could be argued that the increase in home ownership facilitates this tendency. Women are under more ideological pressure to maintain a perfect home in owner-occupied property, where standards are seen to be the individual responsibility of the owners, rather than being outside a tenant's control as in rented property, although of course women in all forms of accommodation are subjected to these pressures. However, those in the worst housing experience the greatest difficulty in meeting the norms of good housekeeping.

Individual nuclear family units not only provide the maximum number of outlets for commodity production, but also facilitate social control. The growth of new housing estates, with their anonymous corridors and large barren spaces, and the destruction of the old terraced house communities with their adjoining gardens, have inevitably led to more isolation of family life. Inevitably it is women, as housewives particularly, who bear the strain of this.

Formulating demands around housing design and quality are particularly problematic for feminists. We have already discussed the contradictions involved in demanding more roomy kitchens and better working conditions in the home. However, the structure and design of houses are very important, and if feminists do not argue for better standards, women will be subjected to working in rotten conditions, bearing the brunt of the cuts in housing expenditure, greater costs of heating, more accidents in the home and endless other problems. As feminists we must demand control over the planning process, in order to overcome the isolation of domestic activity and individualised childcare, and to achieve better conditions in the home.

### Conclusions

What does all this imply for the feminist struggle around housing? First we must begin to recognise that a very real division is incorporated into the existing structure of housing between the public and private sectors, where the public sector is increasingly just a residual back-up for single-parent families, minority and ethnic groups. Demands around housing therefore must be seen to be as politically central as demands around the wage and employment, and not simply be seen as a matter of individual choice, which for women in particular it is not. Both access to housing, and the quality of housing available, structure not only the material divisions between the rich and the poor, but also sexual divisions between men and women. Indeed, housing crucially determines the parameters of our social relationships, as well as our physical well-being.

In formulating any alternative housing policy, feminists need to consider both the availability and provision of low-cost adequate housing, and the form in which they are provided. For instance, housing units should not only be available for the planners' notion of the traditional nuclear family, but for a range of different relationships. It must also be recognised that 'housing need' will vary at different periods of women's and men's lives. Equally, it is important that far more thought should be given to creating communal conditions and facilities for those who want them. For any real change to take place, therefore, there has to be a massive increase in government expenditure on public housing, so that this sector can be greatly extended. This demand has to be made in conjunction with demands for greater control over public housing, by those who inhabit it.

Finally then, as feminists, it is vital that we raise these issues in our trade unions, our work, our political parties and at local grass-roots level, insisting that feminist demands are incorporated into the general political strategy and so broadening the socialist perspective. Only then can there be a truly integrated socialist feminist strategy and analysis of housing which demands decent and secure housing for everyone, and allows us a choice in the way we live.

# The Women's Room

## MARILYN FRENCH

Mira's experience was so different. She had completely settled into her new, easier life. The mornings were bad. She hated to get up. Norm had to call her, then shake her, and she would stagger downstairs and hang like an exhausted alcoholic over a clutched mug of coffee.

The children were unhappy in the morning, like her. They would argue and complain about the breakfast. They refused to eat an egg that was cooked too long or not long enough. They no longer liked this cereal. They wanted English muffins, or they wanted toast. She left the kitchen to dress while they lamented their miserable existences, and more often than not, she came back from driving them to the bus stop to throw their breakfasts in the garbage.

After her return, after that heart-sinking moment of coming back to the greasy frying pan and the littered table, there was cleaning. The afternoons, though, were better. Money was plentiful despite all the loans, and one thing Norm was willing to spend it on was the house. So Mira's afternoons were spent in an orgy of planning decor and buying furniture, rugs, draperies, lamps, pictures. Slowly the house filled up. It got to be hard to handle, so she bought herself a small file box and some packages of 2 × 3 cards. On each card she wrote one task that had to be performed, and filed them in sections. The section headed WINDOW WASHING would contain cards for each room in the house. Whenever she washed the windows in one room, she would mark the date down on the card, and place it at the end of the section. The same was true for FURNITURE POLISHING,

*Source*: Marilyn French, *The Women's Room* (Sphere, 1973), pp. 208–11.

RUG SHAMPOOING, and CHINA. Regularly she removed all the dishes from the dining-room china closet, washed them by hand – they were good china, not to be entrusted to the dishwasher – and returned them to their freshly washed shelves. She did the same in the kitchen; she did the same thing with the books, removing them, dusting them carefully, and returning them to clean, wiped, and waxed shelves. She did not make cards for ordinary, daily cleaning, only for the large, special tasks. So each day, after the small chores of cleaning kitchen, making beds and cleaning the two main bathrooms, she would also perform a thorough cleaning of one room, washing mirrors and windows, waxing any visible wooden floors, cleaning the small ornaments, dusting ceilings and walls and furniture surfaces, and vacuuming. She would then mark on the appropriate card the large task accomplished. That way, she reasoned, she would always keep up. It took her two weeks to go through the whole house – ten working days. She did not clean on weekends. And extraordinary tasks, like cleaning every dish in the kitchen and pantry, she did only twice a year. The same was true of the curtains. It was good housewifery, performed in the old way. Mira's mother cleaned this way, although without the cards. And had scrubbed sheets and shirts on a scrub board, and walked two miles each way to the market. The Wards' house was always shining and smelled fresh, of lemon oil and soap.

Mira would feel tremendously satisfied when she finished her morning's work. She would bathe then, using expensive bath oil, and smooth an expensive lotion all over her body when she was through. She felt luxurious. She would stand in the door of her enormous closet in a thick velour robe and choose her outfit for the afternoon. She chose her perfume and make-up to complement the outfit. She would walk through the house, dressed to go out, relishing the silence, the order, the shine of polished wood in the sun. Her mother-in-law had given her a clock similar to one she owned, an old-fashioned clock with a great glass dome over it, that struck the hour with chimes, the quarter hours with little bells. It ticked loudly: you could hear it in most of the downstairs rooms. She walked listening to its ticking, feeling the order and the peace, the cleanliness, the comfort. She would walk to the kitchen; the morning light had slid away, and the paler light shone on the old hutch, making the clean china pieces, old pitchers and cups, charming unmatched plates standing on end on the shelves, gleam and reflect. The beauty was her doing. The clock ticked.

She would go out then on a shopping expedition, or to do errands, or on an infrequent visit to one of her friends. The boys were older now; she could tarry a bit, and not get home until four. But she was usually annoyed when she did get home. There was always something, it seemed: muddy footprints, finger marks on a clean wall, a blackened towel. She would rage at the boys; they largely ignored her. They did not understand, she knew that. The cleanliness and order were her life, they had cost her everything.

When she came home, it was usually to go out again: the boys had appointments with the dentist, the orthodontist, games with Little League, Scout meetings, Clark had violin lessons, Normie, trumpet lessons. On Saturday mornings she took them for riding lessons, waited and took them back, while Norm went out to play golf. Her nights were calmer than they had been. Norm was very busy these days, and often did not come home for dinner. She fell into the habit of feeding the boys early, and continued it even on nights when he did come home. It was better: they could eat and go off and do homework and then watch TV, or on summer evenings, go out and play ball for a while before baths and bed. Norm was more pleasant at the dinner table when the boys were not there. After about nine o'clock, she was free. Norm would sit watching TV, she would glance up at it and back at her book, but he tired early and went to bed. She liked sitting there alone, listening to the silence of the sleeping house, the night noises outdoors – a barking dog, a car starting up – all measured by the ticking clock.

In nice weather, she worked in the garden. She would drive to the nursery in the spring and pick up boxes of spring flowers, pansies, violets, crocuses, iris, lilies of the valley, daffodils, and jonquil, and set them lovingly in the damp sweet-sour earth. The air was soft and a little wet, and she enjoyed feeling the cool, damp dungy earth in her hands. She stood, looking around, planning the garden. She would buy white wrought-iron pieces with delicate tracery, and set them there, by the rock garden. She bought lounges for the patio, and glass-topped tables. She hung a bird feeder.

When Norm did not come home for dinner, or when he ate and went out again to a meeting, Mira would spend the evening reading. Then, at about eleven, she would pour herself a drink and turn out the lights and sit and think. He never came in very late, always by twelve, and he always tripped on the doorstep from garage to kitchen hall, and he always yelled out complaining, 'Why the hell don't you keep a light on?' Still, she never left it on.

# Housework in a Slum

## KEN COATES and RICHARD SILBURN

Certainly, in St Ann's, the condition of the houses bears immediately on the lives of the people. Englishmen widely believe in a thing they are pleased to call a 'private life'. You can live something like it in a commuter suburb, where if you have a blazing row with your wife, neighbours will only get to know about it if she tells them. Private lives require a sturdy minimum of investment in bricks and mortar: there are, for sure, numerous disadvantages in such private lives, but these are disadvantages which many people in St Ann's might well like to taste. In some of the streets of St Ann's nothing is personal unless it is whispered. The shape and structure of the houses project even the most individual activities into the social domain. If you go to the lavatory, you meet your neighbours in the yard. If you want to make love you may well feel it discreet to listen for your neighbour's snores before you start the bed-springs rattling. Even when the houses were brand new, they were suitable only for people who lived very similar lives, and whose conduct varied very little from a fairly restrictive norm. Eccentricities of behaviour are immediately noticeable in such places. Badly insulated, they transmit noise, smells, heat, cold, and personal secrets with complete impartiality. This is true of well-maintained houses in St Ann's as well as decrepit ones, but openness to the wind and rain do not mitigate the difficulties of life under such conditions.

All these deprivations add up. Their sum is back-breaking toil and hardship. And these pains are suffered in houses that are too

*Source*: Ken Coates and Richard Silburn, *Poverty: the Forgotten Englishmen* (Penguin, 1970).

small, too densely concentrated together; houses that are in various
stages of dilapidation and decay; houses that lack the basic
amenities taken for granted by most people. You get dirty in St
Ann's quite easily, but it is hard to get clean. It is often damp. It is
often cold. It is never easy to make it dry and warm. Any one of
these drawbacks would, on its own, constitute at least a serious
irritation, but a combination of all of them, compounded in so many
cases by material poverty, becomes well-nigh intolerable. The
heaviest burden falls upon the housewives, whose task it is to raise
their families in these circumstances. The one thing that makes
decent family life possible in these unpromising environments is
stark drudgery; the role of the wife and mother involves an endless
round of unremitting, indeed, heart-breaking, but thankless,
labour. Such toil could easily be made unnecessary if a little social
effort and investment could be applied. The household linen hang-
ing on the clothes-line stretched across the backyard is certainly
clean and white when it is first put on the line to dry. The children's
clothes are clean before they go to play in the street. The municipal
wash-house, with its heavy ranks of steel basins, its fantastic sculp-
ture of steaming pipes, and its forbidding scales of drying racks, is,
seen from St Ann's, a vital addition to the local amenities. Seen
from outside, it is a symbol of the housewives' enslavement. But this
dichotomy is, itself, a great deal of the trouble in St Ann's. Things
can appear to have a different significance if you view them from a
different vantage-point.

Human beings are almost infinitely adaptable, and provided that
they are ill-treated consistently, they are apt to regard ill-treatment
as 'natural'. If the lavatory leaks a little, and always has leaked a
little, one comes to regard the leak as 'normal'. If the roof blows off
such a lavatory, of course one will expect to be annoyed. But all the
myriad petty discomforts can too easily be borne with remarkably
little complaint. Damp, cold, rot, decrepitude are as 'natural' in St
Ann's as is the smoky atmosphere: for all most people know, they
have been sent by Providence and must be endured. Indeed, since
Providence has never sent anything else, what other response would
be possible? Only *exceptional* damp, *unusual* cold, *excessive* rot, and
decrepitude to the point of collapse are felt to be legitimate subjects
of discussion. If you hang your washing out in the yard to dry,
normally it will be attacked by numerous little black smuts: you will
not normally complain. But when a particularly sulphurous bath of

smuts burns holes in all your clothes while they are on the line, then you will complain. In the same way people mute their criticisms of what others would regard as intolerable housing amenities. This, and not a fear of exaggeration, is the hazard we have to be aware of when interpreting the remarks of the people of St Ann's about these housing conditions.

While this complex of overcrowding and decay colours the lives of all who live in St Ann's, it has a special significance for those who are in poverty as well. Everyone finds necessary household maintenance and repairs an unwelcome financial burden, but for the poorer such expenses may be quite nightmarish. Indeed, here one can detect a good example of how rich one has to be to be poor: precisely because a poor family cannot afford expensive but once-and-for-all repairs (assuming such repairs to be feasible), household maintenance must either be neglected, or undertaken in a cheap but piecemeal fashion, where any improvement is partial and temporary in its effect. In the long run, of course, not only is this inefficient, but it costs more than the single, substantial investment. To neglect maintenance, however, is only to shift the burden from one part of the household budget to another. An ill-fitting window-frame which lets in draughts and damp will, during the passage of a season, considerably inflate the heating bill. To fight dirt costs more if you have only a gas stove on which to heat water. The cost of hot water is reduced in relation to the capital expenditure which can be undertaken, so that an efficient boiler system is more costly to install than a simple immersion heater, but cheaper to run. To lack even the rudiments of a hot-water system is to pay more per pint of hot water than anyone else has to pay. To fight damp when it is constantly present means laying out vast sums of money on coal or coke, which become more expensive because small quantities have to be purchased for want of ready money to meet large bills. To air clothes when there is no airing cupboard is not only a chore, but an expensive one, while to fail to air all the unworn clothes is frequently to write them off to mildew. This was vividly illustrated in one household we visited where the bedroom was so damp that clothes stored in the cupboard had to be removed daily and spread on a clothes-horse in front of the fire to dry out. The man who lived there showed us why this was necessary; he produced a pair of trousers mouldered beyond recall, obviously now only suitable for the dirtiest of tasks. These trousers had fallen from their hanger, and had laid unnoticed in the wardrobe bottom for a damp week. To buy food for a day at a time because there is no pantry in which to store it is to meet higher bills at corner stores than would be involved in larger purchases from supermarkets. It would be valuable, if people had the spare cash, to line damp rooms with some form of insulating material before wallpapering them: for want of that small capital outlay, they may spend more on frequent re-decoration than they otherwise might have saved: but since the outlay in papering a room three times a year is piecemeal, it is possible, while root-and-branch solutions to the problem are not. The less you have, the more you need to spend. Low wages are conjoined, in this picture, with atrociously bad houses in which money is eaten away far more voraciously than would ever be thought conceivable in suburbia.

The expense of necessary heating and drying is not only considerable, but is ultimately hopeless – it is not a tax which in any way augments a person's living standards, but, like protection money, merely staves off for a little longer an absolute loss. Yet the poorest and neediest must spend substantial proportions of their scant resources in these negative, and, it should surely be added, demoralizing, ways.

To be poor is to pay more, and to pay more often. And there is no slum problem which is not at the same time a poverty problem. The conventional image, still current in some quarters, of the rehoused poor 'putting coal in the bath' is very sour in St Ann's, because for all too many people it might be nice to have the option of putting the coal they can't afford in the baths they haven't got.

# III

# Women and Education Policy

# Introduction

It is almost at the level of cliché to make the point that education at school is, outside the family, the most important means by which children are socialised. At the same time, in a society based, in theory at least, on ideas of social mobility and achievement, education is also a means whereby individual children are given the intellectual resources to travel upwards in class terms and outwards in environmental terms. Thus education, like health care and social security, is both an important means of transmitting ideology and, at the same time, constitutes an important resource for individual children. Within all the social services, but especially within education, it is often necessary to argue for increased access to the material resource of the service while simultaneously suggesting that there are aspects of the service, particularly the ideology transmitted by it, which one deplores (see Sections I and IV). Much of the literature on women and education tends to make this kind of distinction, arguing *both* for greater equality of access for girls *and* for changes in what are claimed to be inherently sexist curricula and values put over in school.

However, unlike social security and, to a lesser extent, health care, education comes differently packaged for different kinds of children. In other words, individual children have very different educational experiences, both at an ideological and at a resource level. In this country much of that experience is differentiated along class lines: crudely, the very well-off use the predominantly single-sex public and boarding school system to accustom their children to an elite future, and the middle class ensure that their neighbourhood state school reinforces the values of their children's socialisation at home and that, in a streamed system, their children are all in the higher streams; meanwhile, working-class children are largely concentrated in the less well-resourced state schools, are often in the lower streams, and are frequently regarded by their teachers and even encouraged to think of themselves as 'no-hopers'. But class is not the only basis on which education is differentially packaged. As Rosemary Deem makes clear in the article reproduced here, deliberate and formal distinctions between the education of boys and girls have been made until very recently and only brought formally to a halt through the 1975 Sex Discrimination Act. Until that legislation came into force, boys and girls were often deliberately taught different curricula such that boys more often took 'academic' subjects while girls took 'vocational' subjects, and girls were sometimes formally limited in their access to further and higher education by the operation of quotas (e.g. at medical schools). The result of both explicit and covert discrimination was that boys were far more likely to succeed at public examinations and to enter higher and further education (Wilkin, 1982).

Sex discrimination legislation in itself probably does little to alter the balance between boys' and girls' achievement, or bring their curricula nearer together. The legislation was introduced as part of a more general swing in the climate of opinion which has almost certainly contributed to changes that have taken place in the recent past: girls' achievement, while still below that of boys', has nevertheless begun to catch up. For example, in the mid-1960s less than a third of the students at university were girls; that figure has now risen to over 40 per cent and is probably still rising (Blackstone, 1983). Nevertheless, the class factor remains important: according to Wilkin, women undergraduates are more likely to be from the middle class than men (Wilkin, 1982).

There are, however, broad brush constraints, many of them policy-determined, which tend to counteract these other progressive changes. Deem gives the example of cuts in teacher training, which had the effect of reducing the opportunities that had previously been available to large numbers of girls who had been considered by their teachers to be, as they put it to Michelle Stanworth, 'not university material'. Women are much less likely to read science subjects than men (Wilkin, 1982), and this is a severe disadvantage at a time when government is determined to push teaching and research resources into sciences while simultaneously cutting back severely in the social sciences and the humanities. The reductions in university places, just at the time when girls are beginning to gain something like equal access, may have the effect of decreasing the absolute numbers of girls in universities even if they manage to catch up with boys proportionally.

Deem's concern is to explain these policy changes and to place them within their economic and political context. Not only does economic change ultimately determine social policy change, but also, she suggests, there are particular features of capitalism and the labour market within it that are dependent on the promotion of a particular ideology about women. The education system is an important tool in the promotion of that ideology, and as ideological needs alter so, she argues, do the values taught in school. (For a critique of Deem's emphasis on the relations of capital rather than those of patriarchy, see Nava, 1980). But can policy change be translated quite so well and quickly into the schools? Deem herself acknowledges that the match between policy decisions made at one level of government and what actually happens in the classroom may be less than perfect. In an earlier part of the article, which is not reproduced here, she says:

> just as policy has to be interpreted by local authorities and individual schools, so ideologies have to be translated into specific policies and practices, and this may lead to inconsistencies. Hence, for example, in the case of the educational system, we should not assume that dominant ideologies about women necessarily give rise to uniform practices in schools and amongst teachers.

As with all the social services, it would be foolish to assume that executors of policy on the ground are always the obedient poodles of those who think up grand designs. Be they housing visitors, social workers, doctors, or, as in this case, teachers, all these personnel will have ideas which do not necessarily conform to the views prevailing within higher echelons of power. Often the executors of policy will be resistant to change and conservative in their outlook, stoutly defending views that went 'out of fashion' some considerable time ago. The piece extracted from Michelle Stanworth's study of classroom interaction partly demonstrates this inherent conservatism. The teachers appear to operate a very rigid model of the dual labour market and seem to make no effort to encourage their girl pupils to struggle against it; on the contrary, they take positive steps to encourage passivity in the face of obstacles. Nevertheless, the converse may also be true: where increasingly conservative views prevail at the more central locations of political power, it is still possible for individual teachers to take a more liberal and even radical stance. The development of women's studies courses in higher and further education, despite a context of severe cutbacks, is an important example of how highly motivated teachers can act with some considerable independence (Thompson, 1983).

Perhaps the most important lesson to be learnt from Stanworth's study is the way in which teachers, often quite unconsciously, impose sex-role stereotypes on their pupils in such a way that girls, again quite unconsciously, absorb a sense of their own inferiority and are rendered, literally, anonymous and invisible. This so-called 'hidden curriculum' is claimed by many feminists to be at least as important in child development as the formal curriculum (see, for example, Byrne, 1978), and has been subject to intensive study (e.g. Spender and Sarah, 1980). Overcoming such discrimination is difficult, particularly if many teachers – women as well as men – are unaware of what they do. A start might be made by women teachers coming to recognise how they themselves are subjected to sex-role stereotyping in the educational hierarchy, and by making links between their own position and that of their girl pupils. But a handful of feminist teachers are hardly likely to have a radical effect on the entire educational milieu. Indeed, Valerie Hannon suggests that there is little point in trying to tackle the 'hidden curriculum' since 'our potential to change [it] . . . is very slight' (Hannon, 1976, p. 113). Instead she suggests that the content of the formal curriculum should be entirely overhauled: 'for girls to become a more powerful group, they must be given some understanding of females' past powerlessness . . . in other subject areas, like English literature, social studies, art, biology and – where it is taught – psychology, there is a similar need to examine what girls are learning about women's abilities and potential, and therefore what they should (realistically) expect for themselves' (Hannon, 1979, p. 115).

It (almost) goes without saying that all curricula, whether at primary school level or at universities, should be similarly scrutinised and overhauled. This book, along with all the other recent publications that have attempted to insert women into the knowledge taught within educational institutions (e.g. Spender, 1981), is part of that effort. But all these books will almost exclusively be read within the context of the largely middle-class institutions of further and higher education. For women of all social classes to be further liberated, *both* access to those institutions *and* the content of what is taught there should be increasingly woman-centred in order to gain the ground that until now has been very largely occupied by men.

**Additional reading**

Two important books not mentioned in this introduction are Miriam David's *The State, the Family and Education* (1980), and Rosemary Deem, *Women and Schooling* (1978), both written within a Marxist perspective. *Gender, Class and Education*, a collection edited by Stephen Walker and Len Barton (1983), contains a number of useful articles on the interaction between class and gender in education and, in particular, has an interesting discussion by Madeleine Arnot of the feminist issues surrounding co-education and single sex schooling – an issue which, for reasons of space, I have not been able to refer to in this section.

# State Policy and Ideology in the Education of Women 1944–1980

## ROSEMARY DEEM

### The 1944 Education Act and after

The 1944 Education Act, in theory, was supposed to widen the educational chances of the working classes through the provision of free secondary education for all. In practice, as Halsey, Heath and Ridge (1980) have recently shown, this has not been the case even for working-class boys. For working- and middle-class girls, the benefits have been even smaller. This is not surprising, as the Norwood Report in 1943 stressed the importance of relating boys' education to the labour market, but emphasised that girls' schooling must relate to their eventual place in the family. Despite the demonstration, for instance, by conservative researchers like Douglas (1967) that after 1944 girls in primary schools consistently demonstrated their academic superiority over boys, there is little evidence that this superiority followed girls into their secondary school. There are a number of possible explanations for girls' superior primary school performance. First, the kinds of academic skills important in primary schools – especially reading and writing – are those for which girls' earlier family socialisation may have prepared them better. As the Newsons' researches on child-rearing demonstrate (Newson and Newson, 1968, 1976) young female children are more likely to be encouraged by their parents to remain indoors, to talk to adults (especially their mothers), to be unadventurous. Secondly, primary schools have a much more 'familial'

Source: extracted from Rosemary Deem, 'State Policy and Ideology in the Education of Women, 1944–1980', *British Journal of Sociology of Education*, Vol. 2, No. 2, 1981, pp. 131–43.

atmosphere than secondary schools; there is a predominance of female teachers, an emphasis on pastoral care, 'family-group' learning, and less emphasis on cognitive development and formal academic skills. Thirdly, primary schools tend to have little formal curricular differentiation between the sexes, except in physical education (Plowden Report, 1967). Furthermore, in the period after 1944 when selection for secondary schools through the 11 + examination predominated, girls' 11 + performances were weighted differently to boys' performances so that girls achieved fewer places than their examination results indicated, and boys achieved more places than their results merited. So girls in many areas had less chance of a grammar or technical school place than boys. And even where girls were successful in obtaining grammar school places, they were much more likely, as the 1959 Report on Early Leaving showed, to leave at age 15, before any public examinations had been taken, thus losing one of the 'benefits' of a grammar school education. Further, as Byrne (1975) has shown, the allocation of resources in secondary schools quickly took on a pattern which favoured boys rather than girls, with limited provision of science and technical subject facilities in mixed schools, and minimal provision of these in girls schools.

Although there was a great deal of debate about education after 1944, much of it up to 1951 focused on the eradication of class differences, not gender differences, in an endeavour to build a more buoyant economy and develop a substantial welfare state. Similarly, social policy continued to emphasise the importance of motherhood and the family, even though women had begun to enter production industry in large numbers during the war, and despite a post-war increase in the numbers of married women doing paid work. So, for example, many of the nurseries opened during the Second World War were closed down after the war. Hence women's domestic role continued to be stressed both ideologically and in state policies, so that where women did engage in waged labour, they did so primarily in low-paid, unskilled jobs.

**Upskilling and dual roles for women 1951–1963**

By the early 1950s, the period of post-war reconstruction was coming to an end, rationing had ceased, wages were beginning to rise, and people were being encouraged to spend more money.

Increased numbers of women were already working in manufacturing industry, and by the mid-1950s the process of 'upskilling' had
begun in other sectors of the labour market. This process meant that
more and more of available jobs were said to require higher
technical skills or educational qualifications, and it also altered the
context in which debates about education were taking place, because the economy increasingly demanded labour power in the
secondary and tertiary sectors. Other debates and ideologies,
originating both from state apparatuses and from capital, talked of
affluence and a consumer spending boom, and more education was
seen as part of the route to yet greater affluence. Hence the
participation of women in the labour market was both 'allowed' by
the concerns with economic growth and made more possible by the
improved educational opportunities offered to women. Changes in
family size with the increased availability of contraception also
enabled greater number of married women to enter or re-enter paid
work. At the same time, the welfare state and associated social
services continued to grow, and relieved women of some of their
former domestic responsibilities.

But despite greater participation by women in the workforce,
ideological emphases on women's place in the home remained
strong, albeit tinged with some acceptance of women's secondary
place in the labour market. The Birmingham Feminist History
Group (1979) have argued that although notions of women's
equality were important in the 1950s, nevertheless: 'Ideologies
about women in the fifties are underpinned by the notion of equal
but different – men and women have their special spheres; and
women bring different qualities' (p. 150). And the notion of
women's dual roles (paid work and the family) was overwhelmingly
applied only to middle-class women. So, for instance, the Crowther
Report of 1959 on the education of 15–18-year-olds talked about
the likelihood that middle-class girls would combine a career with
motherhood and marriage and the necessity for them to receive an
education which prepared them for this future dual role. A similar
argument was presented in the 1963 Robbins Report on higher
education, although it was couched in terms which spoke of untap-
ped pools of ability (women and the working class) who could be
drawn into higher education if more places were available. Robbins
also related to the upskilling debate – the expansion of education
and the high birth rate of the immediate post-war period, for

example, had given rise to a shortage of qualified teachers especially in primary schools, and changes in the numbers of white-collar jobs available to women had also given rise to a demand for better qualified and certificated female labour.

However, for working-class girls the emphasis within education remained largely on the preparation for marriage and a family, with little account being taken of their equally likely long-term participation in the labour market. Certainly a slight shift of emphasis was taking place during this time – so that, for instance, it was recognised in the Crowther Report that girls might need to be aware of scientific and technological developments, but, it was assumed, in different ways and for different reasons from boys. The 1963 Newsom Report on 'average' and 'below average' child says this in a most emphatic way:

A boy is usually excited by the prospect of a science course ... he experiences a sense of wonder and power. The growth of wheat, the birth of a lamb, the movement of clouds, put him in awe of nature: the locomotive he sees as man's response: the switch and throttle are his magic wands ... the girl may come to the science lesson with a less eager curiosity than the boy, but she too will need to feel at home with machinery. (Newsom Report, p. 142)

## Social democracy and the comprehensive school 1964 – 1970

This period, under the banner of a social democratic ideology, having its roots in the increased economic growth and general affluence of Harold Macmillan's 'never had it so good' ethos in the previous period, but also in the contradictions this brought about, saw a massive extension of the social services, intended to attack the structural roots of inequality and poverty, which had interestingly been 'rediscovered' despite the country's apparent wealth. However, this extension of the welfare state was double-edged, because as well as offering services it also involved a measure of control over those who were the recipients of those services. The state reforms of the 1960s arose both from working-class and union pressures but also from capital itself, anxious to restructure Britain's economy in the face of greater overseas competition, industrial disputes and falling profits (Gough, 1980). Partly because of the pressures from capital, there were, as Jessop (1980) notes, no moves to redistribute income, which might have effectively attacked class inequalities; instead welfare services were used as palliatives. Consequently, Jessop argues, the extension of the welfare state had no effects on deprivation but rather encouraged the politicisation of various groups in urban areas, for example squatters, tenants' rights and welfare rights groups. It should also be recognised that the emerging women's movement of the late 1960s was part of this politicisation process.

In education there was during the 1960s a gradual shift towards comprehensive secondary schooling partly prompted by a (false) belief that such schooling would help eradicate the worst inequalities (class, not gender) of the tripartite system, as shown by researchers in the sociology of education (see Finn, Grant and Johnson, 1978). But this shift was also brought about by an apparent consensus about education in the country as a whole. The growth of the comprehensives brought with it a significant expansion in the curriculum content of secondary schooling, which should have been helpful to girls, except that in many schools expansion meant typing or shorthand or child-care for girls, and quite different subjects for boys. For working-class girls (unlike middle-class girls, for whom comprehensives potentially offered them the academic education denied to many under the systems of 11 + weighting) comprehensives probably made little difference. The Labour government's priority from 1964 onwards was the servicing of the economy in response to demands made on them by capital; in so far as working-class girls could have contributed to this, it would have been only in those unskilled jobs for which greater or better education was not required. Hence, one of the potentially most damaging consequences of the shift to comprehensives – the closing or amalgamating of many single-sex schools – passed almost unnoticed. Yet as Shaw (1980) has argued the assumption that mixed schooling is preferable on academic grounds is not well supported by educational research. R. R. Dale's (1969, 1971, 1974) three-volume study focuses mainly on the social advantages, and it is possible in any case to challenge the nature of the superior social development of girls which is argued to accompany mixed rather than single-sex schooling, since one of the things it may involve is breaking down girls' resistance to the imposition of various stereotypes of femininity to a greater extent than is found in single-sex schools.

Recent research (DES, 1975, and Fairhall, 1979) suggests that girls' academic achievements are higher and that they are more likely to make untypical choices of subjects (physics, chemistry, etc.) in single than in mixed-sex schools. Furthermore, as Shaw (1980) suggests, in a mixed school, boys may use girls as a negative reference group for their own academic performance, with consequent effects on girls' own performance.

In primary schooling the Plowden Report of 1967 found little existence of overt sex discrimination or differentiation in the curriculum except in games. But it is clear that Plowden relied heavily on examining the form rather than the content of schooling (and even then missed many of the subtler forms of discrimination). Otherwise it might have paid attention to the representations of girls and women found in many primary school texts. In any case the apparent absence of discrimination in primary schooling seemed, on the evidence of Benn and Simon (1970), not to follow through into the secondary school. Those writers found that over half the comprehensive schools studied by them restricted some subjects to one sex only. In the absence of any DES or local state guidance to the contrary on this, such restriction is unsurprising, because of limited resource provision in many schools for craft and science subjects (Byrne, 1975). This period did, however, see some improvements in the educational opportunities available to women who had already left school. For example, the establishment of the Open University (Griffiths, 1980); and the provision of special training or refresher courses for married women taking up or returning to teaching. Nevertheless, the intentions behind these policies almost certainly owed more to the demands of the labour market than to any notion of women's rights.

Nevertheless, the 1960s represented a continuation of the shift begun in the 1950s towards ideologies about women and related state policies which recognised the increasing role being played by women in the sphere of wage labour. And as the Birmingham Feminist History Group (1979) recognise, the tensions of women's dual roles which were accepted in the 1950s were increasingly being challenged in the early 1960s as more and more women experienced the difficulties and problems of being both wage workers and wives/mothers, and as the development of the contraceptive pill started to decrease the possibility of unwanted pregnancies. By the late 1960s those challenges to the predominance of women's role in the family over their role in the labour market were being made more strongly by a new feminist movement in Britain, and the ground was being well-prepared for the passage in 1970 of the Equal Pay Act (even though this was to take six years to implement).

## 1970–1974: the breakdown of consensus about education and the decline of social democracy

Even before the election of a Conservative government to power in 1970, an attack had begun to be mounted by the Right against many of the educational policies of the Labour Party. As Finn *et al.* (1978) says: 'during the late 1960s, the Right came to identify education as an important causal factor in the "moral crisis" of the period' (p. 188), and so began to attack comprehensive schools for failing to maintain standards of literacy and numeracy. This was only part of a more general move to cut welfare expenditure and restructure social relations. From 1970 onwards the new Conservative administration concentrated its efforts on undoing much of what Labour had done in the field of social policy, but also focused much of its educational policy on returning 'freedom of choice' to that small minority of parents whose children might go to a grammar school. Signs of an economic crisis were increasingly present, and the previous open encouragement of married women to leave the home for the labour market rapidly disappeared. The Equal Pay Act was also encouraging employers not to employ women or to regrade their work, so that it was no longer comparable to men's work. This gave an indication of the kinds of policies that might be adopted with regard to the education (or non-education) of women. No overt moves were made either to increase or decrease the amount of discrimination faced by women in schooling, but David (1980) argues that the James Report (1972) on Teacher Training suggested changes which in practice would disadvantage women student teachers and women teachers. For example, the Report recommended that the first cycle of teacher training might take place in polytechnics (already heavily male-dominated institutions) and in universities and further education colleges where there were still far fewer females than in the traditional colleges for training teachers (which were a female stronghold in higher education). Also, David continues, although the Report made provision for the retraining of married women returners, it did so in a context which assumed that child rearing was of no relevance to a career in teaching, and that years so spent were wasted. This view presents an interesting contrast to the then prevalent assumption that (primary) school teaching was an extension of women's role in the home. Similarly, the 1973 Russell Report on Adult Education noted that women were prominent students in adult education institutions, but neither adequately considered why this was so nor made special recommendations about how adult education provision for women might be improved and made more accessible to them.

If the previous Labour administration had only been dimly aware of the importance of redressing women's inequalities, the Conservative administration of 1970–74 was even less aware of the problem. It was preoccupied with the problems of capital accumulation and deteriorating relationships between capital and the working class, and state intervention in the economy increased. But women were seen to play only a minor role in that economy, even though this misrepresented their actual participation and despite the existence of an increasingly powerful feminist movement and greater general discussion of women's oppression in society. And women's education gained only a low priority. Hence when in 1973 the Conservatives grudgingly introduced a Green Paper on sex discrimination in public life (pressurised by the House of Lords and a private member's bill) the proposed legislation did not even cover education.

## Discrimination legislation without action, and the collapse of social democracy 1974–1979

This period presented the Labour Government of 1974–79 with quite serious problems in respect of its educational policies, not only in terms of the mounting attack on educational standards by the Tories but also because of the deepening economic crisis, which meant that education could not continue to be expanded but indeed had to be cut back, as had many other parts of the welfare state. Yet at the same time it was responsible for the passage of a Sex Discrimination Act (at the end of 1975) which was to be applicable to education. However, no resources were to be made available to remedy existing discrimination. The Sex Discrimination Act did not in any case promise to be very useful in relation to education. As well as a cumbersome procedure for complaints involving the County Courts rather than tribunals, it focused mainly on ending discrimination in entry to mixed schools and on direct discrimination in the kinds of courses offered to pupils, without considering other elements of the form of schooling or, for example, the whole issue of how gender and gender relations are represented in the curriculum. The record of the EOC in education has also been a poor one, showing reluctance to tackle the major areas of discrimination which might involve real political confrontation, rather than the contained disputes of the courts which have the advantage of a patriarchal hierarchy. The Great Debate of 1976/77, which may be seen as a response to what Finn *et al.* (1978) call the breakdown of educational consensus, did certainly consider the issue of women's education, and discuss the importance of preparing both boys and girls for roles in both the home and the labour-market, but in the absence of any positive follow-up to this in terms of actual educational policy changes, the Debate remained a not very effective exercise in democratic participation to which few people were actually invited. And it is certainly apparent that the Great Debate was primarily concerned with questions of educational standards and the relation between schools and working life rather then with gender and gender relations within schools or outside them. And even in relation to the discussion about preparing children for life there was no adequate consideration of the failure of many schools to prepare *girls* for wider forms of social, economic and political participation. Since the period from 1976 marked also an ideological shift towards emphasis on the importance of family, the general reluctance to implement non-discriminatory policies in schools is not surprising. The strengthening of the family was seen as a way of re-establishing and re-structuring social relationships in a period of economic and social as well as political uncertainty. And women's position as domestic labourers and rearers of children within a restrengthened family was seen as of crucial importance.

Hence even in the attempts to deal with the increasingly serious problems of youth unemployment, the schemes offered both in the Job Creation Programme and in the Youth Opportunities Programme which superseded it, made no recognition of the fact that the often inferior schooling of girls rendered them as much in need of help in entering the labour market as boys, if for different reasons.

The EOC report on the Job Creation Programme in 1978 showed that on all schemes girls formed a minority. And the failure to recognise the entry of girls into the labour market as a problem for education as much for other agencies was made apparent in the consultative paper on *Education and Training for 18 year olds* (DES, 1979) published early in 1979, which made no mention of the special needs for girls.

Reductions in public expenditure during Labour's period of office hit women's education particularly hard, as if to underline further the inconsistencies between the existence of legislation against sex discrimination and specific policies of different state apparatuses upholding that discrimination. Teacher training received one of the largest cuts at a time when it was still one of the major avenues for women's higher education, especially in certain geographical regions (many women are not as mobile as men and cannot travel as far for their post-school education). Reductions in adult education provision (in some cases complete closure) also affected women more than men. For women are the largest consumers of adult education. And the virtual ending in many areas of discretionary grants for post-compulsory education also reduced the opportunities and financial independence which might otherwise have been afforded to some women. The break-up of the social democratic settlement adversely affected the working classes as a whole, but women in particular. But at the end of this period attempts to eradicate gains already made by women were still being heavily resisted, particularly by the feminist movement.

**The dawn of Thatcherism 1979–1980**

The election of a Tory government in 1979 brought many changes in both policies and ideology, since Thatcherism combines an authoritarian populism appealing to national rather than class interests with a return to nineteenth-century liberalism and an emphasis on the responsibility of individuals. As Gough (1980) notes, a central feature of Thatcherist policy has been an attack on the welfare state and an attempt to return to the private sector many aspects of education, housing, health care and other social services. The alarming rise in unemployment figures as firms feel the effects of high interest rates ... has gone side by side with the attempt to make individuals less dependent on state services. In education, policy has concentrated on selective and private schooling, the curriculum, parental choices and school meals. Moves to project or increase women's educational opportunities are unlikely; the Tory party see itself as a staunch defender of the family unit (Mrs Thatcher said at the Tory Party Conference in 1977, 'We are the party of the family', *The Guardian*, 21 March 1980, p. 12) and various Tory spokespersons have made clear the view that women's real place is in the home, not in paid employment or public life. For example, Patrick Jenkin – Social Services Secretary – said in a BBC Radio 4 discussion early in 1980: 'the balance between the national needs for women's directly productive work and the need for them to look after their family is now shifting' (quoted in Barker and Downing, 1980, p. 97).

It is also clear that the existence of 'token women' in the Conservative Party administration offers no encouragement to other women to follow in their footsteps. So, for instance, Jill Knight, Conservative MP for Edgbaston, argues that a strong country is based on the cohesion of the family unit and that women should see staying at home to maintain that cohesion as their primary occupation (Knight, 1980) and sees no contradiction between this advice and her own very different political career.

So we may expect a gradual return to the education of women for domestic labour, emphasis on the importance of motherhood to the economy and the reproduction of 'suitable' labour power (i.e. that which is prepared to accept low wages and discipline) as the need for women's paid work outside the family evaporates. In many areas, girls leaving school will have little possibility of entering employment at all; if they do find jobs, especially in manufacturing, clerical or secretarial work, it is likely that the microchip will soon begin to eat away at that employment. But the state's apparatuses attempt to hide the gravity of the economic situation from women by ideological emphases on motherhood, women's place in the home, and the family, which mask the real problems facing women (an increasing burden of care of the sick, children and the elderly as welfare services contract, few adult education chances remaining, high male and female unemployment rates, competition between women and men for jobs, the attacks on women's control of their own fertility). Most of the advances achieved by women since 1944, both inside and outside education, have occurred in periods of full employment and in the context of social democratic policies and ideology; the treatment of women in education has been closely linked to other social policies and to prevalent ideologies about women's roles. We are already witnessing a return to the ideologies of motherhood which Davin (1978) noted were so prevalent at the turn of the century when the value of a numerically strong and healthy population to British imperialism was heavily emphasised.

The present situation, in which welfare provisions and expenditure on social policies are being drastically cut back at the same time as the central importance of women's domestic and child-caring role in the family is being re-emphasised, is one in which women can clearly no longer rely on the apparatuses of the state to make moves directed at securing their equality and alleviating aspects of their oppression. The present political and economic situation seems to necessitate the organisation of women on a broader political front (with the whole labour movement, for instance) than is possible solely through the feminist movement. This might enable women to tackle not only questions about the centrality of the family to society and the kinds of roles which women should play outside and inside the home, and about motherhood versus parenthood, but also to raise equally fundamental questions about the social and economic threats posed by mass labour-market unemployment and the implications of divisions of labour in the home, the defects of monetarism as a viable economic policy, ways in which the economy might be restructured, questions about law and order and about the quality of education in a period of drastic expenditure reductions. Such strategies might enable patriarchal ideologies and practices to be challenged and considered at the same time and in the same way as the ideologies and practices of state apparatuses. If such strategies are not adopted, then women are likely to bear more than their share of burdens imposed by authoritarian populism and monetarist economic policy because on them fall the care of the sick, the disabled, the old, the problems of replacing school meals, and the disappearance of part- and full-time work for women. Unless women are concerned to work towards the preparation of alternative non-capitalist and non-patriarchal economic and social policies (and this may mean under certain conditions working with men) at the same time as resisting the present direction of state policies and ideologies, then there is no possibility that the conditions for the emergence of a new political ideology, or new economic and social policies, will begin to be shaped in anything other than a patriarchal way. The important message which women both inside and outside formal education must grasp is that if they are both to safeguard existing gains for women in education and seek further change, they cannot confine their protests and political strategies solely to that sector of state affairs but must give their attention to many other aspects and concerns of state apparatuses, as well as to challenging the many capitalist and patriarchal structures which exist both inside and outside the spheres of state influence. Current ideologies and policies are such that challenging them is insufficient: women must also work towards alternative policies, not only for education, but for the whole society and its economy.

# 'Just Three Quiet Girls'

## MICHELLE STANWORTH

**Initial impressions of pupils: 'Just three quiet girls'**

In the early weeks of the academic year, teachers are faced with the arduous task of getting to know not just one, but several, groups of pupils; it is not surprising that it takes a while for the name and face of every pupil to be clearly linked in teachers' minds. What is remarkable is that the pupils who were mentioned by teachers as being difficult to place were, without exception, girls.

*Interviewer:* What were your first impressions of Emma?
*Male teacher:* Nothing really. I can only remember first impressions of a few who stood out right away; Adrian, of course; and Philip; and David Levick; and Marion, too, because among the girls she was the earliest to say something in class. In fact, it was quite a time before I could tell some of the girls apart.
*Interviewer:* Who was that?
*Teacher:* Well, Angie, and her friends Leonore and Helen. They seemed rather silent at first, and they were friends, I think, and there was was no way – that's how it seemed at the time – of telling one from the other. In fact, they are very different in appearance, I can see that now. One's fair and one's dark, for a start. But at the beginning they were just three quiet girls.
*Interviewer:* What were your first impressions of Lucy?
*Female teacher:* I didn't start teaching that class until a bit later, by

*Source*: Michelle Stanworth, *Gender and Schooling: a Study of Sexual Divisions in the Classroom* (Hutchinson, 1983).

which time my mind was dulled. Although I had seen them once a week, she hadn't made any impression on me at all. I didn't know which one she was. She was one of the people who it took me longest to cotton on to her name. She was one I got mixed up, actually, with Sharon, who was equally quiet and somewhat the same build. Now they're quite different, I realise, but at the time I was never quite sure which one it was.

*Interviewer:* So Lucy was very slow to make any impression at all, then?

*Teacher:* Well, a positive impression, yes. I won't say she made a negative impression, but ... well, you see the trouble is that that group had got more girls in it, which makes a difference. The other group had a lot of foreigners, and within a day or two I knew Belinda, who was the only foreign girl. And Dennis had curly hair and Tony had straight hair, so they were well fixed in. In fact, in that group there were only Lyn and Judith who took me a few days to get straightened out, and the rest I knew straight away. Whereas in this group, there were only seven boys and about ten girls, I suppose.

*Interviewer:* So you found it easiest to learn the names of the boys, did you?

*Teacher:* Yes, that's it.

As these quotations suggest, the anonymity of girls is due in part to their reticence. The girl who is mentioned as speaking out early is istantly 'fixed' by her teacher; she has, among the girls, a sort of rarity value. However, this cannot entirely explain the greater readiness with which teachers identify boys, for the few male pupils who were reported by their teachers to be exceptionally quiet in class were, nevertheless, clearly remembered. Teachers' slowness at identifying girls has strong implications for the comfort and involvement of female pupils for, as we shall see later on, pupils take it as a sign of approval if teachers know names right away.

## Advice and expectation

Teachers were asked what advice they would give to particular pupils if they were considering abandoning A levels either in order to get married, or to take a job. Many of the teachers refused to accept that marriage might imply an interruption of studies; as one woman exclaimed (perhaps drawing on her own experience in combining marriage and academic work), 'I don't know why you think marriage is such a disruptive activity!' For the rest of the teachers, the advice offered was often cautionary, and female pupils were warned against giving up A levels as often as males – although, as the first passage below indicates, some men were worried that to advise a girl against early marriage might be taken as a slur on her character.

*Male teacher:* Don't do it. I would say, 'Don't do it.' Don't get me wrong, she could certainly cope with marriage, she wouldn't be an inept housekeeper or a child-beater or anything like that. But if she could get her qualifications before she took all that on, I'd say stay.

*Male teacher:* If Sheila's getting married meant giving up her chance of getting A levels, I'd say it would be disastrous.

*Male teacher:* I'd probably tell Howard the story of my life, how easy it was to get married and how difficult it was to get back. I would remind him of the disadvantages.

*Female teacher:* I think I'd say that nowadays, in her age group, half the marriages will end in divorce by the time they're thirty. And although she may have got a boyfriend whom she feels she's going to love for life, you don't know what's going to happen. I've told some of them in the past, that your husband may die (because accidents do happen!) and you'll have to support the family, and if you don't have two A levels it is much harder to start again.

Largely because of the steadier academic record of their female pupils, teacher were less likely to dissuade boys than girls from giving up A levels to take a job; only one teacher made the point that it might be more risky for girls in general to abandon their studies than for boys:

*Female teacher:* I think I would say no ... The type of jobs girls get offered are rather different from the ones boys get offered. It's likely to be a job lacking in prospects; and it's also quite a lot harder for girls to come back to academic study than it is for men.

The most important point to emerge from this section of the interviews is that teachers tended to find the questions much less credible for their male pupils than for their female ones. When asked about their male pupils, teachers commented that it was very unlikely the boy would contemplate leaving college for employment (in one-third of the cases) or for marriage (in one-half).

*Male teacher:* To take a job? Now? I don't think that's even conceivable. It's like having Alastair McMaster (a teacher noted for being very untrendy) announce he was off to join a rock group.
*Female teacher:* I'd be amazed. I can't imagine Ted thinking of marriage. He's definitely still got the schoolboy atmosphere. I don't think he'd have the kind of maturity to cope with a girl at this stage.
*Male teacher:* Well, it wouldn't arise, would it? Boys don't usually give up their studies when they get married, that's what girls are more inclined to do.

No equivalent comments were passed about girls. It appears that while teachers are equally concerned that girls and boys should avoid a disruption of study due to marriage, and more concerned to prevent the girls abandoning their studies for employment, teachers *expect* such disruptions more often from girls than from boys. In other words, teachers feel at least as strongly that girls should complete their A levels compared with boys; but they combine this with a lower expectation that girls will actually do so.

## Looking to the future

Teachers were asked to predict what each of their pupils might be doing two years, and five years, from the time of the interview. Boys – even those in danger of failing their examinations – were seen in jobs involving considerable responsibility and authority, the most frequent predictions being for civil service or management careers. One boy, for example, of whom his teacher had earlier said, 'His essays are bald, childlike and undeveloped; his statements are simple and naive', was expected to rise to head office:

*Female teacher:* I suppose he might be quite good at summing things up. I don't know quite whether local government or civil service, but I can't just see him pushing paper around. I can see him writing reports on things. Perhaps an information officer, or sales planning, or something like that; something in head office.

Marriage cropped up in teachers' predictions of boys' future only once, in the case of a pupil who was academically very weak, but in whom his teachers recognised exceptional personal qualities; they described him as having 'a warm streak, almost Mediterranean', and 'the gift of communication' (a reference to his sympathetic manner in face-to-face encounters, for he was reported not to speak in class). He alone among the boys is defined more in terms of his personality than his ability, and it may be no accident that he is the *only* boy for whom the future anticipated by his teachers includes marriage and parenthood.

*Male teacher:* I wonder if he's the kind of boy who will marry fairly young, once he's sure of his sexual self as it were.
*Female teacher:* I see him having a frightfully happy girlfriend who's terribly fond of him. So long as she's not ambitious, I think they'll be very happy. He would be a super father. I think children would adore having him for a father, thought I'm not immediately sure what he'd be doing to support his family.

By contrast, the occupations suggested for girls seldom ranged beyond the stereotype of secretary, nurse or teacher. These predictions do not match either the girls' academic standing or their own aspirations. For instance, the girl who is envisaged as a secretary in the following quotation is thought to be fully capable of getting a university degree, and is herself considering a career in law.

*Female teacher:* I can imagine her being a very competent, if somewhat detached, secretary. She looks neat and tidy, her work's neat and tidy, she's perfectly prompt at arriving. And she moves around with an air of knowing what she doing. She doesn't drift.
*Interviewer:* Why would she be a *detached* secretary?
*Teacher:* I can't imagine her falling for her boss at all! Or getting in a flap.
*Interviewer:* What about in five years' time?
*Teacher:* Well, I can see her having a family, and having them jolly well organised. They'll get up at the right time and go to school at

the right time, wearing the right clothes. Meals will be ready when her husband gets home. She'll handle it jolly well.

Another girl, who intends to qualify as a professional psychologist, is predicted, in five years' time to be at home with the children:

*Female teacher:* I don't know what she got in mind, but I can imagine her being a nurse. She's got a very responsible attitude to life. I don't know if nursing would be the best thing for her, but something like that, something which is demanding.

*Interviewer:* What about being a doctor, say?

*Teacher:* I don't think she has quite enough academic capacity for that, but she might go into teaching. A caring kind of vocation, that's what I see her in.

*Interviewer:* What about in five years' time?

*Teacher:* Obviously married. She's the sort of girl who could very easily be married in five years' time.

*Interviewer:* Would she be working then, do you think?

*Teacher:* She might. But she's the sort of girl, I think, to stay at home with the children. She's a caring person, as I said.

Remarks such as this indicate an implicit assumption that girls' capacities for efficiency and initiative will be channelled into nurturant or subordinate occupations (and, of course, into childcare and housework) rather than into other, less traditional spheres.

Marriage and parenthood figure prominently in teachers' visions of the futures of their *female* pupils: teachers volunteered that two-thirds of the girls would be married in the near future. The prediction of marriage was applied not only to girls whose academic record was unremarkable as here:

*Male teacher:* She is the sort of girl who might up and get married all of a sudden and kick over the traces.

*Interviewer:* You mean she might abandon her A levels?

*Teacher:* I'm not saying she would, but I wouldn't be surprised.

*Interviewer:* What do you imagine her doing in five years' time?

*Teacher:* Definitely married.

but also to girls who were considered to have outstanding academic capacity:

*Male teacher:* Well, I'd be surprised if she wasn't married.

*Interviewer:* Is she the sort of person you would expect to marry young?

*Teacher:* Well, not necessarily marry young, but let's see ... 16, 17, 18, 19 years old ... somewhere along the line, certainly. I can't see what she'd be doing apart from that.

In only one instance when teachers anticipated the future was the possibility of early marriage viewed regretfully, as a potential interruption to a girl's development:

*Male teacher:* I should like to see her doing some kind of higher education, and I wonder whether something in the HND line might be more suitable than a degree course.

*Interviewer:* Because it's slightly more practical?

*Teacher:* Yes. This is pure supposition, but it does seem to me that there is a practical vein in her. She successfully holds down a job in one of the chain stores. I can see her making a very great success of management, retail management, because I would have thought she would be very skilled at dealing with people. And though she's a little unsure of herself still, there is a vein of sureness in her. She wouldn't be taken aback by awkward situations, for instance.

*Interviewer:* What about in five years' time?

*Teacher:* Quite possibly early marriage, which I think would be a pity. Not because I'm against the institution of marriage, but because I think that an early marriage would prevent her from fully realising her potential.

Apart from the reaction to marriage, the preceding quotation is atypical of teachers' comments about their female pupils in other respects. First, it is the only prediction in which a management post was suggested for a girl. Second, the fact that a possible career was specified by a male teacher is itself unusual; in two-thirds of male teachers' discussions of female pupils, the girl could not be envisaged in any occupation once her education was complete. In some cases, it is almost as if the working lives of women are a mystery to men:

*Male teacher:* She would be competent enough to do a course at a university or polytechnic, though not necessarily the most academic course.

*Interviewer:* What sort of a course might suit her then?

*Teacher:* I can't say. I don't really know about jobs for girls.

*Male teacher:* She will probably go on to further or higher education. You'd know better than I what a young girl with an independent sort of mind might be doing in five years' time!

The type of futures teachers anticipate for girls seem to be related to classroom interaction in two important ways. First, teachers' views of 'women's work', and their emphasis upon the centrality of family in women's lives, are likely to make high achievement at A level seem less urgent for girls than for boys. To the extent that teachers underestimate the ambitions of their female pupils, they will be reluctant to make girls prime candidates for attention in the classroom. Second – and more pertinent to this study – it seems likely that the current dynamic of classroom interaction does nothing to undermine stereotypical views of appropriate spheres for women and men. The reports gathered here from both teachers and pupils indicate that (whatever girls may be like outside) they are in the classroom quieter, more diffident and less openly competitive than their male classmates. No matter how conscientious and capable female pupils are, they are perceived by their teachers to lack the authoritative manner and the assertiveness which many teachers seem to believe to be prerequisites of 'masculine' occupations.

This interpretation seems to be the best way of accounting for a curious anomaly in the teachers' predictions. One girl who is ranked as the top performer in both her main subjects, and who wants a career in the diplomatic service, is envisaged by her teacher as the 'personal assistant to somebody rather important'. In contrast, the girl with the poorest academic record is one of only two girls to be suggested for a job that is not in the traditional feminine mould. The comments made about these two pupils are reproduced below; they indicate that teachers attach a great significance to assertiveness in classroom situations.

*Interviewer:* And can you think ahead to five years' time, what Clare might be doing in five years' time?

*Female teacher:* I could possibly see her as a kind of committee-type person. She's not a forceful public speaker, you see. She says something rather quietly, and it's absolutely right. The people next to her take it in, but it doesn't have any impact if you see what I mean. I can imagine her as the personal assistant to somebody rather important, dealing with things very competently, and arranging things very competently, and giving ideas backwards and forwards and dealing with individual callers face to face. She's good at face-to-face things, or in small groups, rather than in large groups.

*Interviewer:* What about Alison in five years' time?

*Female teacher:* She could have a professional job of some sort, I think. I can imagine her in publicity or almost anything. She's got a strong presence, and she definitely makes an impression. She's pretty downright and forthright and forthcoming in her opinions. In fact, she is a very good stimulus in the group, though she does make some of the pupils feel a bit antagonistic.

It is, apparently, only when a girl's behaviour in class sharply contradicts the retiring feminine stereotype (a contradiction that may produce antagonism from classmates) that teachers are likely to imagine her in a career at odds with highly traditional expectations.

# IV

# Women and Health Care Policy

# Introduction

A central feature of the present wave of feminism is the focus on women's bodies and the control of their bodies by people – usually men – other than themselves. There are basically two areas of women's lives over which such control is exercised: their sexuality and their reproductive capacity. There are also a number of identified and legitimated people who exercise this control, and in so doing often have the backing of the law. Among them are husbands. For example, on marriage, a woman loses her right to deny her husband sexual access and, in law, rape within marriage does not exist. Moreover, in order to avoid legal action by irate husbands, doctors can insist that a married woman gets her husband's consent to her sterilisation (Coote and Gill, 1974). While many feminists have been concerned with wresting control of sexuality and reproduction away from husbands, modern feminism has also identified another group of authorities, who in developed secular societies in the late twentieth century, appear to exercise, on occasion, even more power over women's bodies than men in general or husbands in particular. These are the qualified medical practitioners, particularly those, such as gynaecologists and obstetricians, who specialise in dealing with women's reproductive capacity.

Early feminist commentary on the control of women by medical practitioners came largely from the United States (see, for example, Boston Women's Health Book Collective, 1971). Some of the American critique reflected the attributes of the American health care system: in particular the special effort by American obstetricians to undermine the practice of midwifery to such an extent that it amounted to the persecution of midwives (Ehrenreich and En-

149

glish, 1979) and the very great specialisation of health care that has been particularly encouraged by the financial organisation of American health care on a private basis (Fee, 1975). Nevertheless, despite differences in health care systems, similar critiques of medical practice developed in this country. The common argument of both British and American literature is threefold: first, that over the past one hundred and fifty years or so, doctors on both sides of the Atlantic have successfully 'medicalised' a number of human phenomena ranging from madness to childbirth, such that, supported by the law, doctors have now almost a complete monopoly over the management of these events. Critics argue that phenomena that are often socially determined rather than pathologically based, and which, in the case of menstruation, conception and childbirth, are wholly natural events for women, have been colonised by doctors who see these human milestones as providing rich pickings in terms of financial gain and professional power (Parry and Parry, 1976). The second and related feature of medical practice discussed in both the British and American literature is the development of the use of medical technology in medical practice. Commentators argue that technology alienates patients from their own bodies and is used by medical practitioners to mystify medical processes (Oakley, 1980; The Brighton Women and Science Group, 1980). Moreover, access to equipment and technological information is carefully regulated by medical practitioners in order to prevent subversion by rival professional groupings (Donnison, 1977). Thirdly, the division of labour in health care systems replicates the sexual division of labour that exists in all other areas of social and economic life (Stacey *et al.*, 1977): doctors are predominantly male, in authority, and endowed with scientifically based propensities to cure and thus forestall mortality; in contrast, nurses are predominantly female, subordinate, and endowed with no special properties other than those of nurturing which anyway come 'naturally' to women (Gamarnikow, 1978) and which, far from magically forestalling mortality, simply make the paths towards death or recovery more wholesome and comfortable. (See also Hearn's article in Section V for a discussion of all these points.)

Discussion of medicalisation, particularly with reference to the natural events of menstruation, conception and childbirth, has been a very important part of feminist critiques of social processes; it has also had practical import in that recently some British hospitals

have made efforts to reduce the amount of technological intervention once used habitually in childbirth. But this discussion has
tended to take place in something of a vacuum, since very little
reference is made to the organisation and financing of particular
health care systems within which this medicalisation takes place.
Given the level of generalisation at which the discussion of medicalisation is pitched, this is not really surprising. If, as Lesley Doyal
points out, doctors have often been identified by feminists as simply
'nasty', then it is immaterial what kind of health care system they
work in.

However, this lack of context can have unintended consequences: if the argument is taken to its logical conclusion, then it is
impossible to defend the National Health Service, since a health
care system which, because it is free, actually encourages people to
use it irrespective of their income simply spreads the 'nastiness' a bit
further. But this is probably taking the argument further than even
the most radical feminist might go. Given the fact that the NHS is a
major employer of women and that it, however inadequately,
relieves women of some of the burden of caring for dependants
informally at home (see Section VI), most feminists, of whatever
kind, accept that if one is going to have medical care at all, then it is
probably best organised along the lines of the British NHS. At least
the principle of being free at the point of consumption means that
the service is – in theory – available equally to all irrespective of
their sex, class, colour or creed.

Moreover it seems at least arguable that medical care is not
always bad for your health, nor does it always involve unnecessary
medicalisation of natural events and socially determined malaise. In
other words, medical care, as well as being a system for reproducing
patriarchal values and controlling women's sexuality, is also a
*resource*. The way in which access to that resource is organised and
financed is of crucial interest to women. Given their relatively low
incomes, a 'free' service makes resources available to many women
which they would not otherwise receive. Moreover, if a health care
system is based on private rather than public funding, then there are
particular incentives to the less scrupulous medical practitioners to
persuade their patients to undergo unnecessary medical procedures. This seems to have happened in the United States; there,
technological intervention in women's lives, including hormone
replacement therapy for the menopause, 'unnecessary' hysterec-

tomies for menstrual pain, and prophylactic breast removal, are among the more extreme demonstrations of incentives to medicalisation in a private health care system. But a publicly financed health care system can also generate problems for women: as Lesley Doyal points out in her article which is excerpted here, in such a system the state, within the limits staked out by medical claims to professional autonomy, has a very direct means of controlling women's reproductive capacity.

The articles selected here are designed to illustrate some of these points and to spark off others. I have concentrated on the topic of abortion because it seems to me to bring together a great many issues. By successfully medicalising a relatively simple procedure, doctors have gained considerable professional power (Bart, 1981). In its turn, by legitimating this power through the law, the state has handed over to doctors enormous control over women's sexuality and life-chances. At the same time, by legalising abortion within the context of a 'free' health care system, the state has made possible free abortion, not quite on demand, but dependent on the discretion of two doctors, both of whom *may* be willing to respond to women's demands rather than regulate and restrict their choices (Greenwood and King, 1981). On the other hand, in a 'free' system where price does not act as a direct allocator of scarce resources, doctors have acquired very great power as 'gatekeepers' to the resource of a bed in a gynaecology ward; in order to restrict access, they operate, as Sally McIntyre demonstrates, all sorts of sex and class stereotypes to distinguish the 'deserving' from the 'undeserving', and those who really 'need' the service from those who, because they are perceived as quasi married, do not really 'need' it. Idiosyncratic factors such as the religious belief of local consultant gynaecologists can also introduce distorted allocation and can even be translated into the overall provision of beds at a regional level. A private sector develops which avoids some of the pitfalls of a system controlled by doctors, and introduces a new and commanding element – the paying customer – into the allocation process. But this, in its turn, reinforces the class inequalities also prevalent in the public sector. While many of the privately funded organisations for abortion are managed by feminists and have a charitable element to them (Leeson and Gray, 1978), others are run by unscrupulous profiteers.

Thus the abortion delivery system, like the rest of the British health care system, is extremely complicated, with strong pro- and anti-woman elements embedded within it. As such, when it comes to the need to defend the health system in general and the abortion system in particular against periodic waves of attack, the basis from which such a defence is mounted is sometimes a shaky and often a compromised one.

## Additional reading

There is a considerable literature on general issues surrounding women and health care, and in this introduction I have tried to refer to some of the more important works. Lesley Doyal's *The Political Economy of Health* (1979) has a useful chapter on 'Women, Medicine and Social Control: the case of the NHS'. For studies of the impact of health care on child-bearing women, readers should refer to all the work of Ann Oakley, who has made the study of childbirth and its medicalisation a legitimate and exciting area for academic study. There is also a considerable literature on the history of health care in this country and the place of women in it; apart from Jean Donnison's work on midwives that I have referred to above, there is also Celia Davies' edited collection, *Rewriting Nursing History* (1980). For work on abortion in particular, readers are referred to the Lane Committee report discussed in the excerpt by Malcolm Potts *et al.* The Lane Committee (having sat for three years) was almost immediately succeeded by a House of Commons Select Committee on the Abortion (Amendment) Bill (HOC, 1975–76). Both the reports of the Lane Committee and this Select Committee are rich sources for depth studies of attitudes to abortion. While the Select Committee was sitting, Victoria Greenwood and Jock Young published a socialist feminist analysis of the politics of abortion in *Abortion in Demand* (1976), while a more recent study of abortion politics within a conventional political science framework is in the book *Abortion Politics* by David Marsh and Joanna Chambers (1981).

# Women and the Crisis in the National Health Service

## LESLEY DOYAL

The factor most immediately responsible for recent developments in the women's health movement in Britain has been the attacks on welfare begun under Labour and pursued with such vigour by the Conservative government elected in 1979 (Politics of Health Group 1980, 1982). The fact that a reasonably effective health service could no longer be taken for granted, served to highlight the undoubted value of the service in meeting some of women's most basic health needs. Thus the NHS could no longer be pushed into the background and its defence became an important priority for feminist health activists. Cut-backs in the NHS have affected women even more seriously than they have men, for three main reasons. First, women are the major users of medical care and therefore suffer most when services are reduced or withdrawn. Moreover, in Britain it has often been the community services, which are used by women and children in particular, that have been defined as 'non-essential' and easily removable. Yet women are also the major producers of health care. They constitute over 70 per cent of all NHS workers, so that reductions in staffing and a deterioration in working conditions affect them most acutely. This is made worse by the fact that most staffing cuts are taking place at the lowest levels of the workforce, where the majority of women are concentrated. Finally, women have always been responsible for the care of the people whom the NHS will not look after. Thus their

*Source*: extracted from Lesley Doyal, 'Women, Health and the Social Division of Labour: a Case Study of the Women's Health Movement in Britain', *Critical Social Policy*, Issue 7, Vol. 3, No. 1, pp. 21–33.

hidden work in the home is now increasing to make up for services no longer provided by the state – a particularly 'neat' solution at a time when the rate of female unemployment is so high (Taylor, 1977; Stacey, 1982). Even more ironically, some of these women are, of course, unemployed health workers, so that they are now doing for nothing or for 'love', work for which they previously received wages.

For all these reasons, then, women have been profoundly affected by the continuing attacks on the NHS and this has had an obvious impact on the practical politics of the women's health movement. The most important change has been the broadening of the basis of political activity to include a concern with the defence of the NHS. Thus women have become increasingly involved with campaigns to save hospitals, jobs and services and to oppose the increasing privatisation of medical care. One of the most significant aspects of this shift is that it has forged a much stronger link between women as providers and women as users of health care. In recent years women working in the NHS have increasingly joined trade unions, and women's health groups have been joined by new groups of feminist health workers – radical nurses group, a radical midwives group, radical health visitors and a group representing feminist doctors and medical students. In 1981, a particularly important step was taken when the Association of Carers was formed as a support network and pressure group for unpaid health workers at home. All these organisations have been involved in one way or another with women's health groups and with health trade unions in resisting the cuts and closures now being implemented in the NHS.

But the involvement of women in these struggles in defence of the NHS does, of course, illustrate the basic paradox facing all socialist and feminist campaigns to defend what are essentially capitalist welfare services. This paradox arises from the contradictory nature of the services themselves. On the one hand, state services can be a source of oppression as the feminist critique has shown, but on the other hand, they do contain elements of considerable value that need to be defended. This is an obvious dilemma, because in criticising services we can be accused of giving support to those who wish to cut them, and our defence of them can seem contradictory and even hypocritical. The answer, of course, lies in a more sophisticated strategy that involves the defence of services in order to maintain those aspects that we really need, while at the same time campaigning for qualitative changes in those services to meet the real needs of both users and workers (Carpenter, 1979).

Feminists have been at the forefront of such campaigns in Britain, and three practical examples of their activities will be given here. One of the most important was a four-year struggle to keep open the Elizabeth Garret Anderson Hospital in London. Founded by Elizabeth Garret Anderson, this hospital for women had been staffed by women for over a century. In 1974 it was scheduled for closure, providing one of the first targets for reductions in public expenditure. Women's groups campaigned with trade unionists to keep the hospital not just open but also providing new services in which women would have a real say in the care they were receiving. The campaign met with only partial success, but some of the hospital's services have been retained. Secondly, some groups of general practitioners have been trying to use the relative freedom offered by their contract with the NHS to set up services organised along feminist lines, *within* the health service. Thus they are setting up practices with non-hierarchical working relationships and the active involvement of users in the running of the organisation. Within this context, they have concentrated particularly on the provision of 'well women clinics' to avoid the identification of healthy women as sick patients (Gardner, 1981). A final example is provided by the campaign to influence the way in which women are allowed to give birth. Here, women concerned with their rights as patients have joined with male supporters, and with groups of radical nurses and midwives, to campaign both for greater freedom of parental choice in how and where births should be conducted and also for the protection of nursing and midwifery skills that are often ignored or eroded in the pursuit of what is defined as 'technical excellence' in obstetrics.

It should be clear, then, that feminists in the women's health movement are now active participants in the defence of the NHS – though it must be said that their approach has sometimes brought them into conflict with the more orthodox defensive strategies of male-dominated trade unions. Indeed, the experience of health struggles over the past few years has shown that the presence of feminists is essential if these campaigns are to go beyond mere defence of the status quo towards a critical re-evaluation of the beliefs and practices of Western scientific medicine.

This shift in the political priorities of the women's health movement has been accompanied by a growing sophistication in the understanding of women's experiences of the NHS. These new developments in theoretical analysis have been informed by the continuing debate within the women's movement about the relationship between patriarchy and capitalism (Fee, 1975; Barrett, 1980). While this debate has usually been conducted in fairly general terms, it is of obvious relevance for any discussion of the relationship between women and medicine. Put at its simplest, radical feminists argue that the oppression experienced by women can be explained simply in terms of patriarchy – the universal tendency for male domination – though they would see the form of patriarchy changing with historical circumstances. They therefore see the major division in society as that between the sexes, claiming that the situation of women has to be understood in that light. Socialist feminists, on the other hand, argue that the position of women is also directly affected by the mode of production – understood in a Marxist sense. Thus in a society such as Britain, women's oppression is said to be explicable not just in terms of the existence of a patriarchal and male-dominated culture, but also in the light of the *capitalist* nature of British society, making both gender and class divisions of analytic and strategic significance.

This debate is very important for feminist health politics. It will be argued here that patriarchy alone cannot provide an adequate explanation of the complex and multi-faceted nature of medical sexism. Furthermore we will show that socialist feminists are right to raise serious doubts about how far the women's health movement can succeed while remaining largely outside the wider political arena. Socialist feminism has provided the potential for a more coherent understanding of medical sexism – of the ways in which medicine oppresses women. This makes it possible to move beyond the simple explanations of 'nasty' doctors sometimes found in early feminist writings, or the belief in the ahistorical universality of male domination suggested by some radical feminists. In this way, we can achieve a more structural understanding of why women are treated as they are by most orthodox medicine, as well as formulating more effective strategies for change.

The concept of 'reproduction' has been central in many areas of the socialist feminist analysis of women's oppression, and it is particularly useful in looking at the relationship between women and medicine. However, we need to begin by distinguishing between two very different uses of the term – the ideological and the biological. At the *ideological* level it is clear that medical knowledge and medical practice are part of the means by which gender divisions in society are maintained (Doyal and Elston, 1983). In other words, although sexism is mediated through the actions of individual health workers who have particular beliefs about the nature and duties of women, their behaviour also contributes to the overall process of maintaining the sexual division of labour that has come to be characteristic of advanced capitalism. Indeed, it seems clear that the institution of scientific medicine does not merely *reflect* the discriminatory views of women held in the wider society, but plays a particularly strategic role in actively creating these stereotypes and in controlling women who may deviate from them (Ehrenreich and Ehrenreich, 1978; Smart and Smart, 1978; Hutter and Williams, 1981). In this sense, then, medicine is involved in the reproduction of a particular view of the nature of women, and with the socialisation of women in accordance with that ideology. Thus, in Marxist terms, medicine plays a part in the overall reproduction of the relations of production, and for socialist feminists this is an important point, both theoretically and strategically.

But there is also a more common-sense use of the term 'reproduction' which applies to the biological reproduction of the species. Radical feminists have paid particular attention to the question of biological reproduction, since for them it is the capacity of women to give birth that is *in itself* the source of much of their oppression (Firestone, 1979). However, these arguments have been criticised for being biologically reductionist, and leaving little possibility for change. Socialist feminists, on the other hand, would argue that male attempts to control biological reproduction – often carried out by means of organised medicine – not only have to be set against the background of a patriarchal culture, as radical feminists rightly assert, but also have to be seen in the context of a capitalist mode of social and economic organisation. Thus while much sexual repression is clearly related directly to an ideology of male domination, it is also clear that if social relations are to remain basically unchanged and capital accumulation is to be maximally facilitated, then some degree of social control has to be exercised over women's sexuality, over who gives birth and under what conditions (Gordon, 1977). The size of the population, for instance, or the maintenance of a particular family structure have both been deemed matters of general social concern at different historical periods. Under such circumstances the medical care system functions as a mechanism by which state policies are translated into practice. Moreover, it is important to recognise that women's access to fertility control will have profound implications not just in an immediate biological sense, but also in terms of their other social and economic roles. Thus governments can significantly affect the degree of freedom women have over their own lives, and the part they are able to play in the wider society by controlling their access to abortion or birth control. While the idea of 'patriarchy' gives us some lever on explaining these processes, it cannot *in itself* account for the historical changes that have taken place in society's attitude towards women, sexuality and reproduction. Nor, however, can a simplistic Marxist view that sees all such changes as attributable to the economic base.

So far, we have examined different ways of analysing women's experiences as users of medical services. However, socialist feminists in particular have also emphasised the fact that women are not only 'patients' or consumers. As we have seen, they are also the major producers of health care. But women are not evenly distributed within the health labour force, and recent research has emphasised the ways in which women's work in the health sector reflects the sexual division of labour in the wider society. In Britain, only about 25 per cent of doctors are female (Elston, 1977) and most women health workers are to be found lower down the hierarchy, especially in nursing and ancillary work which involve both the traditionally 'female' skills of caring for the intimate needs of the sick, and the domestic duties of cooking, cleaning and laundering. Most health work is therefore 'women's work' – indeed, in the NHS much of it is also 'black women's work' (Doyal *et al.*, 1981). This sexual and sometimes racial stereotyping is reflected in the low pay, low status and unpleasant conditions that characterise many jobs in the health sector, mirroring women's jobs elsewhere in the economy. Finally, and very importantly, there has been a growing recognition of women's unwaged and often unseen work both in caring for the sick and disabled at home, but also in maintaining the health of their families through their daily domestic labour. In both theoretical and also more practical terms, there has therefore been an important shift away from a concentration on the role of women as consumers towards an understanding of their role

as producers of health care. In particular, it has become clear that
the use of women who have been socialised into seeing themselves
as 'carers' and who have a weaker position in the labour market, has
played an important part over the years in maintaining a low cost
health sector in Britain.

# The Working of the 1967 Abortion Act in Britain

## MALCOLM POTTS, PETER DIGGORY and JOHN PEEL

In 1974 a Committee chaired by Mrs Justice Lane reported on the first four years' experience of the working of the 1967 Abortion Act. This chapter draws on the Lane Report (Lane, 1974) to a great extent. In addition, it outlines the political and administrative consequences of the Act, the sociological effect on its beneficiaries and on the medical profession, and provides some additional data that have become available since the Lane Report went to press.

### 'Antenatal' influence of the Act

The Abortion Bill, in one form or another, was under discussion in Parliament from November 1965 to October 1967, and a further interval of six months elapsed between the passage of the Act and its implementation. Throughout the whole of this period, a fierce debate by and between the public and the medical profession produced enormous changes in public and professional attitudes. The number of hospital abortions increased steadily (Figure 1) and public opinion became more liberal, as demonstrated by a systematic series of opinion polls over this period.

An immediate and constructive effect was to encourage family planning legislation. Mr Edwin Brooks (Labour, Bebington) had achieved a high position in the 1966 poll for Private Members' Bills. Initially he had considered a Bill to amend the abortion law but,

*Source:* Malcolm Potts, Peter Diggory and John Peel, *Abortion* (Cambridge University Press, 1977).

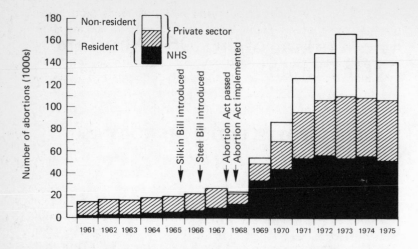

**Figure 1**   *Legal abortions in England and Wales (1961–75). (Virtually all non-resident women are treated in the private sector.)\**

when this was taken over by David Steel, he turned his attention to contraceptive legislation. What would normally have been a controversial measure was passed with remarkable ease. 'The intensity of the lobbying against the alleged "murder" of the foetus,' wrote Brooks later, 'was itself sufficient to absorb the energies of those involved, but there was also the difficulty of denouncing abortion yet at the same time appearing to be hindering the extension of contraceptive services which would help reduce the need for terminations' (Brooks, 1973). During the debate on the 1967 Family Planning Bill, the Speaker of the House of Commons was forced actually to solicit opposition speeches, although no major disagreement arose on the measure.

While the Abortion Act was being discussed, individual members of the Abortion Law Reform Association, and a few other concerned individuals, foresaw that the National Health Service (NHS)

\* *Editor's note:* For more up-to-date figures, see *New Society*, 27 October 1983. The number of legal abortions per year between 1975 and 1982 has remained fairly steady (between 130 000 and just over 150 000). Since 1978 there has been a slow rise in residents of England and Wales getting NHS abortions and a slow fall in residents getting abortions in the private sector.

would be unable to meet potential national needs, and began planning to set up charitable bodies to help women seeking abortions. The Birmingham Pregnancy Advisory Service, under the leadership of Dr Martin Cole and Mrs Nan Smith, came into operation on the first day of the new Act in April 1968. A non-profit-making organisation, charging only a small fee to cover the cost of its professional services, it counselled and referred women seeking abortions to carefully selected private gynaecologists who agreed to restrict their fees to a relatively modest level. Before the end of 1968, they acquired a nursing home, the Calthorpe, and employed their own surgeons to perform first-trimester abortions, for an inclusive fee of £65 ($130). In London, a similar pregnancy service arose under the leadership of Mr Alan Golding, and later established an exclusive relationship with the Fairfield Nursing Home, London, where surgeons were employed on a salaried basis, instead of receiving payment case-by-case. Two businessmen, Mr T. Heathcote and Mr R. Reynolds, advanced the initial capital involved in both nursing homes. The two pregnancy advisory services have performed an increasing share of the non-NHS abortions in England and Wales.

## Implementation

In tracing the workings of the Act, it is appropriate to distinguish three types of service: (a) the private sector, (b) the charitable pregnancy advisory services and (c) the NHS.

### Private sector

The initial effect of the 1967 Act on the private sector was to reduce the total number of operations and possibly the total number of surgeons operating. The Act required that operations were only to be performed in licensed nursing homes, which had been inspected and approved by the Ministry of Health (later to become the Department of Health and Social Security – DHSS). The process was a slow one and the Ministry was strict in the application of its criteria. Prior to the Act, a number of abortions had taken place in doctors' surgeries and in small specialised units, neither of which were approved after April 1968.

Despite the slow beginning, there was a rapid recovery in private-sector abortions. In non-charity private nursing homes approved for termination, the beds were intensively used and sometimes women were discharged within a few hours of the operation. A new group of rather inexperienced surgeons entered the field, and while the 1967 Act cast out some devils in the form of backstreet abortionists, it also allowed in a few medically qualified goblins. Some individual abuses were well publicised and caught the attention of the public. The Society for the Protection of the Unborn Child (SPUC) and the Abortion Law Reform Association (ALRA) remained in existence, following up on conflicting stories of successes and abuses in the Act. As summarised in the Lane Report, adverse criticisms fell into three main categories. It was claimed that the Abortion Act was interpreted too liberally, that women seeking abortion in the private sector were financially exploited, and that the standard of service was sometimes low.

It was predictable that important differences of philosophy would arise between the private sector and the NHS. In the UK, the NHS, both at hospital and general practitioner level, is financed out of taxes. Hospital consultants receive a basic salary, general practitioners are paid a fee for every patient on their list, whether sick or well. Doctors are often poorly informed about the detailed costing of any therapy. NHS consultants are allotted a fixed number of in-patient beds with relevant nursing care and ancillary services, but no particular annual budget. In the private sector, the motivation for work and the appreciation of cost of the individual procedures are similar to those in private practice throughout the world. Obviously there is an interest in the fee, although in practice there is virtually always a commitment to the underlying needs of the patient and fees may be reduced or waived in cases of hardship. The abuses that did arise in the private sector probably involved very few doctors. The Lane Committee commented, 'in consequence of the Abortion Act a situation has arisen in which a very small number, of perhaps about 20 or 30 members, of the medical profession and those associated with them, have brought considerable reproach upon this country, both at home and abroad'.

Those opposed to the operation created a doubly complex image: by emphasising the dangers, they turned a simple operation, appropriate for a properly supervised general practitioner to perform, into one that only the most experienced gynaecologist was supposed to conduct, and then they criticised the level of fees paid. Abortion has inflamed emotions to the extent that it seems almost as if, unlike delivering a baby or performing routine surgery, no professional fee or reward should be asked.

*Pregnancy advisory services*

Both services have grown since their founding. The Birmingham Pregnancy Advisory Service opened several referral centres in other towns, purchased a number of clinical facilities, and changed its name to the British Pregnancy Advisory Service (BPAS). By the end of 1974, it had completed over 100,000 abortions, whilst the PAS in London had counselled 50,000 women. Both services reduce fees, waive them altogether, or make loans to women who are too poor to pay the £65–£67 ($130–$134) requested. Unfortunately, both services have been inhibited by the DHSS from providing daycare facilities, which would enable them approximately to halve their fees.

By 1970 the two PASs were performing 15 per cent of all registered abortions, or 33 per cent of all private cases. However, whereas a quarter of private abortions in that year involved women from overseas, the PASs dealt almost exclusively with British residents, amongst whom they have come to perform over four out of every ten non-NHS terminations. In fact, by the 1970s, the total number of abortion beds available in hospitals and clinics was probably equal to, or slightly in excess of, needs. As a consequence, some clinics in the private sector began to draw in more and more women from continental Europe.

The London-based private sector has always dealt with the majority of overseas patients (see Figure 1). The volume of European women seeking abortion in Britain has grown with time, and the profile of country of origin has also altered. France has supplied many women; even in the first quarter of 1975 over 7000 women travelled to Britain. However, while West Germany supplied over 13000 cases in 1971, its contribution had fallen to one-third of that figure by 1975. Conversely the number from Italy and Spain has risen steadily (1001 and 949, respectively, in the first-quarter of 1975).*

---

* *Editor's note*: Since this article was written, the areas from which foreign women came to this country for abortions have radically changed. In 1982, out of 34500 non-resident women getting legal abortions here, 21000 were Spanish, 5100 were from Northern Ireland and the Irish Republic, and 3800 were from France (*New Society*, 27 October 1983).

*The National Health Service*

A woman seeking an NHS abortion has two hurdles to clear. First, she must convince her general practitioner that her case falls within the provisions of the law. It is unlikely that she will have canvassed his opinion on abortion before she accidentally became pregnant. Originally, she may have selected and registered with him as the nearest doctor when she moved house or when her children first had measles. Should she discover that her doctor is hostile to abortion, she has the right to transfer to another general practitioner, but such a process is time-consuming and requires considerable determination; in practice the option is rarely exercised.

Wherever the woman seeking abortion lives, her general practitioner is likely to refer her to the local hospital, where there may be from one to four consultant gynaecologists. Her general practitioner will know the attitudes of these local gynaecologists towards abortion and this enables a sympathetic doctor to select a sympathetic gynaecologist and conversely a hostile general practitioner to play at sending his patient for abortion whilst actually referring her to a gynaecologist he well knows will not agree to perform the operation. Apart from the possibilities of much chicanery, it may well be that, in a given district, the only available gynaecologist, or all the gynaecologists, are basically hostile to abortion. In such districts, few NHS abortions will be performed and we shall show later that the most important factor in the situation is the attitude of the gynaecologist. Unfortunately, although gynaecologists are in general willing to see women from outside their normal catchment area, this rarely applies to women referred for consideration of abortion. All NHS gynaecologists have a waiting list of patients requiring less urgent operations. Any woman accepted for abortion must be given priority over this list and, in addition, if a given gynaecologist who is liberally inclined towards abortion works alongside one who is hostile, it will rapidly follow that the liberal gynaecologist finds himself performing large numbers of abortions and providing a delayed service to his other patients – because of which delays, the routine and possibly also the fascinating gynaecological cases are referred to his illiberal colleague who is refusing to share the abortion load.

Unfortunately, the problem of varying medical attitudes is aggravated by wide variations in gynaecological facilities within the NHS.

The Lane Committee called attention to the fact that in 1971, the number of gynaecological beds per 100 000 women varied from 52 in East Anglia to 91 in the South-West Metropolitan area. Strangely, such wide variations in available facilities are not in any way correlated with the number of abortions performed; in the instance given above, there were 72.4 abortions per 1000 women aged 15–44 years in East Anglia and only 58.3 in the South-West Metropolitan area. To show even more clearly that medical attitudes are more important than facilities, one may contrast the Newcastle and Liverpool areas, which have almost identical facilities but were performing respectively 79.6 and 41.6 per cent of the abortions of women resident in these two regions (Figure 3). To complete the contrast it should be noted that the *total* number of hospital bed-days per million of the population devoted to therapeutic and 'other' abortions was greater in Liverpool (31.3 per million) than in, say, East Anglia (24.1).

Ultimately the actual numbers of beds available may be virtually irrelevant. Buckle and Anderson (1972) in Lewisham first showed, almost as soon as the Abortion Act came into force, that more than three-quarters of women could be aborted safely on an outpatient or daycare basis. King's College and St Mary's, both London teaching hospitals, and the teaching hospital in Nottingham also went on to establish very successful daycare abortion facilities (Hull *et al.*, 1974; Lewis *et al.*, 1971). It is probable that many general, provincial NHS hospitals would have followed this lead but for financial starvation (Maresh *et al.*, 1974). Daycare abortion facilities were only established at Kingston Hospital on the outskirts of London when the Pregnancy Advisory Service made the hospital a grant of £2000, which was sufficient to buy essential equipment to start a unit capable of performing up to 600 operations per year (working only two days per week). This was the first unit where assessment and out-patient abortion is performed by trained general practitioners working within the NHS.

As a result of differing interpretations of the 1967 Act by general practitioners and consultant gynaecologists, the NHS abortion rate varies two- to threefold in different parts of England and Wales (Figure 2).

The range of variation has remained roughly constant since 1968. After four or five years the so-called 'conservative areas' came to perform NHS abortions at the rate which the 'liberal areas' had first

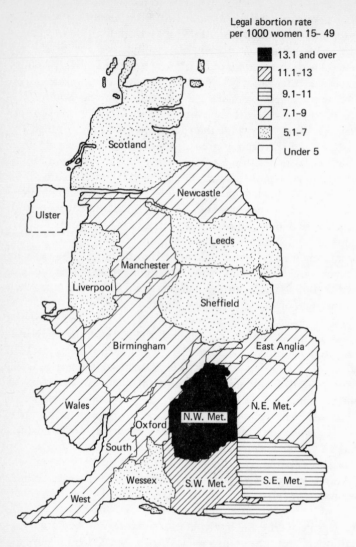

**Figure 2** *Legal abortion rate per 1000 women (15–49) by residence in 1971. (The map of Britain is drawn so that the area of each NHS region is proportional to the population of that region. N.W. Met. etc. = London and adjacent counties, as far as the coast.)*

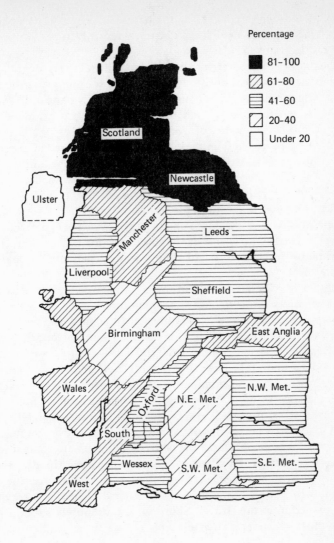

**Figure 3** *Percentage of resident women in each NHS region who obtained an abortion in NHS hospitals of their home region in 1971 (See also Figure 2.)*

adopted, although by that time, the latter had moved on to permit even higher rates. Few facts illustrate the arbitrary nature of medical decisions so clearly.

The pattern of general practitioner, consultant gynaecologist and consultant psychiatrist decision-making has been analysed in depth in Aberdeen* and is partially understood in other parts of Britain. In Aberdeen there was a ten fold variation between individual consultants in the number of women they 'approved' for abortion. Refusal was more likely in the case of single than married women. In various parts of Britain, consultants tend to refuse a fifth to a third of women referred for abortion by general practitioners (Parry Jones and Grimoldby, 1973; Eames *et al.*, 1971; Williamson, 1972), although many of those refused on the NHS seek, and obtain, non-NHS abortions. Todd (1971), reviewing experience in Glasgow, commented, 'it is likely that restriction of the criteria for termination in general would simply lead to patients "shopping around"'.

Ingram (1971) has described the treatment of women seeking abortion under the 1967 Act as *abortion games*. He describes what he terms 'Pontius Pilate' and 'Bounced Cheque' manoeuvres by uncertain or antagonistic referring doctors (the 'Bounced Cheque' involves delaying the woman's referral until it is too late for the surgeon to operate). The 'Big White Chief' and 'Little Indian' games revolve around dominating senior gynaecologists who impose their views on a whole hospital, town or even region. The 'Plumber' game is played by a doctor who asks others to tell him what to do and is the reverse of 'Amateur Psychiatrist' or 'Young Dr Kildare'. Ingram concluded 'the concealed function of all abortion games is to abolish or minimise personal responsibility for decisions made for or against termination, whether by patient, doctor or society'. In ethical terms it is hard to decide if this is a serious condemnation of the British Abortion Act, or merely a reflection upon those who operate it at all levels.

**Northern Ireland**

The 1967 Abortion Act specifically excludes Ulster, which continues to operate the 1861 Act in its unamended form. The Criminal

---

* *Editor's note:* see Sally Macintyre's study excerpted in this volume; also G. Horobin (ed.) (1973).

Justice Act (Northern Ireland) 1945 does permit infant destruction in the third trimester when it is necessary to save the woman's life. That is, Ulster perpetuates the paradox that the baby may be legally killed at seven months, but that it is illegal to destroy the embryo seven days after the missed period. This same anomaly applied in England between 1929 and 1967.

Women from Ulster and the Republic of Ireland are allowed to travel to England for a legal abortion if they can find the money and make the contacts. An Ulster Pregnancy Advisory Association was founded in 1971 (Compton *et al.*, 1974). Through this and other channels, in 1974 1100 women a year travelled from Ulster (1968 – 36; 1969 – 96; 1970 – 199; 1971 – 649; 1972 – 775; 1973 – 1093). The age and marital status of women seeking to have a legal abortion performed in England are identical to those of English residents. Among those referred by the Pregnancy Advisory Association, 20.7 per cent were Roman Catholic. Thirty-five per cent of the Ulster population are Catholic, but the proportion of Catholic women seeking legal abortion is rising year by year. More Catholics were unmarried (72.2 per cent as compared with 65.1 per cent of Protestants), were somewhat younger, and came slightly later in pregnancy. Middle-class urban women appear to be setting the pace for those from across the Irish Sea who seek legal abortion. In 1973 1200 women from Eire obtained abortions in England and in the first nine months of 1974 about 1450 had already availed themselves of the same facilities.

**The medical response**

The volume of medical opposition to induced abortion lessened as more and more doctors came to face the visible reality of the problem of unwanted pregnancy among their patients (Cartwright and Waite, 1972). As the Lane Committee was to comment in 1974, 'From the evidence we have received it appears to us that there has been some change of opinion within the medical profession towards a readier acceptance of abortion as a means of preserving health'. While recognising the need for abortion for mixed medico-social reasons, doctors contrived to rationalise their actions within the traditional framework of curative medicine. In the first year of the new Act, 72 per cent of abortions were registered as being performed on grounds of 'risk of injury to the physical or mental health of the woman', while only 4 per cent of cases were registered under the much-contested medico-social indications.

By 1970, the chairman of the British Medical Association, Dr H. Gibson, and Professor Sir Norman Jeffcoate, soon to become president of the Royal College of Obstetricians and Gynaecologists, felt able to express their support for all the main clauses of the Act (*The Times*, 12 February 1970). They still believed that the operation is best performed under the supervision of a consultant in the NHS, or by a doctor of equivalent status. But an amendment to this effect attracted insignificant support in a parliamentary debate in February 1970, and was talked out by its own supporters. Addressing a meeting of the Royal College of Obstetricians and Gynaecologists in 1969, Dr T. L. T. Lewis, Secretary of the College, said, 'We thought there would be a slightly more liberal attitude towards the problem for that, after all, was the purpose of the new law. How wrong we were. I am afraid we did not allow for the attitude of, firstly, the general public and, secondly, the general practitioners' (Lewis, 1969). Three months later, a *Lancet* editorial commented,

> Things were certainly easier for the gynaecologists before the public and Parliament made their wishes known in the Act – but they were much harder for women. There is a minority of gynaecologists who, though making no claim to religious or conscientious objections, unhappily retreat from an awkward situation behind a barrier of moral disapproval and take little part in the operation of the Act. They thus deprive patients of emergency treatment to which they are entitled and increase the strain on their NHS colleagues. (*Lancet*, 26 April 1969).

The grounds for sustaining continued opposition are mixed, and range from a reasoned concern for the ethical problems posed by abortion to peevish arguments about overloaded departments, lack of government assistance and reducing doctors to the 'role of technicians'. The ethical consideration of the problems reached their nadir in a BBC discussion on *Morals and Medicine* in 1970, when Professor Jeffcoate laid bare the muddled motivation of, at least some, doctors who opposed the Act.

> One can understand some women, with their new emancipation, taking the view that they themselves should decide whether their pregnancy should be terminated or not; that they should have the

right to demand its removal. If there were an acceptable method of inducing abortion which they themselves could employ I can see no reason why they should not be free to do so, providing they appreciated the risks. There may come a time when an efficient oral abortifacient is discovered. A woman might then choose to take this, just as she can now elect to take oral contraceptives or to smoke cigarettes, despite any hazard involved. Meanwhile, however, abortion necessitates an operation, carried out by a skilled team, consisting of a surgeon, anaesthetist and nurses. These are all motivated by a strong ethical code and are dedicated to protect life and health. Only they can form a detached and professional opinion as to what are the best interests of the patient. (Jeffcoate and Foot, 1970, p. 29)

The members of the British Medical Association continued to resist the Act after it was passed, as they had during its passage. They set up their own enquiry into the working of the Act in 1971 and appointed Professor Ian Donald as Chairman. (A few months earlier, Professor Donald had stated that, as a result of the liberal abortion law, it was becoming difficult to find enough doctors to act as 'executioners' in the NHS.)

The Royal College of Obstetricians and Gynaecologists remained cool. The evidence it presented to the Lane Committee was vague and often biased.

The attitude of surgeons in private practice has frequently been pilloried, but observations by consumers, women attending NHS hospitals, can also be harrowing. The history of a woman aged 41 years with four children and a recent episode of tuberculosis was passed on to the Lane Committee. She reported being 'submitted to the most humiliating interview in which the NHS gynaecologist expressed his personal distaste for carrying out terminations and succeeded in making me feel both irresponsible and immoral, so that I came out in tears – as had the patient ahead of me' (ALRA, 1972).

The high percentage of sterilisations accompanying abortions within the NHS (over 50 per cent of married women having NHS abortions in 1968–69 were sterilised)* may reflect a punitive attitude among some NHS gynaecologists as well as a genuine answer to the need for fertility control.

* Personal communication by P. Keatelman to the authors, 1970.

The response of the nursing profession shadowed that of doctors. Some welcomed, most accepted, but a few protested bitterly. For some young nurses the operation can present a particular challenge and a wise surgeon will be careful both to listen and explain. When young nurses care for women seeking abortion, and have the opportunity to talk at length with them, they commonly come to take a sympathetic view. The Lane Committee concluded that the Abortion Act had little or no effect on nursing recruitment. It also commented that morale was often very high in clinics doing only abortions, because the nurses employed clearly believed in the value of the work they were doing. In 1969, the Board of Social Responsibility of the Anglican Church gave it as its view 'that it would be wrong and useless for matrons and nurses to attempt to interfere to delay co-operation in a case actually under treatment. Responsibility must be allowed to rest where it is placed by the Act' (i.e. with the certifying doctors).

In December 1970 the Catholic Nurses' Guild of Scotland issued guidelines to its members. 'Nurses who objected to abortion', they pointed out, 'should always demonstrate their charity to patients having abortions'. Concerning cases in the wards, the guidelines suggested that Catholic nurses 'should be prepared to look after these [i.e. *abortion*] patients in all neutral matters, giving pain-relief and comfort, and post-operative care'. It was suggested that in the theatre 'Catholic nurses may not give essential assistance, such as handing over instruments or sutures. Standard sets of sterilised instruments and towels may be provided on a trolley, as these are equipment for gynaecological operations and are morally "neutral"'.

Whatever nurses and their spokesmen say about the Abortion Act there is no doubt that, as a group, they are heavy users of its facilities. Diggory (1969) and Ingham and Simms (1972) as well as others have shown that, when women seeking abortion are analysed according to occupation, nurses are over-represented.

# Gynaecologist/Woman Interaction

## SALLY MACINTYRE

The process of deciding about abortion applications has been described as follows by MacGillivray and Dennis:

> Although no two cases are quite comparable, it is possible to sift them in broad categories, and for most gynaecologists it was a matter of collecting the basic facts to determine the group into which the patient fitted and then making the decision. (1973, p. 53)

This raises the questions of what basic facts are seen as relevant, and how decisions based on them are reached. Neither the law nor medical training contain clear guidelines for adjudicating on the indications for termination. Both the search procedures and decision rules used may therefore rely on clinical experience (which, as Becker *et al.* (1961) have pointed out, is often accorded higher status than scientifically verified knowledge) and on common-sense lay experience. In classifying patients into groups for which abortion is or is not indicated, gynaecologists must rely on their knowledge of features of normal social life as well as of the medical sphere narrowly defined (see Macintyre, 1973, 1976).

The gynaecologists studied all used very similar search procedures, but their decision rules varied. The question addressed by all the gynaecologists was, 'In what ways would continued pregnancy be problematic?' While single women are called upon to justify having babies (falling pregnant and keeping their babies), both law and public opinion call upon them to justify surgical

*Source*: Sally Macintyre, *Single and Pregnant* (Croom Helm, 1977).

175

termination of pregnancy rather than, for example, marriage or adoption. As one gynaecologist pointed out, termination is not the same as not having become pregnant. Both the fact of the gynaecologists' search for justification and the decision-making procedures they used were dictated not only by the requirements of the Abortion Act but also by their own personal attitudes. Dr Innes, for example, stated that he wished that no abortions need ever be performed: from the perspective of his position as parent and obstetrician, he regarded them all as tragic.

The gynaecologists' concerns were similar to those of the GPs, topics on which they focused being the relationship with the putative father, past contraception and the possibility of marriage. As with the GPs, these items were collapsed into general typifications of patients' characters and current situations in the light of their past behaviour and relationships.

Their first concern was with the question of the possibility of marriage. Abortion and marriage were perceived as mutually exclusive. If marriage were impossible, on grounds reasonable to the gynaecologist, then abortion could seriously be considered. If marriage were possible, then other indications would have to be very compelling indeed. In all the referral letters mention was made of the impossibility or improbability of marriage, but these were usually brief statements not indicating any reasons: 'She fears she cannot be married at the present' (Dr Baxter about Faye); 'There is apparently no question of marriage' (Dr Gibson about Grace); 'Apparently the question of marriage does not arise' (Dr Gibson about Diana).

The gynaecologists, therefore, all questioned the women about why marriage was impossible. A simple statement that marriage was impossible was insufficient at this stage: good reasons had to be adduced. Thus, Dr Innes fleshed out Dr Gibson's skeletal comment about Grace's relationship with the putative father (see above). He ascertained that Grace had broken off with him when he was imprisoned for fraud, and that neither she nor her parents wished the relationship re-established, that she had been going out with him for a few months when she had intercourse with him, that she had not known of his previous criminal record when she was going out with him, and that she had a new boyfriend who would break off the relationship if she continued the pregnancy. Similarly, all the others were asked detailed questions about their relationships with the putative fathers.

Some of the questioning was designed to establish the circumstances in which pregnancy occurred, and the woman's character in the light of this. For example:

*Eileen:* Oh, yes, Dr Nicoll asked me questions. Who was the father of the child and where was he and all that. He said to me, 'Were you not intending marrying him when you had ...?' I said, no, not really, it was just a friendship that we knew wouldn't last all that long. It was going to be a thing that would only last for so long.

In his account of her to me, Dr Nicoll said:

She has been having intercourse with random friends – and having become unstuck after the carry-on, looks to the National Health Service to pick the chestnut out of the fire. She tells me that she does not see anything wrong with her type of sexual relationships, either inside or outside of marriage.

When he asked her about the possibility of marriage, she told him that the putative father was leaving the country the next day. Like Dr Baxter, Dr Nicoll did not believe this – 'I think this young lady is a good actress and spins a good story about the circumstances associated with this pregnancy' – although he did believe marriage to be impossible because of her promiscuity. He used her sexual and contraceptive history to make inferences about her character, inferences which he then used to predict her likely response to continued pregnancy: 'I think her conduct – by my standards, immoral – show the sort of girl she is. If I refused she might crack up because she hasn't got the moral or mental courage'. Eileen had considered the possibility of embroidering her story to make herself appear more respectable, but had rejected it. She was aware of the sorts of circumstances she could describe to save face:

I just said that quite a lot of people had relationships like that – I don't know whether he was expecting me to say, 'Oh, yes, I was going to marry him', or not. I don't know. Maybe he just wanted to find out whether I was going to be truthful. Maybe he was expecting me to say, 'Oh, yes, he was going to marry me, and then he ran away'.

As with the GPs, the best account seemed to be one that indicated that marriage was impossible either because the woman had succumbed to casual sex or had been deserted by the man. Grace's account was acceptable and saved face for her: she had gone out with a man in good faith, and only after she was pregnant did she discover that he was a 'thoroughly bad lot'. She was thus not open to the same imputation of immorality as was Eileen, because, unlike Eileen, at the time of intercourse she was considering marrying her boyfriend. If the boyfriend had not deserted the woman and marriage therefore seemed at least possible, the gynaecologists questioned the women closely about why they were not intending to marry. Kate and Barbara both cited their wish to finish their studies and become established in socially useful professions, and their, and their boyfriends', lack of money. Annabelle similarly stressed her wish to complete training and also cited her boyfriend's bad reputation and her parents' disapproval of him. While Jenny could not appeal to her training or career, she could cite her youth, being only 17, and the heavy responsibility of marriage and motherhood at that age. These arguments about not getting married at that stage all seemed 'reasonable' to the gynaecologists.

Faye, however, could offer no such definite reasons: she simply said that she did not wish to marry and have the baby then, even though her boyfriend was keen for her to do so. Her application was refused:

*SM:* Did Dr Simpson give you any particular reason?
*Faye:* Well, in a way he did, because I was intending carrying on going out with my boyfriend and he didn't see why we couldn't get married. Of course, I just told him I thought we weren't ready for it. That was just my reason, but he wouldn't accept it. Obviously.

It appeared to be assumed that if a woman were going to marry in the near future it would be unreasonable to terminate her pregnancy unless on compelling medical grounds. If a woman were not going to marry she would face the problems of single parenthood or those of continuing her pregnancy to full term term prior to adoption. Particularly for the students, the latter course was seen as potentially injurious to mental health since it would curtail their studies. In justifying not marrying, therefore, the women were also justifying abortion, since similar reasons could be adduced for both; for example, lack of money, curtailment of training, or extreme youth. It being assumed that 'normal as-if-married women' will continue their pregnancies, women cast in such characters but who wished abortion had to produce acceptable reasons for not marrying.

Like the GPs, the gynaecologists paid more attention to occupational careers for those who were students than for those like Diana or Faye who were clerks, or like Caroline, unskilled workers. The students were asked how their studies were going, how much they were committed to them, what they intended to do when they had completed training, and in what ways continued pregnancy would interfere with these plans. By contrast, beyond establishing Diana's, Caroline's and Faye's occupations and incomes, the gynaecologists did not question them further about the costs to their occupational careers of continuation of pregnancy. The students appeared to be seen has having careers which would be adversely affected by continuance of pregnancy, with consequent effects on mental health, in a way that unskilled or white-collar workers were not.

The gynaecologists were also concerned with care arrangements during pregnancy and for the baby. Thus women were asked about their incomes, their parents' occupations and incomes, whether they lived with their parents, in digs, flats, or student hostels, and what their parents' reactions were or would be to the pregnancy. Annabelle, for example, was able to cite not only the impossibility of marriage but her precarious financial position (being on a grant and never having paid insurance stamps), her parents' poor financial position, the problem of finding somewhere to live during and after pregnancy, and the distress she would feel about hurting her parents. The question of parents' reactions was seen as relevant not only to the amount of support the women would receive as single parents or newlyweds, but to the amount of support the women could expect during pregnancy.

While the gynaecologists asked similar questions to each other, the decision rules based on these differed. Drs Innes and Lawson in general refused very few cases. They felt their task was to establish that the women had come to a decision in the light of proper consideration of all the alternatives, and to ensure that the women were absolutely certain that they wanted an abortion:

*SM:* Are there any questions that you routinely ask of termination referral cases?
*Dr Lawson:* Oh, a lot . . . I always ask them who they've talked the

problem over with – to elicit if they had been in touch with their parents or the man concerned ... and obviously make sure that they've talked and thought about it sufficiently and had the value of the conversation to elicit what they really feel about it ... The nature of the relationship, and if they're proposing to get married – not that that necessarily means a final decision one way or the other, but it helps them ... to see the whole thing in perspective ... By and large I don't feel I'm the arbiter of whether they should be done or not – just help them make the decision.

Dr Innes always asked patients whose idea the abortion had been, whether they had thought about it themselves or had it suggested by others, as he was concerned lest women had abortions under pressure from others. He was also concerned with women's possible ambivalence, e.g. Grace said: 'Well, he says, "I'm just wondering why you left it so long. Is it because you're not sure whether you want the termination or not?"' Both Drs Innes and Lawson stated that they asked about past contraception in order to establish what method would be most appropriate after an abortion or birth:

*Dr Innes:* I always ask about contraception not because this has any relevance to the decisions at hand – but in order to know what's best for the women concerned ... My questions are oriented to the future – I don't care about the past, and I think her deserts or worthiness are irrelevant.

The other gynaecologists did tend to think themselves to be arbiters of the decision, and used these search procedures to establish whether it was reasonable for the pregnancy to be terminated. For them a major contra-indication was if the woman were going to marry the putative father. In attempting to predict the likely relative effect of continuance or termination of pregnancy on the women's mental or physical health the question of moral character was important. Dr Nicoll agreed to terminate Eileen's pregnancy because he regarded her moral character as extremely poor and her as therefore being unable to cope with continued pregnancy or motherhood, but he felt little sympathy for her. This appeared to be an extreme case: both GPs and gynaecologists were usually most reluctant to terminate the pregnancies of those seen as 'bad, promiscuous girls'. They were most likely to agree to terminate the pregnancies of those they saw as 'nice girls who had made mistakes', such as Caroline, Hannah and Lynn. For example, in accounting for his decision to terminate Hannah's pregnancy, Dr Oliver said: 'If she is relieved of her present difficulties she assured me that in spite of the fact that she is engaged she will not expose herself to risk of a further pregnancy'. They were also reluctant to terminate the pregnancies of those seen as 'normal-as-if-married women', such as Faye: women who knew this then had to produce accounts that placed them into the 'nice girl who made a mistake' category, as did, for example, Jenny.

# V

# Women and the Personal Social Services

# Introduction

Women, as distinct from men, bear two relationships to the personal social services. Women predominate as providers of these services, and, with some qualifications outlined below, they are, as consumers or 'clients', more frequently in direct contact with the services than are men.

With very few exceptions, and then only in the higher grades, women rather than men are the home helps, the staff in residential homes and day centres, the cooks and distributors of meals on wheels. In other words, there is a distinct sexual division of labour in the personal social services. This pattern is repeated in social work, where women predominate amongst those social workers in face-to-face contact with clients, while men predominate in managerial positions in social work. For example, in 1977, 83 per cent of all social work assistants and 64 per cent of all social workers employed by local authorities in England were women; in contrast, 71 per cent of area directors and 91 per cent of Directors of Social Services were men (Popplestone, 1980). As Hearn points out in the article reproduced here, the pattern of gender divisions within social work closely parallels development in those other 'semi professions' that are largely concerned with reproductive and emotional life. He argues that the process of professionalisation allows for and encourages the penetration of men at the higher levels of the career structure. Simultaneously, the commodification of emotional life allows for the introduction of theoretical concepts (e.g. systems theory) and practice goals (e.g. efficiency and effectiveness) borrowed from the world of capitalist business enterprise.

The second relationship of women to the personal social services – namely as the predominating sex amongst consumers of the services provided – is less easily quantified but nevertheless is the case. There are a number of reasons for this, some related, crudely, to women's special 'needs' and other reasons that are more closely related to an ideology of femininity and, more particularly, motherhood. For a start, women live longer than men and amongst the population of the elderly severely handicapped and impaired they are the predominating sex. Although only a very small proportion of the elderly are in residential institutions (about 3 per cent), elderly women of all ages over 70 are proportionately more likely than men to be in long-term residential care (Moroney, 1976). At younger ages, too, women are more likely than men to cross the paths of social workers and other professional care-givers. Given their relatively subordinate position in the labour market, and the likelihood that mothers will want to continue to care for their own children even when the fathers are absent, large and growing numbers of women are the heads of single-parent families and dependent on state benefits and social service assistance for their very survival (McIntosh, 1979).

However, another cluster of reasons for the predominance of women amongst the consumers of the personal social services has less to do with straightforward 'need', and more to do with the interpretation and construction by social workers themselves of the role of women within the family. Thus, where children are in trouble, a household in debt, or an elderly person in need of care in the bosom of his or her own family, the first 'port of call' for any social worker involved will almost certainly be a woman who, as a mother, a housewife, a daughter or daughter-in-law, will be regarded as the person most responsible for and pertinent to the solution of the problem. Even where the problem seems to involve at least one other person very directly, as in the case of wife-battering by husbands, social workers are likely to restrict their interviews and 'treatment' to the wife – a practice that lends itself to the implication that the victim is the cause of her own difficulties (Maynard, 1985). But this enforcement of an ideological construction of motherhood and marriage can cut two ways, and in certain respects it can mean that the recipients of personal social services are *men* rather than women. This is particularly the case where the prevailing norms surrounding the domestic division of labour between the sexes appear to be inoperable: for example, in households consisting of a married couple where the wife is physically or mentally incapacitated. In these cases, the surrogate 'housewife', in the form of the local authority employed home help, is more liberally available than she would be to a household containing a disabled husband and a wife apparently capable of carrying out household and personal caring tasks (Bebbington and Davies, 1983).

These two cross-currents, namely the identification of women as the pivotal characters in family life and the preferential allocation of certain social services to men where a woman is, in some sense, 'absent', neatly capture two particular features of the personal social services. These services are, at an ideological level, a form of social control, and yet, at a material level, an important resource for those in 'need'. This dual role of the personal social services, and the contradictions arising therefrom, is one that has been much discussed in recent Marxist critiques (see, for example, CSE State Group, 1979). The existence of these two features also raises an important question about the role of women in the social services professions. Given the ideological underpinning of professional social service work, would it actually make any difference to the treatment of women clients if there were more women in managerial positions in Social Service Departments? Would women in managerial positions be more sensitive to the structural causes of, for example, women clients' depression than professional men are, more willing to treat men and women equally when it comes to providing relief housework and caring services, and more understanding and supportive of women's campaigns to maintain and develop social services such as day nurseries and women's refuges that speak directly to women's needs rather than those of men? The evidence seems to be less than encouraging. As far as social work education is concerned, Daphne Statham points to a deep conservatism embedded within it:

social work teaching . . . concentrates primarily on aspects of theories about masculinity and femininity. The objective seems to be to clarify the nature and genesis of the characteristics of a mother-wife and husband-father-worker. Implicit in this exploration is, in the main, the equation of mature sexuality with a heterosexual preference, of mature femininity with motherhood within marriage. In a very real sense women as persons do not exist in social work literature. (Statham, 1978, p. 70)

(Given what Hearn says about the preponderance of men in the academic teaching of social work, this absence of women 'as persons' in the social work literature is perhaps not surprising and indicates that it is likely to continue for some time to come.) As far as practice is concerned, Elizabeth Wilson also has some pessimistic thoughts. She too thinks it unlikely that, given the individualistic and personal therapeutic style encouraged in social work education, feminist social workers will find it easy to forge links with their women clients and campaign against sexism on a collective basis. Even where feminist social workers have been able to give their support to collective action, as in the outstanding case of women's refuges, she suggests a formidable mixture of motives on the part of the participating social workers, and:

defining their own work as being to do with relationships, many social workers see women's refuges and claimants' unions as merciful solutions to their own overload of cases and thus turn them by default into extensions of the social services. Thus, presumably without meaning to, social workers often find themselves party to the co-option of the alternatives, killing (even if with kindness) their radical potential. (Wilson, 1980, p. 40)

And yet, is it too much to hope that, divided as they are by social distance and professional power, women professionals and women clients can be brought together by their common knowledge of the nature of patriarchy (if not their common experience of its impact), build bridges based on extra sympathy and angry energy, and thereby, each within their own context, become marginally less frustrated and exploited?

**Additional reading**

The literature on women and the personal social services is surprisingly thin, given the predominant role women play within these services. Apart from the reading referred to in the introduction, Ronald Walton's *Women in Social Work* (1975) is a useful study of the history of women's participation in social work, though by no means written from a feminist perspective, and Frank Prochaska's study of *Women and Philanthropy in 19th Century England* is a fascinating study of how women got there in the first place.

# Patriarchy, Professionalisation and the Semi-Professions*

## JEFF HEARN

The development of social policy, and specifically the professions within it, are the product of both capitalist and patriarchal power. However, a much simplified distinction can be drawn between the domination of capitalism over socialised goods and services, and the domination of patriarchy over domestic labour and reproduction. Here the focus is on the significance of the control of reproduction for understanding the professions. Reproduction itself is of various types, including biological reproduction, the reproduction of labour power, and sexual reproduction. The professions are seen as the major way in which the labour, energy and creativity of women in reproduction are controlled by men.

### Professionalisation as a patriarchal process

#### Reproduction and emotionality

On the assumption that patriarchy predates capitalism, the development of capitalism can be seen to have gradually extended from the productive to the reproductive spheres, and from the

*Source*: abridged from Jeff Hearn, 'Notes on Patriarchy, Professionalisation and the Semi-Professions', *Sociology*, Vol. 16, No. 2, May 1982, pp. 184–202. An introductory paragraph by Jeff Hearn has been added to this extract.

\* *Editor's note*: All the original footnotes to this extract have been omitted due to lack of space. Readers seeking the further analysis of the notes should refer to the original article.

simply instrumental to the more elusive emotional. Early capitalism was concerned with the satisfaction of material wants, be they food for the general society or luxury goods for the well-off. For many areas of social life, patriarchy conjoined with capitalism in a mutually reinforcing process of domination. Increasingly particular areas of both reproductive and emotional life became the seat of conversion to patriarchal and indeed capitalist domination – such areas were less amenable to direct capitalist domination and thus to patriarchal domination.

Those areas of social life that were not directly under capitalist domination, yet which contributed to reproduction and were where emotions were especially likely to be unleashed, became clear targets for male domination through professions. Most importantly, these were the very areas that the magic, creativity, indeed healing, of women had enabled them to dominate within peasant society, with women locally acting as the priestesses, the prophetesses, the healers, the wise women, the witches (Ehrenreich and English, 1974). This domination by women certainly applied to biological reproduction, but also to other areas of reproduction, such as the management of life and death in spiritual or social terms.

## *The model of medicine*

The case of medicine is particularly instructive. In the medieval world, the traditional medical role of women was to some extent sponsored by the Church. Indeed, 'for eight ... centuries, from the fifth to the thirteenth, the other-worldly, anti-medical stance of the Church ... stood in the way of the development of medicine as a respectable profession' (Ehrenreich and English, 1974, p. 13).

According to early Christian missionary and Norman practices,

> Ladies were the ordinary practitioners of domestic medicine and the skilled chatelaine could reduce fractures, probe and dress wounds or burns and prepare herbal remedies ... Male physicians were rare, since time and desire for study were almost confined to monks, Jews and others debarred from the supreme masculine occupation of fighting.' (Manton, 1956, pp. 56–7)

Inroads into this pattern were made by men in late medieval times through a combination of Church, state and universities and the men that dominated those institutions (Ehrenreich and English, 1974, pp. 3–5). This was furthered with the rise of science and capitalism. At the end of the seventeenth century:

> There were still women surgeons but women healers were increasingly associated with witchcraft and the practice of the black arts. As medicine became a science, the terms of entry into training excluded women, protecting the profession for the sons of families who could afford education. (Rowbotham, 1973, pp. 2–3).

This process was consolidated, so that

> In ... the medical occupations the seventeenth and eighteenth centuries witnessed an increasing division of labour and a concomitant exclusion of women from the higher and more lucrative branches which were gradually emerging. (Parry and Parry, 1976, p. 164)

The role of education, of both a general and a more specifically professional nature, was indeed central. Clark (1919) in her classic survey of *The Working Life of Women in the 17th Century* describes a similar process in teaching in which governesses cared for children while masters who had undergone more formal training gained professional status. 'By the end of the eighteenth century ... good-class medical practice had closed to women, apparently for ever' (Manton, 1965, p. 61). The barring of women from access to medical schools and the universities effectively prohibited their entry into the medical profession until the end of the nineteenth century.

The domination of the medical profession by men was paralleled and reinforced by powerful sexist ideologies surrounding the very nature of illness, 'complaints and disorders' (Ehrenreich and English, 1973). Of particular significance was the interrelation of sexist medical ideologies and class divisions, with the upper-class female 'invalid' acting as archetype of the ideal client for the male professional. Such ideologies have their legacy in the way women's health and sickness is still often seen to be a 'by-product' of their sexuality, and indeed the dominant forms of psychiatry and psychotherapy (Chesler, 1972).

Despite the opening up of medicine in the early years of this century, the profession remains primarily and excessively in the hands of men (Elston, 1977). Thus the management of health and sickness, originally an area of female specialism, has become almost a male preserve.

## The mediation of conflict

The management of health and sickness became the concern of the medical profession, just as the mediation of disputes and the honouring of life and death had become the domains of the legal and clerical professions respectively. The establishment of the legal, medical and clerical professions is the clearest instance of men coming to dominate particular areas of life, by reference back to some notion of 'neutral' professionalism and service to others. In other areas of economic life, patriarchy developed hand in hand with the growth of capitalism. In the 'settlement' of disputes, pain and mortality, a strict capitalist from of organisation was not viable and a 'professional' form a necessary, but still effective, patriarchal alternative.

Thus Elliott concludes his survey of the historical development of the professions by stating that

> The ideology of professionalism was elaborated in opposition to the economic theories of industrial capitalism, but it was a mediating ideology. It called on business to recognise its limitations but not for the overthrow of the industrial system itself. (Elliott, 1972, p. 53)

Perhaps somewhat surprisingly, a similar theme was taken up by Parsons (1939) when he pointed out the similarities of professional and business in terms of their relationship to particular 'pattern variables'. Both activities are, or aspire to be rational, functionally specific and universalistic. Parsons (1951) later elaborated on this argument when writing on the medical profession. Professions are thereby seen to perform certain tasks formerly performed within the family. Typically these tasks involve the management of social conflict and tension, including illness. According to this kind of perspective the professional may be approached by a client to tackle a problem that previously may have been resolved by one or more of the family members. Typically such tasks are raised in status with their transfer from the private to the public arena; and from women to men.

In terms of the analysis presented here, it is clearly not difficult to impose a critical shift on Parsons' theorising. What is seen by him as social conflict within a reproductive determinism is here seen as sexual conflict within the dialectics of reproduction.

### The gentleman's agreement

Two other points can be added on this first stage of professional development with capitalist patriarchy. First the *domination of men in these early professions was complete* (Reader, 1966). This was not only a numerical domination but a domination of the ethos of the professions, according to which only 'gentlemen' of independent means needed to apply for membership in the first place (Elliott, 1972). A male monopoly or near-monopoly persisted in law and medicine until the last quarter of the nineteenth century. The first 'Law Society' was appropriately named The Society of Gentlemen Practisers in the Courts of Law and Equity and was founded in 1729. Male monopoly clearly persists in the Church of England and Roman Catholic churches and male oligarchy is still maintained in most of the smaller churches.

### Patronising the arts

A second caveat is that in retrospect it is perhaps surprising that the arts have not been more heavily professionalised. True, Renaissance art was tightly controlled by codes and procedures in accordance with the demands of the Church and other patrons (sic); while the numerical dominance of men, particularly in painting, is now catalogued by Germaine Greer (1979) in *The Obstacle Race*. But by and large patriarchy has dominated the arts without direct recourse to a rigid professional model. Of particular interest here is the general counter movement in the arts over the last century from the Impressionists through to the Surrealists and into contemporary pluralism. This provides an important lesson that decentralisation and diversification are no guarantee of non-patriarchal social forms; rather it is a tribute to the strength of patriarchy.

### The control of emotionality

While the mediation of disputes and the management of life and death may in structural terms be instances of reproduction, in individual terms they are a major material basis for the expression of emotions. The nature of emotionality ranges from positive feelings which may actually reinforce the enjoyment of work to negative debilitating grief. Thus in this sense the development of professions is also intimately bound up with the social organisation and control of emotionality.

Emotionality also occurs for other reasons than as an individualistic expression of reproduction. Indeed, at a more abstract level, the very separation of emotionality and instrumentality or rationality can itself be explained by reference to the compartmentalising character of both capitalism and patriarchy. Strangely enough the very duality of rationality and emotionality created by capitalist patriarchy present inconveniences to their maintenance. While large areas of social life are determined by the operation of 'rational' capitalist method, emotions recur in the interstices of capitalist and patriarchal relations. Emotionality created and structured by capitalist patriarchy becomes at once a field for its further elaboration. Capitalist development entails the shifting of control of different types of emotions or different bases of emotionality from merely domestic labour into socialised labour.

**Men in the semi-professions**

Since the development of the 'established professions' monopolised by men, this process has continued apace elsewhere. It is in the so-called semi-professions that this second phase of professional development has taken place. Within nursing, health visiting, midwifery, social work and teaching are the emerging structures by which grief, joy, loss and despair are patriarchally socialised. The semi-professions are thus concerned with incipient and progressive socialisation of emotionality. Activities and experiences formerly performed privately or controlled by women became in this way brought into public control by men, and so subject to the expertise of experts. As such, the semi-professions are symptomatic of a later stage of capitalist patriarchy than that which spawned the traditional professions.

What follows is an attempt to set out the broad types of changes by which semi-professions become more like the full professions, and so become more explicitly dominated by men.

1. *Feminist action*
2. *Initial incorporation*
   (a) Serving a man
   (b) Serving an existing profession
3. *Setting the status quo*
   (a) The patriarchal feminine
   (b) The professional code
4. *Divide and rule*
   (a) Men in the ranks
   (b) Segmenting the market
5. *Takeover*
   (a) Managerialism and men in management
   (b) Full professionalisation

Not all semi-professions are necessarily affected by all of these changes. In some cases one particular process may be dominant, while in another several processes may overlap and interrelate with each other.

## 1. *Feminist action*

Women have been particularly prominent in pioneering the socialisation of emotional experiences through the development of social work, care for the sick and aged, and so on. By forging the socialisation of unpredictable emotions, women have potentially posed a far greater threat to capitalism than men. Indeed, in their earliest forms some of these interventions were potentially revolutionary. This is perhaps best illustrated in the early history of health visiting with its close links with radical and feminist movements (Dingwall, 1977), and the work of Sylvia Pankhurst and other suffragettes in the East London Women's Federation. A rather similar pattern is discernible in the history of social work, rooted in the activism and social reform of women in both Britain and America in the second half of the last century (Walton, 1975; Bolin, 1973). Kravetz (1976) has shown how in America this dynamism continued until the 1920s, with the ratification of the Nineteenth Amendment and the general disintegration of the feminist movement. A rather similar development is described by Gordon (1975) in relation to the American birth control movement. In its early days this represented a bold feminist and socialist innovation, only to be subsequently appropriated by male control in the shape of the medical profession. At the same time, it must be remembered that as soon as this process of socialising emotions began, it increased the possibility for their incorporation by the institutions of capitalist patriarchy.

## 2. *Initial incorporation*

(a) *Serving a man.* If women pose a threat to both men and capitalists by taking on the socialised work of emotionality in the interstices of capitalism, then attempts are soon made to remove the threat. The simplest mechanism to achieve this is for isolated men to take on the control of the activity, as we see with C. S. Loch and his work with the Charity Organisation Society. This is the means often used in the early days of the semi-professions. In effect capitalists are employing men to manage women to work in sensitive areas of economy and society. In turn these women care for and control other men and other women as patients, clients or whatever. Women act as the agents of men. In the case of the Charity Organisation Society the control of women by men was also related to class control. Sexual divisions in such early initiatives were frequently paralleled by both class division and ideological divisions. COS philosophy and development reflected the social position of its members as the professional London elite, with aspirations to form a new urban gentry. This in turn legitimated a progressive confidence in the expert and scientific nature of charity (Stedman Jones, 1971).

(b) *Serving an existing profession.* Though isolated men may be an effective means of control, they are hardly reliable. A more stable and more structured form of incorporation comes from the subservience of particular semi-professions to other full professions. Thus a whole array of paramedical semi-professions have developed to service the full profession of medicine – not only nurses, as catalogued by Gamarnikow (1978), but also midwives, health visitors, radiographers, occupational and speech therapists, and so on. The Ladies Sanitary Reform Association was set up as an incipient health visiting organisation initially, as a parallel to the all-male Manchester and Salford Sanitary Reform Society. The latter concentrated more on the structural aspects of sanitation, while disease resulting from failures in household management and thus requiring practical instruction and home visiting was seen as a woman's concern. Thus a separate ladies group was established, which was later to come under the control of the male-dominated Medical Officers of Health.

Other semi-professions can be understood in this way as serving established professions. Social workers spend much of their time serving, that is receiving referrals from and writing reports for, medics, lawyers, the courts, even the police. Even librarianship is seen at its fullest development when serving men, in universities and other 'places of learning'.

Further intensification of such subordination can often be seen in the physical and institutional arrangements that accompany the semi-professions. Of particular significance for the medical semi-professions is the development of hospital-based medicine, with the form and layout of buildings and the sexual divisions within and outside them reinforcing each other (Versluysen, 1981).

3. *Setting the status quo*

(a) *The patriarchal feminine.* Structural arrangements whereby particular semi-professions service or serve particular professions or particular men may be a major way of defining a space, a territory for the semi-professions, but they do not in themselves act as a very efficient means of controlling the idea and aspirations of the semi-professionals. This necessitates some attention to the realm of ideology.

It has frequently been observed how the sorts of paid work women undertake tend to mirror the domestic tasks of cleaning, food preparation, clothing manufacture, and so on. A similar parallel can be drawn between the social-emotional domestic tasks and the semi-professional areas of specialisation. This element of sex role socialisation I refer to as the patriarchal feminine – feminine as it conforms to the feminine, 'caring' stereotype; patriarchal because in doing so it complements and thereby reinforces the masculine stereotype and specialisation. In this way the ideology of femininity is central to patriarchy in general and the semi-professions in particular.

This ideology is exemplified most clearly in the paramedical semi-professions, with the 'feminine' nurse 'complementing' the 'masculine' doctor (Gamarnikow, 1978; Ehrenreich and English, 1974, p. 38). Carpenter, writing on the historical development of the nursing ethic suggests:

The work itself was not to be tainted with the world of Capital. It was to be carried out as a *service* and pecuniary motives were to play no part, just as home was supposed to be the place where goods and services were provided for love, not money. (Carpenter, 1977, p. 166)

The patriarchal femininity of the semi-professions has also seen more pronounced, even authoritarian, forms. Within nursing the matron has personified a certain reinforcement of patriarchal authority by 'running a tight ship' in the areas left by the medical men. Even more interesting and complicated examples arise within the teaching profession. Indeed, women teachers and headmistresses may both encourage the ideology of femininity amongst their pupils, whilst at the same time emulating their male counterparts.

In its purest form patriarchal authority is reproduced through the class structure of the semi-professions. Nursing, teaching and similar semi-professions have not only provided jobs for a mass of women, but more particularly posts with considerable authority for middle- and upper-class women. This has not only reinforced male authority, but has also brought a divisive class element into the semi-professions. In some senses this class structuring of authority *within* the semi-professions mirrors the sexual structuring of authority *around* and *between* semi-professions and professions. This brings many contradictions, as Parry and Parry (1976, p. 181) comment:

The paradox was that the search for professionalism among nurses was more an expression of the antipathy felt by the status conscious lady-nurses towards those recruited from the working class than it was an effort to establish a self-governing profession of nursing.

This leads us directly onto the question of professionalism and the professional code.

(b) *The professional code.* Another effective form of ideological control (known to all teachers and prison governors) is for the practitioners, the women, to develop their own form of self-control. The principal way of achieving this is by the development of the professional code and professionalisation in general. This in effect masculinises the behaviour of practitioners, with the professional ethic expressing completely 'gentlemanly reasonableness' (Duman,

1979). The professional socialisation of the semi-professionals obliges them to conform to certain norms of behaviour (Theodore, 1971) and establishes the ideology of universalism and exclusivity.

This process has been described by Chafetz (1972) in examining the state of American social work in the post-war period. Attempts to attract more men into a female-dominated sphere have included the development of a more 'professional' base, as part of an effort to, what is misleadingly called, 'defeminise' social work. The introduction of professional codes into the semi-professions may increase the status of individual women, but in its wake brings the practical problem of career continuity, dual roles, dual career families and so on. Most importantly, however, the establishment of professional codes contributes to the possibility of more men entering the ranks.

## 4. *Divide and rule*

(a) *Men in the ranks.* The acceptance of masculinised version of behaviour in dealing with emotionality not only makes such jobs more appealing in themselves to men, but also increases their status in the market. Thus indirectly they become 'more acceptable' to men as careers. The entrance of men into women's semi-professions has been seen in nursing, social work and teaching. Once in, men are available, of course, to enter the more prestigious jobs. This is perhaps most clearly illustrated by the movement of men into first and middle school headships in recent years.

(b) *Segmenting the market.* As men enter the ranks of the semi-professions, they enter in a highly discriminating way. The market is segmented in a number of directions – by status, by specialisation, by stereotype.

Within teaching there are sexual divisions not only between primary and secondary education, but also by subject, with clear divisions between arts and science teaching. A rather similar development occurs within the different specialisms of social work. Women tend to specialise more in front-line casework; men more in community work, research and policy development (Brager and Michael, 1969; Scotch, 1971). The probation service is not only more populated by men than other branches of social work (Walton, 1975, p. 22), but it also has better conditions of service, a flatter organisational hierarchy, and arguably a more reliable source of finance from the 'law and order' sector. Within psychiatric social work men have an influence out of all proportion to their relatively small numbers (Timms, 1964, p. 74). A more subtle and yet perhaps more significant discrimination is between practitioners and theorists, with men again tending to dominate the 'academic' section of the semi-professions, including social work (Rosenblatt *et al.*, 1970).

All of these various discriminations by specialism can be seen both in strictly economic terms as well as in status terms. Mennerick's (1975) study of organisational structuring by sex within travel agencies has the important double lesson that 'creaming' may take place not only between agencies of different status, but also within agencies. Within most of the semi-professions there is the strange contradiction of women occupying the majority of posts, as well as being diverted into the more specialist areas of work away from the centre of the profession (Mackie and Pattullo, 1977, pp. 90–1).

## 5. *Takeover*

(a) *Managerialism and men in management.* The differential promotion of men and women in the semi-professions culminates in the progressive separation of the semi-professional managers and the semi-professional practitioners. Not only are the managers likely to be largely or exclusively men,[1] but the management ideology is heavily male-orientated.

The semi-professions can be seen as one relatively easy route by which men can reach managerial positions (Kadushin, 1976). This is particularly so in the context of British local government, where almost all departments other than social services are traditionally heavily male-dominated. The position for women is exacerbated by management's preference for full-time rather than part-time senior staff. There are, for example, very few part-time social workers above basic grade level. In many ways managerialism represents a further reinforcement of the male-orientational ideology of professionalism. Furthermore, the managerial takeover links the patriarchal ideology directly with the capitalist restructuring of these activities. For example, Gough (1979) claims that the spread of managerialism within the welfare state in recent years is one way in which priorities and services can be altered to the disadvantage of the working class.

A detailed account of the onset of managerialism in nursing,

particularly since the Salmon Report in 1966, has been provided by
Carpenter (1977). He sees that Report as an implicit critique of
*female* authority in nursing, and in this way sexist. He writes:

> Female nurses are viewed as inherently unable to exercise ad-
> ministrative skills. They may be 'meticulous in details on which
> the life of a patient depends' ... 'but when, on promotion to posts
> in Matron's office they venture on to "administration" many
> seem unable to take decisions'.

The outcome of this criticism and the subsequent reorganisation
was the creation of more posts in nursing management, 'made ripe
for male capture'.

A comparable pattern has occurred within social work. Walton
has commented:

> In almonering, psychiatric social work and child care, women
> formed a spearhead for professional development and it is a great
> irony that in a profession so long fought for over many lifetimes
> by women that there should be the prospect of long-term subjec-
> tion to men and the fact that principles carefully nursed may be in
> danger of disintegrating from mechanical managerial and plan-
> ning systems (Walton, 1975, p. 263).

Although managerialism is often linked with bureaucratisation
and thus contrasted with professionalism, the dichotomy is surely a
false one. In fact in the cases of both nursing and social work, a
so-called 'new professionalism' has followed close on the heels of
the 'new managerialism'.

(b) *Full professionalisation.* Full professionalisation comes when
the activity is fully dominated by men – in both management and the
ranks. It is the fate that awaits the semi-professions. Full professionalisation is also signalled by the monopolisation by men of the
particular area of emotional life, free from competition from other,
probably more female-dominated occupations.

The process has come full circle. While semi-professionalisation
indicates partial patriarchal domination, full professionalisation
indicates full patriarchal domination. Once this has been accomplished, further areas of life can be opened up for sponsorship;
further semi-professions can service the professions.

## *The case of midwifery*

Before continuing onto some concluding remarks, it may be useful to consider, albeit briefly, some of the historical changes that have affected the semi-profession of midwifery. In connecting back with earlier comments on reproduction and emotionality, midwifery is clearly a crucial area. Midwifery is a semi-profession at the point of biological reproduction. Just as within Marxist analysis the point of production is crucial, so patriarchy can be usefully analysed by reference to the specific points of reproduction, sexual, biological, social. Similarly birth is one of the most emotional experiences, if not the most. Midwives, and subsequently health visitors, monitor these emotions, though not necessarily explicitly or even consciously. More importantly, they translate them from private into public terms. Birth is acknowledged as producing a certain amount of emotion, but not too little and certainly not too much. If either extreme occurs then further steps may be taken by the semi-professional to place the case within a more socialised context, that is, to bring it to the attention of other professions and senior members of semi-professions, and therefore men. In this sense the semi-professions can act as spies on behalf of men.

Interestingly enough until the seventeenth century childbirth was effectively 'women's business', the province of the midwife. However, controls had been operative during the sixteenth century in the sense that midwives had to take an oath not to use magic when attending pregnant women (Rowbotham, 1973, p. 5). From the beginning of the eighteenth century the delivery of babies became for male doctors a means of entering increasingly lucrative family practice. The right to use instruments was essentially part of the monopoly of surgery enjoyed by men. This led to a division of the market, with doctors' skills reserved for those who could pay and midwives continuing to provide for the poor.

This situation persisted until the second half of the nineteenth century, with increasing interest from feminists in extending employment opportunities. In Britain the Female Medical Society was founded in 1862 and shortly afterwards it instituted a Ladies' Medical College for instructing women in midwifery and medicine. This was largely superseded by the London School of Medicine for women set up in 1874. By 1886 the Matrons' Aid Society was working under the bolder name of The Midwives' Institute. By the

1890s the relationship between the women midwives and the men doctors was becoming more fraught. In particular two issues dominated the political arena: the questions of inter-professional authority and midwife registration, which was pressed for by the Midwives' Institute in particular.

A number of Parliamentary Bills for registration were prompted during the 1890s culminating in the successful Bill of 1902. Since then there have been a whole series of further intense divisions around foetal monitoring, amniocentesis, hospital inductions, the use of chemical pain relievers, home confinements, the role of fathers (as 'surrogate doctors' or otherwise) and so on.

Several conclusions can be drawn from these events. First, and most important, is that in the professionalisation of midwifery, the contending parties were more clearly defined by sex than in other semi-professions. The closer one approaches the point of reproduction the more marked are sexual divisions of the related workers. Secondly, changes that took place have to be interpreted as of a dialectical nature rather than as fixed or evolutionary. Thus feminist pressure within the ranks of the midwives did not simply arise in the early days of semi-professionalisation, but continued at each point, especially to fend off the various compromises on offer. Indeed, the Act itself had complicated and apparently contradictory implications. On the one hand it represented a partial setback to the male medical monopoly, following the Medical Registration Act of 1886. On the other it meant midwives were 'unique in being subject to the licensing procedures of a local government (and) could be struck off from the . . . register for a wide range of ill-defined and petty ethical misdemeanours which even included minute regulations governing their dress' (Parry and Parry, 1976, p. 180).

Versluysen concludes her historical survey of midwifery:

> female midwives found their subordinate status confirmed by the . . . Act which put a majority of medical men on the council responsible for the training and registration of midwives, thereby making clear that neither skilled women nor mothers could regard birth as their own concern anymore. (Versluysen, 1981, p. 43).

The case of midwifery acts as an important reminder that changes towards greater professionalisation should not be seen as part of some remorseless evolutionary process. Rather professionalisation is merely a shorthand term for a variety of processes by which men move into and increase their influence on the semi-professions.

## Concluding remarks

So far I have surveyed some of the ways semi-professions become more dominated by men and so more 'fully professional'. According to this analysis the professions, both established and emerging, are both fully and partially dominated by men, and indeed the whole process of professionalisation is one of the bastions of patriarchy. This is particularly so in the sphere of reproduction and the control of emotionality, areas of life that present difficulties for capitalist organisation and patriarchal domination.

The major purpose of this paper has thus been to demonstrate the impact of the professions in the maintenance and development of the patriarchy. It is in the context of this relationship that the semi-professions, staffed mainly by women, managed mainly by men, in turn assumes a greater significance than is usually attributed to them. The traditional professions have grown to dominate important areas of reproduction. Indeed medicine, the Church and the law effectively control the management of life and death, in biological, spiritual and social terms respectively. They operate close to and with jurisdiction over the various points of reproduction. They are concerned with the socialisation of what were formerly private, emotional experiences around the points of reproduction.

In contrast to the overarching role of the professions, the semi-professions have a much more limited area of interest and work. They either act as the 'handmaidens' of the professions in performing specific duties, for example radiographers, or they focus on particular points of reproduction, for example midwives, or they assist on extending professional concerns into new areas, for example psychotherapists. The male-dominated professions define the limits of action and ideology and so control both reproduction and the semi-professions indirectly, almost without having to be there. The female-dominated semi-professions do particular types of, often arduous, work and control particular aspects of reproduction directly. Indeed, the closer one approaches particular points of reproduction, whether sexual, natal or whatever, the greater may be the ideological need to demonstrate apparent control by women, through the semi-professions, although the greater may be the material need to exert actual control by men, through the professions. The semi-profession of midwifery is clearly crucial, particularly in terms of the sexual division of occupations in relation to the points of reproduction, in this case that of birth itself.

A final, more speculative, point is that professionalisation, already analysed as patriarchal, is one of the major ways in which two apparently disparate realms, institutional science and personal sexuality, are linked. The church, medicine and the law still effectively define sexual limits. Sexuality may yet become more fully 'scientised' through the action of professionals.

## Note

1. See introduction to this section of this reader – *ed*.

# VI

# Women and the Informal and Voluntary Sector of the Social Services

# Introduction

Policies for 'community care', as Finch and Groves point out in the article reproduced here, are not particularly recent phenomena. However, in recent years there has been a considerable growth in attention given to such policies, both from politicians and policy-makers and from feminist commentators. On the one hand, politicians and policy-makers have come to recognise that there are inevitable problems, now and on the horizon, arising out of demographic trends and the inexorable growth in the proportion of the population who are elderly and dependent (see Family Policy Studies Centre, 1984, for a useful summary of these trends). At the same time, politicians have also recognised that there are sources of manpower, and more particularly *woman*power, that have traditionally provided caring services for the dependent population for nothing, either 'informally' within the family or within the context of the voluntary social services that use volunteers. During a period of severe cut-backs in social service expenditure, at a time when there are also increases in the 'need' for social services, it is clearly in the politicians' and policy-makers' interest to encourage the provision of these free services and to persuade even more people to come forward as 'informal' and 'voluntary' carers. Feminists, on the other hand, are highly critical of these policy trends, for they see them as yet another form of the exploitation of women. After all, they argue, 'caring' is in many ways very like common or garden housework (Ungerson, 1983) except that it has particularly depressing and debilitating features (see, for example, Flew, 1980; Bayley, 1973), and recent research from a variety of sources has confirmed that the majority of carers (though by no means all) are women

209

(EOC, 1982a; Charlesworth, Wilkin and Durie, 1984; Wilkin, 1979; Finch and Groves, 1983). Moreover, despite changes in women's participation in the labour market, there seems little sign that women will be less likely to take on 'caring' in the future:- it is far more likely that women will add to their burden of labour by working in paid work in such a way that they can combine paid employment with the unpaid tasks of caring (Ungerson, 1985).

Much of the support for policies of 'community care' is couched in 'naturalist' language. Mrs Thatcher's speech reproduced here is a typical example. Such language is used to maintain the view that the two (undefined) institutions of 'family' and 'community', and altruistic relations within them, are 'natural' and therefore inevitable. However, a central feature of the most recent wave of feminism has been an attack on 'naturalism', both in its use within the biological sciences (Sayers, 1982), and as the notion has been co-opted by policy-makers (Rose and Rose, 1982). As part of this critique, key institutions such as 'family' and 'community' have been re-analysed, both to refine their over-simplified and ideological definitions, and to unpack the different roles of men and women within them, and demonstrate the way in which those roles are socially, as opposed to biologically, constructed. Moreover, as Finch and Groves show here, one of the important determinants of the differential social roles of men and women is social policy; policies for 'community care' which rely increasingly on services provided within families, with only sporadic support from social and voluntary services, make it inevitable that the main task of caring for the nation's dependants will fall upon women, since it is they who have traditionally given of their domestic labour for no formal monetary reward.

Mrs Thatcher is concerned not only with services provided within the family, but also with the services of volunteers working within the context of nationally based voluntary organisations and locally based neighbourhood associations. She sees such voluntary activity as complementary to state-financed and organised social services, and at one point suggests that voluntary services should be the chief providers and the statutory services the stop-gap and co-ordinators of voluntary effort. The context of the speech and the language she uses both imply that she also expects that most of the people manning (sic) these services will be women, working in a voluntary capacity. Indeed, at one point in the speech Mrs Thatcher says that 'voluntary service enables the individual to express *her* personality,

imagination and ingenuity' (my italics). But is volunteerism necessarily compatible with or substitutable for state-funded and organised social service activity? And is it necessarily exploitative of the
goodwill of women? It is important to remember that 'voluntary
effort' can mean a wide range of activity, from work that complements state activity (e.g. meals on wheels) to work that is designed
as a critique of and counter-balance to state activity. As far as
women's interests are concerned, women's refuges, rape crisis
centres, and some self-help health groups are examples of volunteerism which is oppositional rather than complementary to the
state. Moreover, all these organisations *insist* that their voluntary
workers are women on the grounds that 'women's problems' arising
out of male sexism can only be appropriately handled by women.
Respectively, such organisations present a critique of, and an
alternative to, the services of local authority social service and
housing departments, the operations of the police in cases of
violence by men against women, and the treatment by doctors of
women patients. (See Curno *et al.*, 1982, for examples of other
kinds of oppositional voluntary activity, or, as they term it,
'women's collective action'.)However, as the article by Hilary Rose
points out, these organisations are often run on a knife edge,
balancing between solvency and insolvency, charismatic leadership
and non-hierarchical collective management, and, particularly
where state funds are received and there is co-operation with local
social service agencies, balancing between feminist struggle and
feminine philanthropy. As Jan Pahl has put it, in an article describing the way in which language can be part of these balancing acts
and ambiguities: 'Does the movement for women's refuges work *for*
women, or *with* women? ... Is Women's Aid a charity or a pressure
group? ... Are refuges social provision, or part of a social movement?' (Pahl, 1979).

These kinds of question indicate that it is impossible to generalise about voluntary activity; it is neither necessarily exploitative of
women, nor is it necessarily feminist. Clearly there are many
different intentions and styles, some 'reformist', some 'radical',
some 'complementary', some 'subversive', some 'elitist', some 'par-
ticipatory'. For feminists, whether academics or activists or both,
the problem is to refine definitions of volunteerism such that the
styles and purposes of voluntary action can be categorised, and their
relation to the liberation and exploitation of women better understood.

**Additional reading**

The growing literature on volunteering tends to forget the sex of the
volunteers under discussion and thus manages to omit any reference
to gender issues. An exception to this general feature is a sym-
posium edited by Stephen Hatch on *Volunteers: Patterns, Meanings
and Motives* (1983) where at least the sex of the volunteers is
identified in most of the articles and considered as a variable in the
analysis. In 'The Working-Class Family: a Marxist perspective',
Jane Humphries (1982) documents the defence of the family by the
working class in the nineteenth century, and, in particular, working-
class support for informal care within the family in preference to the
state provision for dependency through the residential institution of
the workhouse. The statements of Mrs Thatcher and the parallels
she draws between being Prime Minister and being a mother are
fascinatingly drawn together in Tony Fitzgerald's article on 'The
New Right and the Family' (1983).

# 'Facing the New Challenge'

## MARGARET THATCHER

It is a heartening fact that there are now more older people being looked after in their own homes than ever before. You wouldn't always think that but it is true. Indeed I think it's remarkable that 95 out of every 100 retired people live at home, and only 5 in every 100 are in residential and hospital care. And ladies and gentlemen, that couldn't be achieved without some marvellous voluntary work on the part of organisations like the Women's Royal Voluntary Services. I go round one Saturday every year before Christmas to the house-bound. I may say that is a day which I enjoy tremendously and learn a great deal from. I know just how much is done to help those people to stay living at home, and I know that the most important thing in their lives is to go on living at home with their own familiar things surrounding them. They're also so very cheerful. Sometimes they can keep you in absolute stitches with some of the things they tell you about their previous life. This year only one person I saw was under the age of 90. And some of them told me about life in their young days. And as I came away from one or two of the houses or rooms where they were living I just had a feeling that the things they were telling me about belong to a very wholesome society in some ways, in the relationship between people and the generosity shown one to another. But that's just a little bit of what I do almost every year, especially in my own constituency.

But it all really starts in the family, because not only is the family the most important means through which we show our care for

*Source*: extracted from the Prime Minister's speech at the Women's Royal Voluntary Service national conference, 'Facing the New Challenge', 19 January 1981.

others. It's the place where each generation learns its responsibilities towards the rest of society. You stressed the family, Madam Chairman, and I want to stress the importance of the family here at this conference because I know that almost everyone here will recognise as I do the debt we owe to the example set within our own families. That certainly is where I learnt it at home with my parents. And our own involvement in voluntary work is so often the outcome of the example and training of parents and relatives who expected us to want to do something for others. Not only to do it, but to do it happily, because that was the way we lived. And those who set us on our way certainly knew none of the jargon phrases and would never have spoken of 'informal caring networks' when they meant family and friends, relatives and neighbours. Yet those who set us on our way, they understood the fact which our society is only now rediscovering. That the only effective way to reach all those who need help is through the voluntary service of millions of individuals who do what they can because they want to. And however much money we have and however rich Britain becomes, there's no way and no budget which could produce statutory services to meet the needs which as volunteers you now satisfy. And in the end, real neighbourliness and understanding care comes most naturally from those who choose to give it, and it comes most effectively from those who are neighbours and friends of those they help.

So this enthusiasm for voluntary help is therefore not the need to reduce Government spending. The fact is that it's as important in times of expansion and economic growth as it is during a recession. There are those who come and imply that the volunteer is just a cheap substitute for a salaried staff, but quite the contrary. I believe that the volunteer movement is at the heart of all our social welfare provision. That the statutory services are the supportive ones underpinning where necessary, filling the gaps and helping the helpers. Yes, they are vital in sorting out the logistics, but the army in the field is overwhelmingly made up of volunteers like you. Of course, to many of us this is to restate the home truths by upbringing and experience we've learned. But it makes it all the more exciting to see the way in which this view is increasingly widely accepted. Accepted even among those who once thought that voluntary action was only a stop-gap, for the state found the resources and trained the experts to run the thing in what they would have called 'their properly professional way'. But that view is particularly old-fashioned, and I'm very encouraged by the way in which local authorities, directors of social services, the social work profession and the specialist press are increasingly determined to shift the emphasis of statutory provision so that it becomes an enabling service, the statutory provision enabling the volunteers to do their jobs more effectively.

And, of course, that also gives the statutory service a key role to play. And what I'm trying to show is that in the kind of society in which we are privileged to live, it depends first on doing what we should do at home and looking after friends and families. It depends then on joining together to see that things are looked after in the community, and that too depends upon having good statutory services to see there aren't any gaps, upon getting everything well organised to see that we go where help is needed and to enable us to do our best.

It really all locks together. It isn't that any one group is in competition with another. It is that all are necessary to the way of life in which we live. And so therefore the statutory services do have a key role to play. The full-time professional can ensure that voluntary groups are used to the best advantage, and they act as a catalyst where voluntary effort has faded or volunteers are few. And above all the statutory services can support the supporters. They can ease the pressure on the volunteers with professional help and advice. I've always thought that one of the very best examples of everyone helping and pulling together to give the very best possible service is the Meals on Wheels Service. It tends to be taken for granted: it shouldn't be. As I went round your exhibition one of your people told me that last year the WRVS provided 17 million meals, and what a welcome they must have been to the people to whom they were taken. A welcome not only because it was a hot meal, but the welcome shown on their faces as they welcomed the people into their homes, and welcomed tremendously the social contact which that gave them. Many many congratulations on the things which you do day in and day out for which perhaps too little thanks are given.

But I think the statutory services can only play their part success-fully if we don't expect them to do for us things that we could be doing for ourselves. There is, as you know, a growing army of self-helpers, kinds of informal grassroot groups dedicated to meeting local need in individual ways. And here is where there is a very real new hope. These are not great national bodies, but they are groups of people getting together where they see a local need. I met several of them. You'll find sometimes in a village that someone who's had an idea that people living alone may not be able to demonstrate that they need help. So they've put bells in their homes. When that bell is pulled the bell rings outside and everyone in the village knows that that person needs help. You'll find the churches issuing cards, and the moment a card goes in the window everyone knows that someone needs help. I will have groups in some of my housing estates who are getting together and looking after mothers who need babysitting for children, who need help with children, getting together to help the old people. Another group is going around to try to ensure that there is access in the main shops for wheelchairs of people who are disabled.

These are the smaller self-help groups called forth when there is a local need by them spotting a local need and filling it themselves. And I know how very much those groups depend on the more formal structure of the WRVS and others to provide them with the advice which they need to carry on their job. And that really is one example of volunteers in the great national body helping other volunteers called forth in these local groups.

And I don't think any of us should feel put out because some other group is tackling problems in a different way from us. Because really variety is one of the glories of the voluntary movement. And very local and even spontaneous effort can be given continuity and material help by the national organisations. Volunteers who may not join a national body can often join a local group, and yet the bigger voluntary organisations can give substance to local initiative and help to foster and extend it. There need therefore be no conflict between those newer forms of voluntary effort and older established organisations like yours. They've all a place in meeting the needs of our varied society. And it's only by recognising that there are many things that we can't do as effectively as others that we free ourselves to do things that we can do best.

That really is a lesson that Governments have to relearn the whole time because we politicians and administrators mustn't forget that the state has a limited role. Yet it is so easy for people to expect the state to do more than it ought to do. And there are always very real temptations for politicians to pretend that they're able to do more than is ever possible. And that's why I welcomed the way in which we in Britain recognise that it's right for Government to help independent voluntary bodies financially, because those bodies can do things which the Government can't or they can do them a lot better. And last year the Government, which is merely the instrument of the taxpayer through the taxpayer, gave about £85 million in grants to voluntary organisations. Very well spent money indeed. Much of it called out matching contributions from industry and individuals.

And it makes the partnership between Government and the voluntary organisations easier. Also the last budget included a £30 million package of tax concessions designed to increase income from charitable giving. Again that wasn't proposed as a means of saving taxpayers' money. Government help to voluntary bodies has not been reduced: indeed it's been increased. It was intended to increase the independence of charities and the variety of their response to the problems they face. If too much of the money were to come from Government, then too much of the direction of activity would be dictated by priorities of Government and too little by the demands of the situation on the ground, which you know better than anyone else. The vitality of voluntary organisations would be sapped if they were ever to make themselves creatures of Government. So our role, with the voluntary organisations, is to help you to do the administration and work of mobilising this enormous army of volunteers which can do the work throughout the community in a better way than anyone else can.

Sometimes in your pamphlets but always in the demonstrations of the work you do, you show that the voluntary principle is important for reasons which are far beyond economics. Yes please do clap; it is extremely important. The willingness of men and women to give service is one of freedom's greatest safeguards. It ensures that caring remains free from political control. It leaves men and women independent enough to meet needs as they see them, and not only as the state provides. And that's why voluntary organisations such as ours can only exist effectively in a free society.

# Community Care and the Family: A Case for Equal Opportunities?

## JANET FINCH and DULCIE GROVES

### Equal opportunities: legislative commitment and policy implications

The concern of this article is to examine some of the unacknow-ledged consequences, for women in particular of community care as a way of coping with the needs of frail elderly and severely handi-capped individuals who might otherwise be in residential care. It is argued that the primary care of these groups will fall increasingly on female relatives. Community care has increasingly been viewed as an auspicious policy option in the past decade and the election of a Conservative government in 1979 is unlikely to reverse that trend. But the enthusiasm with which the idea has been taken up has not always been matched by clear thinking about its likely consequ-ences.

Any assessment of the implications of relatives being carers needs to take into account the degree of handicap or disability experi-enced by the dependent person. Many elderly, handicapped and convalescent people are sustained in their own homes by limited family or neighbourly assistance, supplemented by such volunteer help, paid good-neighbour schemes or domiciliary or medical ser-vices as are available and appropriate. But the most frail and handicapped people need continuous assistance or supervision or nursing. If social policies are concerned, where possible, to keep this

*Source*: very slightly abridged from Janet Finch and Dulcie Groves, 'Com-munity Care and the Family: a Case for Equal Opportunities?', *Journal of Social Policy*, Vol. 9, Part 4, October 1980, pp. 487–511.

group out of residential care, primary care by family members seems (except in unusual cases) to be the only alternative.

Discussion of the likely outcomes of the continuation of present community care policies is based on certain assumptions – that major cuts in public expenditure will continue, that the numbers of the very old will go on rising to the end of the century, and that levels of unemployment will remain high. It is also assumed that legislation which signals a commitment to 'promoting equality of opportunity between men and women', as in the Sex Discrimination Act 1975, will remain in force. Although it is beyond the scope of this article to discuss the concept of equality of opportunity, which remains somewhat enigmatic, nevertheless some notion of positive promotion is clearly implicit.

The juxtaposition of sex discrimination legislation with policies designed to promote community care for the very frail and the handicapped illustrates a situation outlined in the [1974] White Paper, *Equality for Women,* which suggested that although 'there is a role, limited but indispensable, to be played by legislation . . . there are wide areas in which the government itself can do little. This position sets the scene for an absence of positive promotion of equal opportunities, in which certain public policies, while not appearing to have a direct bearing on equality between the sexes, could be counter-productive to this goal and could actually negate the effects of such equal opportunities legislation as is already enacted. Community care policies could be a case in point.

Furthermore, sex discrimination legislation does not at present directly enter the sphere of the family, despite the fact that various policies of successive governments have implicitly embodied and actively reinforced certain models of the sexual division of labour and other family relationships, as Land and Parker (1978) have clearly demonstrated. Much of British social and financial legislation of post-war origin which impinges on domestic arrangements reflects a fairly traditional concept of family roles which may not now accurately portray some contemporary domestic arrangements (Donnison, 1978).

The purpose of this article is to demonstrate that current community care policies cut across a legislative commitment to equality between the sexes. If the principle of equal opportunities is to be taken seriously and if public policies are to promote that principle, then community care policies, among other policies, must be rigorously examined, and steps taken to ensure that the burden of care in the future will be open to equal sharing between the sexes.

## The community care bandwagon

It can be argued that the principle of community care was recognised by central government as far back as the National Health Service Act 1946 and the National Assistance Act 1948 (Titmuss, 1968, p. 106) and that the legislation of that period gave local authorities most of the powers (albeit permissive ones) which they needed in order to develop community care in the personal social services (Moroney, 1976, pp. 51–2). The Mental Health Act 1959 gave a considerable spur to public interest in developing community care as a major policy option. However, with respect to the care of the elderly, the Phillips Report (1954) had already discussed the role of domiciliary services aimed at keeping people in their own homes for as long as possible. The subsequent history of the development of community care as a major policy aim is well documented (Jones *et al.* 1978; Sainsbury, 1977; Bayley, 1973), with particular emphasis usually being laid upon the impetus given by the Seebohm Report (1968).

Over this period, the meaning of 'community care' has changed considerably, and has moved well beyond what was implied by those who advocated it in the early 1960s. At that time, the emphasis seemed mainly to be upon replacing large and often geographically remote institutional facilities with smaller units of residential provision, located in built-up areas which would, if possible, be familiar to individual residents (Kushlick, 1967). Soon, however, the concept of community care was being given a rather different meaning, as the Skeffington (1969) and Seebohm Reports introduced the idea of citizen participation in local social services and the Aves Report (1969) underlined the possibilities for the use of volunteers in the social services. Thus, by the early 1970s, it was possible for Bayley to make his key distinction between care *in* the community and care *by* the community (Bayley, 1973). Although the earlier emphasis was more upon community care in the sense of the community simply being the location for the care of dependent groups, by the mid-1970s Bayley's work had shifted the emphasis towards care *by* the community, incorporating some notion of 'the community' actually doing the caring. Recently, there has also been a growth of interest in 'the informal network of support provided by family friends and neighbours' (Wolfenden, 1978, p. 15), and in the possibilities for the further development of these relationships and their integration with statutory services. The recognition of the quantity of caring provided by this informal sector leads, in a time of public expenditure cuts, to the view that it is more realistic to develop social services by further mobilisation of the informal sector: 'If we are concerned that adequate services should be provided for those who need them there is . . . no choice but to seek to develop a new style of provision that interweaves statutory and informal care' (Bayley, 1978). Community care indeed has come a long way from the simple notion of providing small residential units in normal surroundings.

Despite widespread enthusiasm for community care as a concept, in practice the picture is discouraging. Although the Mental Health Act 1959 committed central government to the development of services along the lines of community care, in the intervening twenty years the allocation of resources has not necessarily reflected this priority. The provision of day care, for example, is well below target: by March 1979, only 2 local authorities (out of 107) had achieved the target for day care places for the mentally ill laid down in the 1975 White Paper (DHSS, 1975a)[1], and 27 provided no day care places at all.[2] In fact, the provision of a whole range of domiciliary services which would facilitate the home-based care of various groups of the frail and the handicapped is well below even the targets set for them by official policy documents: in 1976, current provision of domiciliary services was commonly at about half the level recommended by the guidelines of the Department of Health and Social Security (DHSS) itself (DHSS, 1976).

There seems to be no sign that these trends will be reversed in the foreseeable future, especially after the election of a Conservative government in 1979. The DHSS appears to be firmly committed to a policy of community care across the board, as its thinking on resource allocation has indicated. Its response to public expenditure cuts has been to stress the twin priorities of economy and rational-isation and, above all, the virtues of using 'low-cost solutions', wherever this can be done without damage to standards of care (DHSS, 1976, para. 1.20). The concept of the low-cost solution must be acknowledged as problematic, not least because, in the context of community care, it may simply mean a failure to calculate the personal, financial and social costs which fall upon individuals rather than institutions (Macintyre, 1977).

The history of community care to date appears to be character-ised by an enthusiasm in rhetoric and in policy documents which has not been matched by a willingness to commit resources to the provision of the kinds of services which might facilitate its develop-ment, and the gap between rhetoric and resources has increasingly been seen as one to be filled by volunteer labour. A consideration of likely future developments in social policy gives little ground for optimism that this gap will be closed: indeed, given the background of the existing DHSS commitment to community care as a low-cost solution, there are good reasons for believing that the present trend will not merely continue, but will accelerate in the next decade. These reasons relate in particular to three assumptions about the conditions which will govern further developments in social policy and about their likely outcomes:

1. Further extensive cuts in public expenditure will make local authorities, as well as central government, search all the more assiduously for cheap alternatives. One possible consequence, as Moroney has argued (following Titmuss), is that, just as in wartime certain people were asked to forgo resources because other groups were seen as more important, so in times of perceived economic crisis, certain groups may be asked to bear a disproportionate burden:

> The mentally handicapped and the elderly were required to pay a disproportionate cost during the 1940s. Who will be requested to make the sacrifice in the 1970s? Will the sharing be more equitable? Following the government's policy of general re-trenchment, families caring for the handicapped in their homes receiving little support during the expansionary periods of the 1960s, are likely to receive less in the near future. (Moroney, 1976, p. 102)

2. The predicted increase in the numbers of one dependent group in particular, the elderly, will render some form of domiciliary provision a perceived necessity, even for the comparatively small numbers of the elderly,[3] whose condition has previously rendered

them eligible for residential care, since further real expansion of residential care is taken to be out of the question. In the provision of such care, the voluntary sector does play a not insignificant part, but the statutory sector is still by far the major provider of residential care: in 1976, out of 115 111 elderly people in residential care in England, 99 027 were in local authority accommodation (DHSS, 1977). The DHSS has acknowledged that long-term residential care will continue to be necessary for the frailest old people, but if this facility were to be made available to the same proportion of elderly people as at present, the numbers of places would have to expand considerably to meet the expected growth in the numbers of the elderly, especially in the oldest age groups. It is estimated that the numbers in the eighty-five-or-over age group (who make the heaviest demands on services), which have already increased by 133 per cent in twenty-five years, will rise by a further 75 per cent by 2011, bringing the anticipated numbers in this age group to 904 000 (OPCS, 1978a). A much smaller increase is expected in the seventy-five-or-over age group, with the peak coming in 1991. The DHSS statement of priorities in 1976 did envisage the need to increase residential provision in the light of the increasing numbers of the elderly, but, given the overall resource constraints, community care is constantly emphasised. An expansion of domiciliary services is also envisaged, but the expansion would be small: 6 per cent per annum for home nursing, and only 2 per cent for home helps and meals (DHSS, 1977b ch. 5). Not surprisingly the range of non-statutory resources for caring is seen as a major contributor. The recent DHSS discussion document on services for the elderly envisages the use of family resources, volunteers, and 'informal effort' wherever possible rather than the expansion of statutory domiciliary services (DHSS,1976).

3. Continuing high levels of unemployment, accelerated in the immediate future by the economic policies of the present government and in the slightly more distant future by the increasing impact of micro-electronic technology, will maintain the existence of a pool of people who are unemployed either for a long term or permanently. Predictions about future unemployment are hazardous, and there is much disagreement about the possible effects of micro-technology. However, it is very likely to affect areas such as banking and insurance, and since two in every five women who work are in clerical jobs, such women may be particularly at risk to job displace-

ment in the future. Moreover, it is certain that employment in the public sector, another major area of women's employment, will contract as a result of present government policies.

If these assumptions about future developments in social policy are correct, the demand for care in the future, particularly from the increasing numbers of the very elderly, will far outstrip the commitment to develop such statutory provision as would make available either residential or community services. If the demand for such services greatly exceeds the supply, the existence of large numbers of the long-term unemployed may well come to be equated with the availability of a pool of carers: in particular, it might be argued that it would be desirable for some people at least to be kept usefully occupied in caring for frail or handicapped members of their own families. From this position it would be but a short step to the identification of certain groups of paid workers as meriting a transfer from 'employment' to 'occupation', so as to reduce competition for scarce employment. Married women and anyone working beyond the age of entitlement to a state pension would be especially at risk in this context. This could be seen both as a 'low cost solution' to the question of how to provide care and as a means of reducing the pressure for paid work.

The rest of this article examines some of the assumptions upon which these likely future developments are predicated, and spells out their implications for women in particular.

### Reality and the double equation

An examination of the reality of community care, in a situation where there is minimal input of statutory resources, reveals that the provision of primary caring falls not upon 'the community' but upon identifiable groups and individuals, in a way which is not necessarily equitable. Indeed, this can be best expressed in terms of a double equation – that in practice community care equals care by the family, and in practice care by the family equals care by women. Although there are exceptions, the validity of this double equation can be demonstrated by reference to the evidence about the provision of care and by an examination of the utilisation of the key concepts of 'community' and 'family'.

The meaning given to 'community' by advocates of community care is often not specified, and appears to rest upon certain unexamined assumptions. This meaning is especially crucial when care by the community is being advocated, because this requires the assumption that there exists some kind of grouping of people who are both able and willing to take on active caring on a consistent and reliable basis. Used in this context, the term 'community' seems inevitably to denote some kind of geographical basis for this grouping, despite the fact that the Seebohm Report (1968), for example, does recognise the force of the argument that links between individuals who form a non-geographical 'community of interest' may be stronger than relationships made on the basis of locality (para. 476). Nevertheless, it is difficult to see how 'community' can avoid a geographical connotation, when it is used in the context of community care: if it is a question of bathing an elderly person or doing shopping for the house-bound, a degree of proximity does seem rather necessary.

Thus, despite the denial of the Seebohm Report that its thinking stems from a 'a belief that the small, close-knit community of the past could be reproduced in the urban society of today and the future' (para. 157) it does tend to assume precisely that. Recent writers no less than earlier ones are obliged to postulate the existence of some kind of localised network through which services flow. Hadley uses a geographical model when he writes about informal helping networks which 'must depend to a considerable extent on the *stability of the community* in which they are embedded. If there is redevelopment, re-housing, a loss of job opportunities or a reduction in local transport facilities, then the stability of the community may be endangered and informal networks damaged or destroyed' (Hadley, 1978, p. 524).

Since contemporary writing about community care does appear to presume the existence of locally based 'communities' which already provide helping services, it is still pertinent to heed Titmuss's warning that public policy can be described in idealistic terms representing what one would *like* to exist masquerading as present reality. Titmuss saw a danger in the attraction of community care, in that it 'conjures up a sense of warmth and human kindness, essentially personal and comforting', so that 'what some hope one day will exist is suddenly thought by many to exist already' (Titmuss, 1968, p. 104). A belief in the existence of mutually caring relationships, especially those formed in the urban context, has a long history in the sociological enterprise. Nisbet (1967), for example, identifies the rediscovery of 'community' as central to the development of sociology, and, more recently, Pearson (1975) has identified this sociological pastoral' as one of the key principles underlying the development of welfare ideologies.

Influential as this kind of imagery has been, if major social policies are to be based on the assumption that communities or caring networks do indeed exist, then it is important to go beyond imagery and examine the evidence for the existence and the frequency of the particular quality of social relationship implied by the imagery. Abrams (1977), having done precisely that, suggests that available research indicates the significant bases for social caring as, first, kinship and, secondly, 'moral communities' (for example, churches and occupational associations) rather than territorial groupings, and he argues that research is urgently needed to establish whether and in what circumstances *proximity* can become a basis for care. Moreover, he suggests that, from what we know about the settings which foster active community care, they are either fast disappearing or socially undesirable on other grounds.

It seems, then, that there is a serious possibility that community care policies are postulating the existence of a form of social organisation for which there is little evidence, except perhaps in the case of a small minority of people. Moreover, when one looks more carefully at the evidence of communities providing care, it appears that most of the caring is being done either by the immediate family or through a wider kinship network (Abrams, 1977, p. 134). From the point of view of networks which provide caring services, it looks as though communities are effectively extended kinship groupings, and that kin links provide the channels through which most services flow. That community care effectively means family care is demonstrated, for example, in Bayley's study of the mentally handicapped: it is clear that the major burden of care is borne by the immediate family of the handicapped person, primarily by the mother (Bayley, 1973).

The first half of the double equation, that community care effectively means family care, is hardly surprising, in that the obligation to care has traditionally been laid upon the family both culturally and legally. Historically the family has been regarded as the first line of support for dependent individuals, (Wilson 1977, pp. 89–90), and Abrams argues that an underlying assumption in much contemporary talk about community care is that the family should be (and if necessary should be persuaded to be) the immediate setting wherever possible. This seems to be borne out by the assumptions of the DHSS priorities statements, which see living 'at home' as the only alternative to residential care; in other words, the family setting is seen as the location for caring. That family members should be the ones to provide primary caring for the highly dependent is not simply a matter of practical convenience, but is reinforced by the legislation covering the payment of the Invalid Care Allowance. This benefit is payable to someone of working age[4] who stays at home to care for a disabled person, but it can be claimed only if the disabled person is a relative. This legislation clearly illustrates that 'community' care of the highly dependent is intended to be kept firmly within the family. The equation of community care with family care is not only demonstrated in practice, but is an assumption of policy thinking, and is reinforced by legislative and financial arrangements, as examination of recent policy documents and political discussions will show.

Since discussion of 'the family' has achieved some political prominence, especially since 1977, it is instructive to examine the implicit models of the family upon which politicians and policy-makers base their thinking. Although, by contrast with some other countries, Britain has never had an explicit 'family policy', Land and Parker (1978, p. 332) have demonstrated that British social policies do contain and promote implicit assumptions about 'the family', which are, in brief that the family should be a private domain, where the state should interfere only in special circumstances; that the family is a fragile institution which needs to be protected; and that a range of social services has to be developed for people who are unfortunate enough to be without a 'normal' family. These assumptions have not been challenged in recent political discussion of 'the family'.

Whatever particular policies they have been seeking to promote, both political parties appear to be in agreement on a central objective – the strengthening of family life. At a conference in October 1978, major speakers from both parties expressed their aims in almost identical terms: David Ennals, then Labour Secretary of State for Social Services, claimed that 'The government ... shares the general concern that public policies should strengthen rather than weaken family life', while Patrick Jenkin, the next (Conservative) incumbent of the same office, stated his hope that 'those many offices of the state which impinge upon the family do so in a way which fosters family life rather than weakens it' (National Children's Homes, 1979). The motivating force behind much of this seems to be the presumed contribution which 'the family' can make to 'society'. Discussions are conducted with reified notions of both family and society, and medical metaphors abound – it is commonly argued that 'A sound and satisfying family life lies at the heart of the well-being of society' (p. 10), or that 'A deep-rooted commitment to the family is necessary if society is to be healthy' (p. 7).

The model of the family which emerges from all this, despite remarks about change and a recognition that occasionally mothers do go out to work, is a very traditional one: the 'normal' family is conceived of as a three-generation family composed of children, parents and grandparents, and stable over the lifetime of its members. Obligations to provide mutual caring are contained within this unit: as James Callaghan told the Church of Scotland Assembly, 'The family is a place where we care for each other, where we feel our responsibilities for each other, where we practise consideration for each other. Caring families are the basis of a society that cares' (*The Guardian*, 23 May 1978). The Conservative party apparently is inclined to agree: Baroness Young states that 'The family that cares for all its members not only helps itself, it is able to help others in the network of the community' (Conservative Party, 1977, p. 78). From all this, it can be inferred that politicians are working on the assumption that obligations will operate on a fairly traditional basis, broadly, one which owes its origins to Judeo-Christian moral codes. In this context, increased opportunities for women can be seen as posing a threat to 'family life': 'We need to be sure that growing and increasing opportunities for men and women, for mothers and fathers, do not begin to threaten the family itself . . . for us Conservatives, the family is, and must remain, the central unit of a stable society' (Geoffrey Howe, 1978). In this kind of model, the caring services which 'the family' is assumed to provide for its members are seen as an outcome of kinship obligations, and the definition of those obligations is never seriously challenged.

If assumptions about caring services provided within the family continue to rest upon a traditional notion of kinship obligations, then equally they incorporate the assumption that most of this care will continue to be provided by women, who have traditionally been designated as the carers in the family.

The cultural definition of women as 'carers' is still strong, and since it is part of a set of assumptions about the sexual division of labour in the domestic sphere, it continues to be reinforced and reproduced by a whole range of social and financial policies which unquestionably embody the notion of women's dependency. Hilary Land's work has been important in establishing that this is the case across a wide range of social policies. In the particular area of family policy, she argues that the overt aim may be to protect the family, but that 'On examination, what is being protected are particular patterns of responsibility and dependencies within the family, and a long-established view of division of labour between the sexes and between generations' (Land and Parker, 1978, p. 332). The converse of the definition of women as carers is that men are not expected to provide domestic and caring services, either for others or even for themselves: Land argues that 'It is clear that men are not expected to look after themselves as much as women, and they are accordingly given much more help from publicly provided support services. Neither is it assumed that they will be able to look after their elderly and infirm relatives' (Land, 1978, p. 268).

There is an important sense in which cultural pressures to provide care apply to all women, but those who are married or cohabiting are particularly vulnerable to such pressures; with the assumption of their financial dependency, their employment is traditionally considered more 'expendable' than a man's. Married women in practice are treated as dependants throughout the whole of social security and tax legislation (Land, 1977b) and if they do give up work to care for a highly dependent relative, they will not even be eligible for the Invalid Care Allowance: a married woman living with her husband or receiving maintenance from him is not entitled to the Invalid Care Allowance, even if she is caring full time for a dependent relative. The assumption clearly is that a married woman's natural habitat is the home, where she is financially dependent upon her husband.[5]

The cultural designation of women as carers in the family setting is reflected in the available evidence about what happens in practice: in terms of primary responsibility, wives care for husbands, mothers for handicapped children and daughters for their elderly parents or disabled siblings. Care is also provided by female neighbours and volunteers. This is not to deny that devoted male carers can certainly be found in each of these categories.

In terms of female caring, it seems likely that many elderly men are being cared for by their wives: far fewer elderly men than elderly women live alone (16 per cent compared to 40 per cent) (Hunt, 1978, chap . 9); 75 per cent of elderly men are married, compared to 30 per cent of elderly women. Elderly women have a longer expectation of life than contemporary males (OPCS, 1978, Table 2.5). Given the tendency for wives to be around the same age as their husbands or up to several years younger and given the traditional division of labour in the home, it seems likely that women are looking after their frail elderly husbands more common-ly than vice versa. In 1977, 79 per cent of men aged from sixty-five to seventy-four and 62 per cent of those over seventy-five were living with a spouse. For women, the corresponding figures were 47 per cent and 19 per cent (Social Survey Division, OPCS, 1979, Table 2.15). Moreover, where elderly people need the help of people outside their household, it is predominantly women who provide it: Hunt shows that elderly people who cannot do their own shopping rely primarily on daughters and daughters-in-law, with neighbours playing a significant part in the case of elderly men, but 'It is noteworthy that none ... say their shopping is done by a son, son-in-law or brother outside the household' (Hunt, 1978, p. 83). As to mothers caring for disabled children, Bayley's study of the mentally handicapped showed that three-quarters of his population were being cared for entirely or primarily by their mothers. Land and Parker also reviewed the evidence on this point and built up a picture of a vast amount of care being provided by female relatives for sick and disabled kin. The traditional support of aged parents has been the single daughter, and the 1966 sample census revealed just over 300 000 single women living with a parent over retirement age, though it is not known how many of these women were 'caring' daughters. The *General Household Survey* for 1977 represents 12 per cent of men and 21 per cent of women over seventy-five as living with their own children or children-in-law (Social Survey Division, OPCS, 1979).

So in practice as well as in ideology, primary caring services located in the family setting are provided primarily by women, which demonstrates the second part of the double equation: that family care effectively equals care by women.

The corner-stone of women's role as carers has doubtedly been a cultural tradition which prescribes women's financial dependence. For this reason, among others, women still occupy a marginal position in the labour force. The adult male is defined as a working male, financially responsible for his wife and dependent children, and not regarded as available to care for handicapped or frail relatives. In the twenty-five- to fifty-four-year-old mature adult age group, more than 97 per cent of the men are economically active, the comparable figure for women being around two-thirds (Royal Commission, 1978, Tables 173 and 175); men of working age appear not to be 'available' to provide continuous care for a highly dependent relative.

## The future context of community care

That community care effectively means that female relatives provide primary care can be demonstrated in the present, but what of the future? Will the same situation prevail in a future in which 'community care' is an increasingly significant aspect of social provision? It seems likely that the expansion of community care at a time of severe financial constraints on resources will mean that women are still expected to carry the major burden of caring, and will often continue to do so in practice. This seems likely because of the strength of the cultural definition of women as carers, because of the institutional reinforcement of that definition and because of future trends in unemployment.

Not only are women culturally assigned caring roles, but policymakers mostly appear to assume that women will continue to be the providers of care in the future. James Callaghan, for example, envisages that many women will continue to devote themselves to the domestic sphere: 'Women who want to become engineers or plumbers, or to buy houses, should not find their sex standing in their way. But equally, those women who choose their families as their life work are equally valuable members of society, and fulfil themselves' (*The Times*, 19 June 1978). Although policy documents now acknowledge more readily that women are commonly in part-time employment, they still tend to assume the centrality of family obligations in determining the life-style of women, especially of wives. The new state pensions scheme, for example, was considered to be 'of particular value to the married woman or the single parent who remains at home while her children are growing up as well as the single woman and others who are obliged to cut short their careers in order to look after aged relatives' (DHSS, 1974, para. 44). Assumptions about a life-style of dependency being appropriate for women are deeply rooted in social and financial legislation, and there is no sign that any political party intends to alter them.

The pressures upon women to provide care will be greatly increased if community care policies proceed in the way which is apparently envisaged at the present time. If the expansion of community care is accompanied by a reduction in residential provision, then numbers of frail or handicapped people who might otherwise have been in residential institutions will have to be cared for by *someone*. Moreover, this will happen in the case of the elderly, even if residential provision remains at its present level, because of the expected increase in that age group. The financial attractions of this have not been lost on politicians: 'Family care is cheaper than institutional care and the burden on the tax payer must be lightened when families themselves can provide the most necessary, and free, supportive system of all' (*House of Lords Debates,* Vol. 400, col. 46). The implication seems to be that elderly or handicapped people will be kept 'at home' or 'with their families' wherever possible, and thus residential care will effectively be rationed by being offered only to those without relatives to care for them, of whom there may well be large numbers, since about a third of the elderly population is childless (DHSS, 1978, p.7).

In his study of rationing in the social services, Judge (1978) suggests that 'service' rationing carried out by social services departments is very much an uncharted area, where 'our existing knowledge of what happens is very limited' (p. 155). In the absence of established criteria for rationing this kind of service, the way is left open for allocation to be operated on some set of 'common-sense' principles, which given the background outlined, are very likely to include the expectation that family members, especially females, will be the main source of caring. There may be an acceptance of the need for residential accommodation where relatives are non-existent or too frail themselves, but what of those whose relatives *do not wish* to take on the primary responsibility for caring? The expansion of community care may well mean that more people will feel that, despite reluctance or outright unwillingness, they have to provide care for their dependent relatives because there seems to be absolutely no alternative. That these people will mostly be women has already been argued, with married women especially vulnerable, particularly if their reason for not wanting to care is that they wish to remain in employment: 'Women must put their domestic responsibilities first, and little account is taken of the financial necessity for any of them to remain in paid employment; even less consideration is given to women who would simply prefer to continue with their paid work outside the home, and shoulder some, but not all, of the responsibility for caring' (Land, 1978, p. 268). This latter choice will be even less available, with the planned reductions in domiciliary support services. Not surprisingly, the Equal Opportunities Commission is already 'concerned that the service which is offered to old people by the statutory authorities tends to vary according to whether a female relative is at hand' (EOC, 1979, p. 9).

The prospect that women will feel obliged to stay at home and care for dependent relatives is increased by the predicted trends in employment in the present decade. There is some evidence that, in the decline of employment consequent upon the introduction of micro-technology, women's employment may be particularly at risk, especially since the expansion areas are likely to be jobs in precisely the scientific and technological areas where women have difficulty in competing. In the future women will find work more difficult to obtain, and the traditional notion that married women's jobs are just for pin-money may accelerate this process, despite sex discrimination legislation.

Thus the present combination of expanding community care and declining employment could well result in strong forces pulling women back into domestic caring roles: one can well imagine its being argued that, since there are not enough jobs to go around, women can be kept usefully occuppied in providing care for their relatives. The ways in which politicians currently support the view indicate that this is a likely outcome, and there is some evidence that the connection between lack of employment and women's domestic role is already being made. Lynda Chalker, a junior minister at the DHSS, is reported as saying, 'Maybe, in years to come, the country will look to the labour market and decide that perhaps it would be better for women with children to stay at home' (*The Daily Mirror*, 3 May 1979).

From the viewpoint of the individual woman, the situation will be that she sees no real alternative to providing care herself: it is an obligation laid upon her by the cultural definition of women as carers and by lack of other provision. Thus community care policies, although they are apparently based on the assumption that structures for providing care *already exist* and simply need to be activated, can very easily become policies which create a *moral imperative* to care, imposed upon women to whom nature and chance have assigned a frail or handicapped relative. Such a situation is clearly disadvantageous to women in terms of the promotion of equal opportunities.

## An unrealistic scenario and radical choices

The forces pulling women back into domestic caring roles, especially in relation to handicapped or frail elderly relatives who need constant care, appear to be an inevitable consequence of present policies. Nevertheless there is a degree of unreality about the assumption that women will be a readily available pool of carers, as they have been in the past. Present community care policies can be seen both as assuming an unrealistic scenario and as forcing women into very radical choices about their own lives. Both of these are a consequence of a failure to question assumptions about 'the family' in the future and about the 'availability' of women for caring.

The assumption that women in the family setting will be available to care for dependent relatives needs to be related to aspects of demographic change. Reduction in family size in this century (OPCS, 1978a, chap. 3), coupled with the current rise in the survival rate of the elderly, means that far fewer adult children are available to care for elderly parents. It is one thing to argue that, in a family with six children, one child may be in a position to offer care; when there are one or two children in the family, a very different situation pertains. In short, as far as the elderly are concerned, demographic change has markedly affected the availability of carers:

Increasingly when people pass the age of 45 they are likely to have one of two elderly parents alive as well as dependent children to care for. Falling mortality rates have already led to an increase in the proportion of middle-aged persons in the population with a very old parent (generally a very old mother) still alive. As these middle-aged people will increasingly be the survivors of generations in which the average family size was small, the responsibility for looking after their aged parents will be shared among fewer of their own generation. (Social Survey Division, OPCS, 1979, para. 7.4.2)

Additionally, where members of the family have been geographically mobile there may be considerable physical distances between the elderly and their children, and very few older people move house to be near relatives.[6]

Where elderly people are being looked after by one of their children, there is a long tradition that this should be a daughter, often a single daughter. However, the supply of single daughters (some of whom may have a 'married' life-style) is now very limited: they represent around 7 per cent of women in their fifties and 6 per cent of those aged between thirty-five and fifty, as compared with 15 per cent in the eighty-or-over age group (OPCS, 1978b, Table 1.1a). Single daughters, therefore, can hardly be regarded as a major pool of carers in the future.

Married women, no doubt, would be seen as an alternative pool of potential carers, but the married daughter does not necessarily stay married. So far, social policies which embody concepts of the nuclear family (with relationships lasting over the lifetime of its members) have singularly failed to take account of current trends in divorce. There has been a 400 per cent increase in divorce over the past twenty years (OPCS, 1978b, chap. 5), and remarriage rates are also rising. Of those newly divorcing now, statistical predictions suggest that one-third are likely to remarry (OPCS, 1979) and that, of those who are under thirty when they divorce, 80 per cent are likely to remarry (OPCS, 1978a, chap. 5). But on the whole men are more likely to remarry than women, with women over the age of thirty-five being, for whatever reason, particularly unlikely to remarry.[7] In the context of this argument, the effects of the Divorce Reform Act 1969 can be seen as reinforcing the unreality of regarding full-time, continuous domestic labour as the normal life-style of the average woman. The increased availability of divorce has created a much larger population of women (highest in the thirty- to forty-five-year-old age group) who have sole responsibility for a household budget, with or without the receipt of maintenance payments. Even if women once regarded marriage as securing their financial future, this becomes increasingly unrealistic as divorce becomes an ever increasing possibility, and post-divorce income is usually inadequate. Certainly, from the point of view of the availability of married women as a pool of potential carers, current trends in divorce and remarriage seem likely to exclude increasing numbers of women, who, even if they are not already in employment, will need to return to the labour market if they can.

Evidence of women's labour force participation rates suggests another reason for questioning the availability of women as carers, since single women have a high rate of full-time economic activity, and the growth of employment among married women, especially in the past decade, constitutes a major area of recent social change. A 1977 survey showed that 52 per cent of women between the ages of twenty-five and thirty-four were working (evenly split between full time and part time), 68 per cent of those between thirty-five and forty-four (28 per cent full time as against 39 per cent part time) and 62 per cent of those between forty-five and fifty-nine, again evenly split. Characteristically, women appear to give up full-time work on the birth of their first child, and to return to part time work before their last child begins full-time schooling (Social Survey Division, OPCS, 1979, Tables 4.1 and 4.7). The part-time activity rates have risen by 30 per cent between 1971 and 1976 (Robertson and Briggs, 1979, Table 4). Thus, being a full-time housewife throughout adult life can no longer be regarded as the norm for women, and a woman who stays at home to care for a handicapped child or who leaves work before the age of fifty-five to care for an elderly parent is adopting a life-style which is increasingly atypical.

Hence, the idea that in the future women can provide care for their relatives because they will in any case be at home, financially dependent upon a man, seems a very shaky basis on which to plan the expansion of community care. Perhaps some women will continue to be available in this way, but whether they will be the ones who happen to have, for example, a frail or handicapped parent needing care is purely a matter of chance. Moreover, this leaves aside important questions about whether the assumption that family members will care for each other bears any relationship to patterns of felt obligation which are actually to be found in contemporary social life; again, there is a disinclination to question the traditional model of the family in relation to the reality of many people's lives.

Notions of mutual caring within the family unit beg some key questions. There is a failure to distinguish between categories of family and kin and to distinguish between different types of family composition; there is also a tendency to equate family with house-hold, and to assume that a marriage relationship is the central feature of every family – all of which serves to obscure important issues. These include, in contemporary social life, which people count as 'family'; what kinds of obligations are attached to given relationships; who endorses these obligations and who does not; how such obligations are reinforced; and whether they depend upon a legal relationship such as marriage. There is a tendency also to ignore the issue of whether women will continue to accept their cultural designation as carers, or whether they will explicitly reject it, in ideology and in practice, in increasing numbers.

Although women's providing care in the family setting seems an unrealistic scenario, because it fails to take account of changes in demography, cultural practice and the structure of employment, it has already been argued that present community care policies will have the effect of pulling women back into domestic caring roles, because they see no other alternative. This raises the very real possibility that women may be expected to and may feel that they have to *give up* work in order to provide continuous care for a dependent relative. Such a possibility is quite consistent with cultural expectations: indeed, one study of single women caring for their dependants found that over half of them had no paid employment, most of them having given up work in their fifties, with no idea of how long caring would be needed (NCSWD, 1975). Many of these women reported that the decision to give up work had been a crucial one for them. It is a situation which can be fraught with conflict, regardless of marital status. If a married or cohabiting couple has decided that *one* of them will have to give up work in order to care, there is a strong chance, on financial grounds, that the woman will be the one to do so, since her employment is likely to be less well paid than the man's, and may well be part-time employment. Women working part-time earned an average weekly wage of £26.20 in 1978, and for the female full-time employee, average earnings were about two-thirds of the male wage (DEP, 1979). Despite the fact that many women may already have had a period out of the labour market in order to care for young children, they can be expected to interrupt their employment, for a second time, in order to care for elderly parents; those who are particularly unlucky may also find themselves retiring early to look after an ailing husband. Despite the 'myth that families no longer care for their kin', which is, as Land has argued, 'as long-standing and prevalent as the belief that the unemployed are mainly work shy scroungers' (Land, 1978, p. 269), in fact, people, especially women, often do take on responsibility for the care of their dependent relatives.

Whatever the expectations and practice in the past, it is clear that, now and in the future, a decision on giving up work to provide care poses a very radical choice, since the consequences of relinquishing paid employment can be extremely serious, both in the immediate and in the long-term future. The immediate consequences of giving up work, where a woman has sole or major responsibility for the household budget, will be considerable financial loss and the reduction of living standards for that woman and her dependants. The immediate consequences for a married part-time female worker are not necessarily less serious, since the contribution of this second wage to the household budget, especially at a time of inflation, can in many cases by no means be regarded as a luxury. Evidence based on a survey conducted in 1974 showed that, out of 11 million couples with a husband under the age of sixty-five, 7 million wives contributed an average of 25 per cent to the family budget, and the earnings of one-third of the working wives constituted 30–50 per cent of family income. Moreover, three times as many families with working fathers would have incomes below the level of supplementary benefits if their wives were to stop earning (Hamill, 1976).

In addition to the immediate loss of income, giving up work in order to care for a dependent relative may be a prelude to poverty in old age for the carer. The current generation of middle-aged women will derive little benefit from recent pension reforms. In the future, carers will by and large be able to qualify themselves for the basic state pension, with some supplement from the state additional pension scheme if they have worked for part of their adult lives.[8] However, it is unlikely that carers will fully enjoy the benefits of an occupational pension scheme, since these are calculated for maximum effect, on a long, uninterrupted period of full-time work, usually forty years. If women give up pensionable employment, deferred earnings are reduced. Although those who stay married may eventually be entitled to an occupational widow's pension, the divorced woman loses her entitlement, and is lucky if she receives anything approaching financial compensation (DHSS, 1976d, chap. 13). A single woman simply could lose years of pensionable service.

If the carer gives up work, but hopes to return to the labour market after the dependent relative has died or has gone into residential accommodation, the current prospects are decidely risky. Unemployment is likely to rise in the foreseeable future and occupational skills can become outdated during a long period out of the labour market. The consequences of this for the single and the divorced are obvious; for the married or widowed woman, they are not necessarily less serious, since she may well already have had one period out of employment to care for young children. The Equal Opportunities Commission has argued recently that 'It is socially unjust that those who perform the vital task of caring for the elderly should have to forefeit employment opportunities and employment rights in order to do so' (EOC, 1979, p. 9).

The argument here has concentrated upon the financial costs of giving up work in order to care, but there are personal costs also. The study of single carers found that the most serious implications for these women were loneliness and exhaustion, along with financial hardship (NCSWD, 1975), and the Equal Opportunities Commission has argued recently that 'Caring for an elderly relative can – and frequently does – impose severe restrictions upon the working, social and family life of the carer' (EOC, 1979, p. 7). Indeed, it can be asked whether, in the case of married women carers, the strains imposed are such as to jeopardise the stable family life which, as we have shown, appears to be so prized by politicians.

In his early paper on community care, Titmuss warned, 'We may pontificate about the philosophy of community care ... but unless we are prepared to examine at (the) level of concrete reality what we mean by community care, we are simply indulging in wishful thinking' (Titmuss, 1968, p. 106). At 'the level of concrete reality', the future development of community care policies which depend upon the provision of primary care by women, mostly female relatives, must be interpreted in one of two ways: either women carers will not be available in the right place, at the right time, or, more likely, such policies, carrying with them a moral imperative to provide care, will pose women with extremely radical choices about their employment, financial independence and future life chances.

## Equal opportunities and community care

In essence, the case presented here is not a case *against* community care, which may be a highly desirable policy aim on many grounds.

The case is that the present experience of community care and the present plans for its future development suggest that it will become increasingly counter-productive to the promotion of equal opportunities between the sexes. The onus, then is upon those, both policy-makers and academics, who advocate such policies to show how they will develop community care *without* disadvantage to women.

Equal opportunities legislation can be viewed as a base from which both men and women can be afforded wider choices in life. Unless one takes the view that no real change can ever be effected in the present political and economic context, it makes sense to monitor public policies in terms of their contribution to equal opportunities. At best, it may be possible to use them to promote equal opportunities; at the very least, it is essential that other policies should not undermine that aim. Like social welfare seen in a Marxist perspective, equal opportunities legislation can be interpreted as a concession wrung from the dominant class – a concession which needs to be constantly defended.

In the context of a commitment to equal opportunities, is it then possible to envisage a development of community care which does not leave women disadvantaged? A 'community care with equal opportunities' policy would need two essential features. First, it would have to create a situation in which women were under no greater obligation than men with regard to giving up work in order to provide care. Secondly, men who wanted to care would have to be genuinely enabled to do so, and would need to be widely accepted in their role as carers. Clearly such a policy postulates some long-term changes in cultural assumptions and practices, though recommendations about this type of social engineering are well beyond the scope of this article. But, in so far as legislation and adminstrative practice can be seen as setting the milieu in which cultural change will be either fostered or hindered, there are some possible steps which could be taken – and, indeed, must be taken – if current trends in community care are not to be counter-productive to the promotion of equal opportunities.

First, the creation of this alternative scenario calls for a greater degree of financial and practical support for those caring for dependent relatives than is currently available, or apparently foreseen. As soon as one envisages men as well as women being the carers, it becomes more obvious that current assumptions about caring do rely largely upon the exploitation of women's unpaid domestic labour in the home. A community care policy which did not depend on it would require a good deal of financial and practical support to compensate for the costly consequences of caring, in both financial and personal terms. Any system of community care which did not rely on women's unpaid domestic labour would by no means be the cheap alternative which it might first appear to be. Ultimately, it would not only involve a large increase in domiciliary services and financial benefits, but it would imply the continued availability of residential care as a choice, with possible innovations in the type of provision and ways of paying for it.

Suggestions about providing a whole new range of statutory services and financial benefits are no doubt unpopular in the present climate, but 'no money' is not a final answer. Land and Parker have already suggested that state-funded caring services could be financed by a reduction or abolition of the married man's tax allowance, by which 'We provide massive subsidies to marriage in its present form' (Land and Parker 1978, p. 131). Such a move would be entirely consistent with the promotion of equality for women. In realistic terms, there may be little alternative to continued commitment to the statutory provision of services; this was recognised by participants in a recent DHSS seminar on social care, where 'It was agreed that any idea of a massive replacement of statutory services by informal caring efforts, or even by voluntary effort, was a "romantic fiction"' (Barnes and Connelly, 1978, p. 100).

Secondly, it is clear that major policy and legislative changes in the field of employment are called for. There are no simple answers here, but it seems crucial to find ways of reformulating traditional expectations about working life and current employment practices to provide for men and women who wish to provide care, without irreparably damaging their future work prospects. At the present time, the notion of full-time work, continuous over the adult life span, is central to the notion of the 'good employee', and is crucially related to appointments, job security, promotions and pensions. The development of part-time work, job-sharing, periods of 'caring' leave and other similar arrangements appear to have something to commend them. Each of these needs to be carefully examined within the context of equal opportunities, but there does seem to be a prima facie case for believing that it would be possible to devise more acceptable arrangements. Since there is likely to be a surplus of workers in many occupations in the foreseeable future, the traditional centrality of work is likely to be called into question in any event.

242 *Women and the Informal and Voluntary Sector*

The opening up of the issue of equal opportunities in recent years has created a situation in which further progress is possible, but the situation is finely balanced, and it is just as possible that other social and economic policies will have the consequences of tipping the balance in the opposite direction. Current community care policies appear to carry exactly that risk. The onus is on any government which leaves equal opportunities legislation on the statute book to demonstrate that the promotion of equal opportunities is a commitment which pervades all its policies, including those relating to community care. Without that intention, equal opportunities legislation represents nothing more than pious hypocrisy.

**Notes**

1. The target for the provision of day care places was 60 per 100 000 of the population.
2. Parliamentary answer, *House of Commons Debates*, Vol. 964, cols 468–71. Of the local authorities which provide no day care places, seven had some provision by voluntary bodies in their area and the rest had none at all.
3. Precise numbers of the elderly in residential accommodation are difficult to cite because of various possible definitions of 'residential accommodation' and of 'elderly' (which, additionally, may be different for men and women). Estimates of numbers in some form of residential accommodation variously suggest 3 per cent (Moroney, 1976); 4.7 per cent (1971 *Census*); and around 5 per cent (Sainsbury, 1977, ch. 5). The proportion in residential care varies considerably according to age: 3 per cent of those aged from sixty-five to seventy-four, 8 per cent of those aged from seventy-four to eighty-five and 21 per cent of those aged eighty-five or over are estimates based on the 1971 *Census*.
4. The Invalid Care Allowance cannot, however, be claimed by married or cohabiting women. See below for further discussion.
5. *Editor's note:* for a full discussion of married women and the Invalid Care Allowance, see Groves and Finch (1983).
6. Hunt found that most geographical moves made by the elderly were *within* an area, and that 'It is comparatively rare for them to move to distant parts of the country' (Hunt, 1978, Tables 12.2.2 and 12.2.3).
7. Among the population of divorced women in the same age group, women aged from thirty to thirty-four remarry at the rate of 184 per 1000, and women aged from thirty-five to forty-four remarry at the rate of 122 per 1000 (OPCS, 1978a, Table 4.13).
8. Under the *Social Security Pensions Act 1975,* calculations of the state additional pension are based on the 'best twenty years' of earnings.

# Women's Refuges: Creating New Forms of Welfare?

## HILARY ROSE

### Women and welfare

The massive expansion of the social services has meant that the state has increasingly penetrated those areas of social activity which are concerned with the material and ideological reproduction of labour power. Activities which were thus once left to the family, now become the concern of the state. Education, housing, health and social security and the personal social services reach in both material and psychological senses into the lives of the population. Feminist writing reminds us that the burden of this reproductive labour, whether unpaid as in the family, or paid as in the lower echelons of the welfare apparatus or capitalist enterprise, is borne by women. Increasingly, feminist sociological writing on welfare (Land, 1976; Wilson, 1977) draws attention to the very clear conception of the relationship between social policy, the family and the position of women which was built into the foundations of the welfare state.

Whilst at first sight Marx as the political economist of *Capital*, and Beveridge (1942) as the architect of the welfare state, would seem to have little in common, nonetheless, social revolutionary and liberal are united in their understanding of the family, not the individual, as the economic unit of consumption. Thus the Beveridge Report seeks to remove inequalities in treatment within

*Source*: extracted and slightly updated from Hilary Rose, 'In Practice Supported, In Theory Denied: an Account of an Invisible Urban Movement', *International Journal of Urban and Regional Research*, Vol. 2, No. 3, 1978, pp. 521–37.

social security between single men and single women, yet overall it emphasises the family as a single economic unit with the husband as the breadwinner and the wife as the housewife. The possibility of women playing a substantial part in paid work outside the home was not really considered. 'The great majority of married women [are] occupied on work which is vital though unpaid, without which their husbands could not do their paid work and without which the nation could not continue' (Beveridge, 1942). Beveridge, therefore, did not treat married women as people in their own right, but as the adjuncts and economic dependants of men. The task of the national insurance system was to make it possible for husbands to provide for their wives in sickness, in health, in unemployment or in old age.

These assumptions for the 1950s and, indeed, most of the 1960s, penetrated both the sociology of working-class culture and the sociology of the family. The influential work of Hoggart (1956) and the Institute of Community Studies held up an intimately affection-ate mirror to the lives of working-class families, facing us with the contradiction that while the work of some such as Townsend was central to the destruction of the myth of the welfare state as the equality machine, at the same time it sustained a myth of the 'naturalness' of familial relations. Thus a discussion by Townsend (1956) of women and social security sees the main difficulty of securing an equitable scheme as 'arising from the responsibilities of motherhood'. He goes on to say that it is wrong to speak of women as the dependants of men 'as the housewife *supports* her husband so that he can go to work', and that 'husbands and wives reciprocate services and are equally dependent on one another'.[1]

The difficulty which underlies both Beveridge's language of 'vital work' and Townsend's 'equally dependent' is that the economic relationship within the family is profoundly unequal, and that its inequality is shored up rather than mitigated by the state. Thus in the context of income maintenance provisions, not only do many married women not know what their husbands earn, but even though their pension rights are determined by the level of his contribution, they have no right to know whether he is fully paid up. What Townsend optimistically saw in the mid-1950s as mutual solidarity flowing from a sexual division of labour, seems in the light of a later, more critical examination of the family to be the enforced cohesiveness of economic dependency sustained by a coercive welfare and wage system. Indeed, while it would be wrong to conceive of the welfare state as a monolith devoid of internal contradictions, it nonetheless protected and preserved a particular ideological conception and a particular economic and social reality of unequal relations of power within the family. It is against this background of inequality that the discussion of violence within the family and the development of Women's Aid as a social movement must be located.

## Family violence as a social problem

Family violence contributes an almost classical case of a phenomenon regarded as 'natural' and essentially unproblematic but which, over a relatively short space, has come to be increasingly recognised as a social problem. While social statisticians have long known that most murders of children are committed by their parents and of women by their husbands, few sociologists have considered what part this violence plays within society. Instead, the terrain has been largely ceded to psychology and has thus facilitated individualistic victim-blaming explanations.[2] Nor has the Marxist perspective on violence been able to deal with the problem that violence against women as an aspect of a control system extends well beyond a specific class and affects all women. Indeed, violence against women and children is an accepted and, in the case of the latter, legalised means of control.

Whilst public anxiety to limit violence against children has long fostered both private philanthropic effort and state action, women have rarely secured such public support. Even in 1977 with the substantial documentation provided by the work of the Parliamentary Select Committee on Violence in Marriage, the well publicised work of the Women's Aid movement, together with a growing body of research, it remains that amongst professional social workers, police, housing officials, doctors and nurses, to say nothing of the general public, the discussion is treated as less real than the discussion of the battered child. In discussion it is not uncommon for an official or professional, when reporting some intensive programme to identify and protect children at risk to justify it in terms of, 'if we can save the life of one child'. At present, such is the anxiety amongst local authorities not to have any child abuse scandals in their area, that programmes which may damage the entire social network of the child are justified in this way. The death of a woman raises no such scandal or concern among officials and professionals at an equivalent intensity.

How then did violence against women become, albeit grudgingly, and with sparse resources allocated, a recognised social problem? If we examine the history of the development of Women's Aid from its pioneering house at Chiswick to its network of refuges up and down the country, the significance of the economic independence of women and their independent access to housing becomes an important policy issue.

The problem of the battered woman and her children and their need for a refuge inaccessible to the husband was, as Hanmer (1977) points out, exacerbated by what was generally regarded as progressive reform within the provision of Part III accommodation for the homeless. Prior to the King Hill Campaign in Kent (Rose, 1971a), which was one of the earliest forays into community action against a welfare state whose emergency housing provision smacked more of the Poor Law than of Beveridge, provision for homeless families all too often excluded the husband. At King Hill, an ex-prisoner of war camp in Kent, families, aided by community activists, occupied the hostel. The husbands, in opposition to the rules of the local authority, entered to live with their wives and children. They used what was then called non-violent direct action, essentially a technique developed and learnt by the activists through their work with the more militant wing of the Committee of One Hundred of the Nuclear Disarmament Campaign. Although in the short term community action seemed to have failed, for the husbands were sent to prison, the defence of the right of families to live together was successful in shifting central government policy even if many local authorities managed to drag their feet in practice (Rose, 1971a). Research into homelessness (Greve, 1964) also emphasised the danger of children being taken into care purely through housing problems and the subsequent difficulty of families coming together again. The more illiberal the provision of temporary accommodation, the greater the danger to children of going into care. Social reformers were thus able to make a double argument not only stressing the disruption of normal family life, but also the diseconomies to the state; the alternative was not merely more humane, it was also cheaper. The gain, however, for those who wished to live as families within accommodation for the homeless, carried with it the unseen consequence that homeless accommodation ceased to be a refuge for women from violent husbands.

It is important not to overemphasise this incidental effect of the reform for an admissions policy which was, during the 1960s, extensively documented by research as being both restrictive and coercive. It was restrictive in that, whereas the original legislation contained within the 1948 National Assistance Act had spoken of 'homeless persons', local authorities had informally chosen to interpret this as homeless 'families' and, indeed, even within the concept of the family acknowledged some families as more deserving of admission than others. The actual problem of the single homeless person, particularly the growing numbers of young single homeless was denied recognition. Greve *et al.*'s (1971) study describing research carried out during 1962 for the London County Council and during 1969 for the DHSS documented both the restrictions and the coerciveness of admissions policy and management practice within Part III accommodation. He reports that 'admission is biased against those (women) whose separation is recent (or imminent) rather than long established'. The applications survey showed that where marital dispute was the immediate reason for the application, the mother was admitted in only 24 per cent of the cases. In all other cases where the mother was alone with her children admission was effected for 32 per cent of the families.

They also note that many women who enter emergency accommodation as the result of marital dispute in practice tend to return to their husbands but, although providing statistics which cast light on this, say little explicitly about the coercion built into both policy and administration concerning the provision of both emergency and permanent housing for women. As part and parcel of what retrospectively may be seen as a high tide of the ideology of the nuclear family, single mothers were automatically and overtly viewed in the official mind as 'unsatisfactory tenants'! (*Unsatisfactory Tenants,* MHLG, HMSO, 1955). There was only a modest chance that women could anticipate being rehoused in permanent local authority housing after the temporary phase. Indeed, the official report notes that in 1954, only somewhat over a third of mothers had even applied for accommodation, feeling that they stood little chance of success. Thus for women who wished to keep their children, the

practical possibilities of their being helped by housing policy was so
remote that returning to an unsatisfactory or even dangerous
marital home was the only option.

The bleak picture built up from the research is of an official
response to a growing problem of homelessness which at the same
time prevented husbands from staying with wives who wished to
care for their children together, separated children from parents
who wished to care for them, and forced women, who were unwil-
ling to lose their children, to return to violent men.

Feminist writing, particularly that most directly associated with
the struggle against male violence, has tended to present the state as
only serving to compel women to re-enter feared relationships with
men. While this is far from incorrect, it presents the state as
monolithic, devoid of internal contradictions. In practice, the state,
whilst advocating the sanctity of the family and the desirability of
patriarchal social relations, at the same moment crushes, without
feeling, actual families. In the case of migrant labour, where the
contradiction is most sharply portrayed, another dimension, namely
racism, has entered, which this paper can only note but not explore.
However, state policy even towards the indigenous population
makes a contract with both the petit bourgeois and working classes
to sustain family life, but only up to a point. Beyond that point,
distinguished by Victorian philanthropy with a rigour which clings
to this day, the undeserving poor are separated from the deserving
poor, and for them, family life, whether between women and men or
parents and children, becomes an uncertain 'luxury', liable to be
withdrawn at the will of the welfare system.

**The first wave**

Knowledge of the plight of women trapped within an oppressive
and even violent relationship by their economic and often
psychological dependency came about in an unplanned but, retrospectively at least, not inexplicable way. Hanmer (1977), citing an
unpublished document produced by one of the original members,
describes how a group of women in Chiswick associated with the
women's liberation movement were running a high street campaign
on prices in 1972. In talking with women about the problems high
prices meant to them, they also learned of the violence which was

the everyday reality of so many women's lives. Sensitised by the critique of family life developing within the movement and the patterns of power and domination in male/female relations, together with a philosophy of sisterhood which commits movement women to seeing other women's problems as their own problems, the Chiswick group found no difficulty in recognising the personal problem as a public issue. What perhaps was distinctive about the members of the Chiswick group was their willingness to act as the first wave of what was to become a social movement.

Amongst the group's members was Erin Pizzey, whose own childhood experience of a violent father made her particularly responsive to the situation of these women, and who with tremendous energy and skill was to play a key role in setting up the first refuge of Chiswick Women's Aid. Her unflagging gift as a propagandist meant that she was able to seize every opportunity afforded by the media, from 'The World at One' on the radio, to television, to the fast written book, *Scream Quietly or the Neighbours Will Hear* (1975), all of which unquestionably helped put the issue of men beating women on to the political map.

The campaigning style of Chiswick was focused on creating maximum publicity; it advertised that at last the unsayable was being said, and that there was a place of safety for women to go. The response was startling, in that women not only from Chiswick or even London, but from all over Britain, simply arrived. The event was turned both into a philosophy of the open door to any woman seeking to enter and also a tactic of causing irritation to the public health authorities. The semi-permanent overcrowding strategy meant that Chiswick was almost always at the centre of a row, thus ensuring a certain continuous news value.

The provision of a place of shelter – often of very low physical amenity, but of continuous practical and moral support – meant that the suppressed need began to reveal itself. In a way policy-makers have always known this, but in reverse. Here the strategy is to refuse to provide some service, or to provide it at punitive conditions, and the need does not and, indeed, cannot reveal itself. It is not unknown for politicians and officials to point to this as entirely satisfactory evidence that there is no need. The achievement of Chiswick was to reverse this, to insist that there was a social problem and, by flouting their original lease and the public health legislation, to point to the possibilities of meeting the need.

## The second wave

To some extent the very individual qualities which had made Erin Pizzey a spokeswoman to be reckoned with, also made it difficult for her to accept the second more collectivist phase of the movement which came with the setting up of the nationwide federation of refuges. Pizzey's skills and political style, amplified by media which are always hungry to create 'personalities', turned her into what the movement was to call a star.[3] The irony was that the skills which had forced battered women into the political agenda and mobilised women to act in their own defence and others defence, became a handicap so far as the second wave of the movement was concerned.

At the first national meeting in April 1974, there were 25 groups helping or planning to help battered women. Pizzey offered to provide a worker paid out of DHSS funds to co-ordinate these and to stimulate the development of other groups. Jo Sutton, who had worked at Chiswick as a social work student on placement, was appointed. Within one year her report to the second national conference in February 1975 spoke of the development of 82 support groups of whom 25 had managed to open a refuge. In addition to pointing out the difficulties the refuges had in getting open and staying open, and dealing with housing and social security officials, the report spoke of the development of an informal organisation. She described how Chiswick was being made *de facto* into the reference point for both information and the receipt of monies. She urged that the conference decide what kind of minimum organisational from it required, to serve an agreed set of objectives, rather than let structures simply emerge.

Nor was the co-ordinator alone in her desire to put the NWA on a sounder footing; 11 of the northern groups brought to the meeting a set of six objectives which they proposed should become those of Women's Aid as a whole.

1. To provide temporary refuge for battered women and their children on request.
2. To encourage the women to determine their own futures and to help them achieve it, whether it involves returning home or starting a new life elsewhere.
3. To recognise and care for the emotional and educational needs of the children involved.

4. To offer support, advice and help to any woman who asks for it, whether or not she is a resident, and also offer support and after-care to any women and children who have left the refuge.
5. To try to change the attitudes and responsibilities of the public, the media, the courts, and other authorities with respect to the battering of women.
6. To stress the fact that the battering of women is a result of the position of women in society and to work towards changing the root causes in society through the women's movement, etc.

The meeting thus was important and stormy; it ushered in the second wave which sought to establish the same non-hierarchical methods of working which characterised the women's liberation movement. Almost inevitably, there was a clash between Pizzey and the newly developed federal structure which would make Chiswick into one house among equals and no longer the reference point of the movement. There was also a plea made at the meeting for there to be 'no stars' to dominate the movement and that instead Women's Aid should build 'a strong base at the grass roots level'. Feeling her relationship with the new objectives and structures to be no longer viable, Pizzey withdrew. The ensuing conflict between Pizzey and National Women's Aid very gradually produced a recognition that there was Chiswick and there was the movement; each had to be negotiated separately.

By 1975 the physical battering of women had suddenly become an issue in several West European countries, and refuges began to be set up by women's movement activists. In America, the response to the discovery of male violence was rather different; here the focus was on the growing problem of rape, so that rape centres became the first activity, to be followed by battered wives' groups. Thus the second wave – explicitly associated with the women's liberation movement and its analysis of the position of women in society and its non-hierarchical methods of organising – was virtually bound to come. While this connection has always been there, both in terms of the common membership and perspectives of key activists, Women's Aid has tended to play down this aspect. It was not until the second conference, for example, that the movement was prepared to accept the document from the northern group which recognised that 'the battering of women is a result of the position of women in society and to work towards changing the root causes in the women's movement'. Until this meeting, Women's Aid, in its anxiety to secure needed material support from the local or central state, played down its women's movement connection – which nonetheless was evident to every commentator, whether friendly or hostile. As one activist wrote, 'we have carried our contradictions on our backs – and for a time nurtured the opposition'.

Initially, Chiswick alone was sustained by financial support from the DHSS and charitable trusts and also by the work of social work students on fieldwork placements. Thus the urgent problem for National Women's Aid was to compel DHSS recognition of their independent existence. Essentially, this pattern has continued. The movement, desperate for resources, has kept its social critique to a publicly visible minimum; even the internal documents of the movement here maintained a very modest key. Constantly, it has had to balance its needs for sufficient resources to survive with the kind of control that even modest support brings. Local authorities may support an application for urban aid, but often seek in return what they call a 'more clear management structure', which seems to look remarkably like an extension of the conventional division between management and the managed. While this is unfair both to the more innovation-tolerant authorities and the more experimentally minded voluntary organisations, there remains a gap between the kinds of supportive and intimate structures Women's Aid seeks to develop and the structures and goals of city corporate management. The political price of securing even this modest funding thus appears constantly to threaten the socially innovatory practice the movement is trying to develop.

Nonetheless, whilst the movement was endeavouring to deal with its own internal contradictions and to keep together the extraordinarily diverse set of groups up and down the country who joined National Women's Aid, the social problem had slowly and reluctantly become recognised. Grants followed official recognition. National Women's Aid established a London office which served to co-ordinate and carry out research and intelligence for the movement. In this their political style was modelled much more on the squatting movement, which had always managed to retain one strand of officially supported activity, than on the Claimant Unions who had always kept to outsider politics.

The Select Committee on Violence in Marriage and the adoption

by several of its members of an increasingly feminist perspective
aided this process. Whilst social service chiefs and housing managers could, for the most part, scarcely be described as enthusiastic
over the recognition of a new social problem which made further
demands on a dwindling budget, field social workers have often
been one of the supports of the refuges. That housing managers and
social service chief officers are predominantly men, whereas field
social workers include very large numbers of women, is not irrelevant. Social workers were present both in the sense of putting clients
in touch with the refuges, rather as they had with Claimant Unions,
and also by working either as full-time activists or within support
groups. Despite their presence, the analysis developed by Women's
Aid and the movement emphasising the common situation of all
women, means that the professional origins of these activists tend to
be de-emphasised. When – as not infrequently happens at a public
meeting when women, both supporters and residents, go to speak –
the audience cannot tell who are the battered and who are the
supporters, then the movement rejoices as their theory and their
practice begin to reach towards one another.

**Running a refuge: theory and practice**

Organisational and political questions such as this are not new to the
movement. While physically most of the refuges look very similar
(this apparent uniformity is brought about by their common lack of
physical resources), there is considerable variation as each of these
houses with a continually changing population seeks to develop its
way of working and yet to learn from the experience of other
refuges. The continuity is provided partly through women who stay
in the home with their children while looking for second stage
accommodation, but mainly through the support group. These are
the women activists who have agreed to work in the refuge, helping
with the day-to-day problems of individual women and the house as
a whole. Their task varies from locating sympathetic lawyers,
helping secure social security payments, helping negotiate with
housing authorities and private landlords, negotiating support services and schools for children, to going back with women to their
homes to fetch clothing and even children who had to be left behind
in the emergency. Many of these tasks are shared equally between

the support group and the residents, but in some refuges only the last task is carried out by activists.

Because some of the men are not just brutal but are potential killers, the group and the home often take on an air of being besieged. Again, because it is almost impossible to make a domestic house physically secure against a determined man who is indifferent to the consequences, the location of the refuge is not publicised, although a telephone number is, and, when a man does find out, it may be necessary to pass a particularly endangered woman and her children from house to house until the man can no longer trace her.

As the women themselves know, the police still exhibit extreme reluctance to become directly involved in family violence, and the protection of the courts remains inconvincing. I remember meeting one young woman holding her little girl very tightly to her, saying how afraid she was that her husband would come and kill her. Urged by the workers to put an injunction on the man, she cited accurately a recent case of a woman who had sought the court's protection and been murdered. For the refuge it is clearly a major defeat if a man breaks in and beats up a woman in the house itself, a defeat which extends beyond the injury sustained by the victim; the sense of safety itself is lost.

The sense of safety and mutual defence, comfort and support is essentially socially created. The physical conditions of refuges vary between the shabby to the scruffy. For while the provision of a refuge is a crucial material precondition of even attempting to support the women, the achievements of Women's Aid can only be explained through its new ways of working together.

Women's Aid is social innovation on a shoestring. The premises are either rented as cheaply as possible, or given on licence by the local authority; sometimes they are even squatted with all the attendant insecurity. It tends to be elderly, worn-out housing awaiting major rehabilitation or even renewal. Furniture is second-hand, given by sympathisers, clothing and toys come by the same route. The houses are not infrequently overcrowded, and the modest facilities are hard used, particularly by the children who after months or even years of living with fear, perhaps witnessing, perhaps experiencing their father's violence, find themselves suddenly torn out of their world of the nuclear family and relocated in a new communal existence. The presence of the children offers possibilities at the social level; at the level of maintaining the houses it multiplies an existing difficulty.

Thus it is the social organisation rather than the physical facility which we must look at with most interest. The support group are very conscious of the unique help that the battered women can and do give to one another, for while the supporters are around during the day, at weekends and also during the evenings, at night in the majority of refuges there are only the battered women and their children. Talking late into the night, when the children have gone to bed, with other women who have direct experience of the same problem, plays a significant part in raising consciousness, particularly for the new arrival, who perhaps has never been able to discuss the routine nightmare of her domestic life. For such a woman arriving at the refuge is not only often the first time to talk about the problem to others who can and will hear, but also the first time that she can examine the situation in which she finds herself, and see the relationship of the violence to her social and economic dependence on the man. It is only possible for her to do this together with other women who share this knowledge from personal experience or from sympathetic understanding. It is her own definition of battering that admits her, not the definition of some expert, so that at each stage her personal experience is acknowledged as legitimate.

Whether the woman leaves, as many do, after a few days and returns to the man, or whether she decides to try to leave him and will, therefore, have to stay many weeks and months, struggling to be rehoused either with another single woman and her children, or on her own, the decision to go to the refuge constitutes the first step in self-determination. For each, it means that she has been able to oppose the violence being perpetrated against her – and perhaps her children. What appears to be running away to the refuge becomes an insurrectionary act in miniature.

There are problems in seeking to generalise about a movement so loosely knit and where each refuge has such a high degree of autonomy. This account has tried to pull out the central characteristics common to the situation all the refuges face. The movement itself is very conscious of these variations, but by their praise of particular methods of working expressed typically as 'such and such place has really got it together', the kind of social theory and social forms the movement is reaching for become more clear.

An account of a meeting in January 1975 of representatives from over twenty refuges discussing the advantages and difficulties contained in different organisational forms, documents this continuous discussion and self-development. The refuges varied radically. In one the management was carried out by a committee which met regularly but which only included the supporters; the residents themselves were supposed to accept the decisions made by others for them – a situation which scarcely offered novelty to women and simply continued their economic and social dependency. Another had a housemother whose task it was to allocate points for general compliance with rules; perhaps not too surprisingly this imposition of girl guide rules and rewards on grown women was dramatically counter-productive, contributing to the eventual closure of the refuge, unable to contain the aggression and violence that such petty impositions precipitated. Another argued that loving care and endless practical support was all that was needed. One Scots refuge was entirely governed by women who shared no part in the women's movement perspective, who saw themselves as helping the helpless. Their construction of this help included a notice with a generous number of rules printed on it, which again was seen in the discussion as mirroring the subordination to authoritarianism which was a constant in women's lives.

A refuge in south London seemed to have found an approach which increased women's self-sufficiency within a collectivist framework. It had only two rules. They were (i) that every woman, whether resident or supportive, should attend the weekly meeting where decisions concerning the running of the refuge were to be taken, and (ii) that no man should enter the house. This seemed to provide the minimum framework within which a democratic practice could slowly take shape and with the guarantee of security against men. Certainly the particular Women's Aid group which developed these two minimal rules achieved a stable and long-lasting house, where women, whose self-confidence as well as their bodies had been battered, began to develop themselves.

While Women's Aid as a whole moves towards these forms of self-management, refuges have passed through phases of being so opposed to hierarchical organisation that they have mistaken non-hierarchical structures to mean no organisation at all. Here, even minimum rules such as requiring attendance at a weekly meeting, or keeping minutes, or ensuring that women who join the supporters' group actually do take their turn on rosters, are felt to be unacceptably oppressive. Lack of any organisational form becomes expressed in both a social and physical level of disorganisation which renders the refuge neither able to work internally very well nor to deal effectively with pressure and hostility from outside. Developing successful non-hierarchical forms of self-management is an intractable task needing continuous self-appraisal by the group. Refuges constantly fluctuate, engaging in a continuous dialogue, both within the house and with the movement as a whole. Pahl's (1978) detailed study of the refuge at Canterbury not only notes this fluctuating process, but recognises the good fortune of her survey in that it was carried out when the house was enjoying a successful period.

Despite this very unevenness of achievement between and within the separate refuges, the whole is characterised by a continuous and painstaking attempt to find the precise shape of these social forms which speak of a new society while at the same time providing a framework within which the struggle against the injustice of the present society can be waged. The juxtaposition, between the enforced dependency and powerlessness of women enshrined within the assumptions and legislation of the Welfare State, and the conception of women as equal and independent beings which infuses the work of Women's Aid, could not be more complete.

The political base of this level of the politics of reproduction is unequivocally weak. Unpaid reproductive labourers have few moments of interaction which are required by the domestic labour process with others sharing the same work. The contrast between the potential conditions for collective action between this occupation and an occupation whose capacity for powerful and sustained collective action is long evident, such as mining, lies not merely in the fact that one is unpaid, the other paid, but in the necessary moments of interaction. Waiting together, an essential 'activity' in the domestic labourer's life, at the laundry, the schoolgate or the well baby clinic, offer some of these moments; otherwise the work is carried out in social isolation, with only the person who is experienced as her oppressor as her sole social contact. Such a work situation does not offer of itself the preconditions of collective action.

In common with other urban movements, Women's Aid has had to contest both material and ideological oppression. Yet this struggle cannot be merely and directly subsumed within a general category of class conflict. Despite the still dominant practice of both Marxist and bourgeois sociologists, a woman cannot be sensibly allocated to a class or class fraction on the sole grounds of her husband's occupation, for class recedes as the sociological base when such a woman is engaged in direct or even deadly struggle against her specific male oppressor. While class considerations play a part in determining which women turn to Women's Aid as a physical refuge and which turn to it primarily for personal support, these considerations are in an important sense secondary not primary. Instead, the material base of the movement lies neither within the sphere of social reproduction nor within that of domestic reproduction, where, to use Engel's metaphor, women constitute the first class; rather it lies in the mounting contradiction of the two – a contradiction intensified by the increasing entry of women with dependent children into the paid labour market.[4]

As women, particularly married women, have increasingly entered paid labour, they have been allocated, within a dual labour market, particularly to service occupations, whether within the private or public sector. The women's liberation movement has with barbed humour constantly drawn attention to the similarities of the labour process for women, so that within or without the home the work they do constantly echoes the domestic labour of housework, and the affectual management of child and male care. Nonetheless, their entry into paid labour, and the minimal but real independence guaranteed by the state provision of cash benefits in the form of family allowance and supplementary benefits, have offered women the possibility of leaving the oppression of being unfree labourers. Within the capitalist society itself, the possibility is born of non-patriarchal relations between men and women.

Women's Aid advances a general feminist struggle by developing this contradiction, or it fails, and is converted from being a social movement of mutual aid into a feminine philanthropic venture of self-help. While its history is not concluded, but continues to be made in the hard terrain of political struggle, the achievements are precious both for feminism and for a new vision of welfare. Not only has the movement made a substantial critique of male violence and offered direct and practical help to its victims, it has served as a prefigurative form embodying new and just social relations, offering a reliable alternative to the dominant bureaucratic and coercive structures of the welfare state.

## Notes

1. Townsend's concept of 'equal dependence' must be seen in its mid-1950s context, as part of an attempt to reform the penurious status of

women, against a tradition where women, the elderly and the disabled were regarded as 'dependants' with few or no economic rights.

2. Notwithstanding the widespread critique of the approach of psychopathology, the tradition dies hard. The explanations of wife-battering in terms of the attribution of blame to the victim flourish.

3. This anxiety over 'stars' has been particularly characteristic of new left movements and above all the women's liberation movement. The technology of mass communication is singularly powerful in helping invent spokespersons and leaders for contemporary social movements. Many of these have been subsequently attacked or even more typically isolated from the main body of the movement. For a discussion of this problem in the context of the Claimant Unions, see Rose (1971b).

4. The Office of Population Censuses and Surveys has reported that between 1971 and 1976 the proportion of women with dependent children going out to work has increased by one fifth. Women's financial contribution to the family budget is increasingly important (*Population Trends*, No. 13. HMSO, 1978).

# Bibliography

Abortion Law Reform Association (ALRA) (1972) *Written Evidence Submitted to the Lane Committee.*

Phillip Abrams (1977) 'Community Care: Some Research Problems and Priorities', *Policy and Politics*, 6 (2), 125–51.

Sally Alexander (1979) 'Introduction' to the Virago edition of Maud Pember Reeves: *Round About a Pound A Week*, Virago, London, first published in 1913.

L. S. Amery (1955) *My Political Life, Vol. 3, The Unforgiving Years, 1929–1949*, Hutchinson, London.

Helen Austerberry and Sophie Watson (1983) *Women on the Margins: a Study of Single Women's Housing Problems*, Housing Research Group, The City University, London.

Aves Report (1969) *The Voluntary Worker in the Social Services*, report of a committee jointly set up by the National Council of Social Service and the National Institute for Social Work Training, Allen & Unwin, London.

J. Barker and H. Downing (1980) 'Word processing and the transformation of the patriarchal relations of control in the office', *Capital and Class*, 10, Spring, pp. 64–99.

J. Barnes and N. Connelly (eds) (1978) *Social Care Research: Report of a DHSS Seminar*, Policy Studies Institute, London.

Michele Barrett and Mary McIntosh (1979) 'Christine Delphy: Towards a Materialist Feminism?', *Feminist Review*, No. 1.

Michele Barrett (1980) *Women's Oppression Today: Problems in Marxist Feminist Analysis*, Verso, London.

Pauline Bart (1981) 'Seizing the Means of Reproduction: an Illegal Feminist Abortion Collective – How and Why it Worked', in Helen Roberts (ed.) *op. cit.*

Michael Bayley (1973) *Mental Handicap and Community Care*, Routledge & Kegan Paul, London.

Michael Bayley (1978) *Community-oriented Systems of Care*, The Volunteer Centre, Berkhamsted.

A. C. Bebbington and Bleddyn Davies (1983) 'Equity and Efficiency in the

Allocation of the Personal Social Services', *Journal of Social Policy*, Vol. 12, Part 3, July.

H. Becker, B. Green, E. Hughes and A. Strauss (1961) *Boys in White*, University of Chicago Press, Chicago.

C. Benn and B. Simon (1970) *Half Way There*, MacGraw-Hill, Maidenhead.

Fran Bennett (1983) 'The State, Welfare and Women's Dependence' in Lynne Segal (ed.) *What is to be done about the Family?*, Penguin, in association with The Socialist Society, Harmondsworth.

Beveridge Report (1942) *Report on Social Insurance and Allied Services*, Cmnd 6404, HMSO, London.

Birmingham Feminist History Group (1979) 'Feminism as Feminity in the Nineteen-Fifties?', *Feminist Review*, No. 3.

Tessa Blackstone (1983) 'Rejoinder to Jenny Shaw', in Mary Evans and Clare Ungerson (eds) *op. cit.*

W. D. W. Bolin (1973) *Feminism, Reform and Social Service: a History of Women in Social Work*, Minnesota Resource Center for Social Work Education, Minneapolis.

Boston Women's Health Book Collective (1971) *Our Bodies, Our Selves*, Simon & Schuster, New York.

G. Brager and J. A. Michael (1969) 'The Sex Distribution in Social Work: Causes and Consequences', *Social Casework*, 50, pp. 595–601.

Irene Breugel (1980) 'Women as a Reserve Army of Labour', *Feminist Review*, No. 3.

The Brighton Women and Science Group (1980) 'Technology in the Lying-in Room', in The Brighton Women and Science Group (eds), *Alice Through the Microscope: The Power of Science over Women's Lives*, Virago, London.

Marion Brion and Anthea Tinker (1980) *Women in Housing: Access and Influence,* Housing Centre Trust, London.

Edwin Brooks (1973) *This Crowded Kingdom*, Charles Knight & Co., London.

George Brown and Tirril Harris (1970) *Social Origins of Depression*, Tavistock, London.

A. E. R. Buckle and M. M. Anderson (1972) 'Implementation of the Abortion Act: Report on a Year's Working of Abortion Clinics and Operating Sessions', *British Medical Journal*, 3, 381.

Sandra Burman (ed.) (1979) *Fit Work for Women*, Croom Helm, London.

Eileen M. Byrne (1975) 'Inequality in Education – Discriminatory Resource Allocation in Schools?', *Education Review*, 27.

Eileen M. Byrne (1978) *Women and Education*, Tavistock, London.

CSE State Group (1979) *Struggle Over the State: Cuts and Restructuring in Contemporary Britain*, CSE Books, London.

Beatrix Campbell (1984) *Wigan Pier Revisited: Poverty and Politics in the Eighties*, Virago, London.

Mick Carpenter (1977) 'The New Managerialism and Professionalism in Nursing', in M. Stacey *et al.* (eds) *op.cit.*

Mick Carpenter (1979) 'Left Orthodoxy and the Politics of Health', *Capital and Class*, Summer.

A. Cartwright and M. Waite (1972) 'General Practitioners and Abortion', *Journal of the Royal College of General Practitioners*, 22, *Suppl.* No. 1.

Barbara Castle (1976) 'The Death of Child Benefit', *New Statesman*, 4 June 1976.

Central Housing Advisory Committee (1969) *Council Housing: Purposes, Procedures and Priorities*, HMSO, London.

Central Statistical Office (1979) *Social Trends No. 9*, HMSO, London.

J. S. Chafetz (1972) 'Women in Social Work', *Social Work*, 17, pp. 12–18

E. Charles (1935) 'The Effect of Present Trends in Fertility and Mortality upon the Future Population of England and Wales', *London and Cambridge Economic Service Special Memorandum*, No. 40, August.

Ann Charlesworth, David Wilkin and Ann Durie (1984) *Carers and Services: a Comparison of Men and Women Caring for Dependent Elderly People*, EOC, Manchester.

Phyllis Chesler (1972) *Women and Madness*, Doubleday, New York.

Ada Nield Chew (1982) *The Life and Writings of a Working Woman*, presented by Doris Nield Chew, Virago, London.

Alice Clark (1919) *The Working Life of Women in the 17th Century* Routledge & Sons, London.

Community Development Project (1976) *Whatever Happened to Council Housing?*, CDP Information and Intelligence Unit, London.

P. A. Compton, L. Goldstrom and J. M. Goldstrom (1974) 'Religion and Abortion in Northern Ireland', *Journal of Biosocial Science*, 6, 493.

Conservative Party (1977) *Conservative Party Conference Debate*, 12 October 1977, Conservative and Unionist Central Office, London.

Anna Coote and Tess Gill (1974) *Women's Rights: A Practical Guide*, Penguin, Harmondsworth.

J. Cowley (1980) *Housing for People or Profit?*, Stage One, London.

Crowther Report (1959) *15–18*, a Report of the Central Advisory Council for Education, HMSO, London.

Ann Curno, Anne Lamming, Lesley Leach, Jenny Stiles, Veronica Ward and Trisha Ziff (1982) *Women in Collective Action*, The Association of Community Workers in the UK.

R. R. Dale (1969) *Mixed or Single-Sex School*, Vol. I, Routledge & Kegan Paul, London.

R. R. Dale (1971) *Mixed or Single-Sex School; Some Social Aspects*, Vol, 2, Routledge & Kegan Paul, London.

R. R. Dale (1974), *Mixed or Single-Sex School: Attainment Attitudes and Overviews*, Vol. 3, Routledge & Kegan Paul, London.

Miriam David (1980) *The State, the Family and Education*, Routledge & Kegan Paul, London.

Leonore Davidoff, Jean L'Esperance and Howard Newby (1976) 'Landscape with Figures: Home and Community in English Society' in J. Mitchell and A. Oakley (eds) *The Rights and Wrongs of Women*, Penguin, Harmondsworth.

Celia Davies (ed) (1980) *Rewriting Nursing History*, Croom Helm, London.

Anna Davin (1978) 'Imperialism and Motherhood', *History Workshop*, 5, Spring, pp. 9–65.

Rosemary Deem (1978) *Women and Schooling*, Routledge & Kegan Paul, London.

Christine Delphy (1984) *Close to Home: a Materialist Analysis of Women's Oppression*, Hutchinson, in association with The Explorations in Feminism Collective, London.

Department of Education and Science (1975), *Curricular Differences for Girls & Boys*, Education Survey 21, HMSO, London.

Department of Education & Science (1979) *Education and Training for 18 year olds: a Consultative Paper*, HMSO, London.

Department of Employment (DEP) (1979) *New Earnings Survey, 1978*, HMSO, London.

Department of Health and Social Security (1974) *Better Pensions*, Cmnd 5713, HMSO, London.

Department of Health and Social Security (1975a) *Better Services for the Mentally Ill*, Cmnd 6233, HMSO, London.

Department of Health and Social Security (1975b) *Report by the Government Actuary on the Financial Pensioners: The Social Security Pension Bill*, Cmnd 5928, HMSO, London.

Department of Health and Social Security, Supplementary Benefits Commission (1976a) *Living Together as Husband and Wife*, SBA Paper No. 5, HMSO, London.

Department of Health and Social Security (1976b) *Priorities for Health and Personal Social Services in England: A Consultative Document*, HMSO, London.

Department of Health and Social Security (1976c) 'Pension Ages' memorandum.

Department of Health and Social Security (1976d) *Equal Status for Men and Women in Occupational Pension Schemes*, Cmnd 6955, HMSO, London.

Department of Health and Social Security (1977) *Health and Personal Social Services Statistics 1976*, HMSO, London.

Department of Health and Social Security (1978a) *Social Assistance: a review of the supplementary benefits scheme in Great Britain*, HMSO, London.

Department of Health and Social Security (1978b) *A Happier Old Age: A Discussion Document on Elderly People in our Society*, HMSO, London.

P. C. L. Diggory (1969) 'Some Experiences of Therapeutic Abortion', *Lancet*, i, 873.

R. W. J. Dingwall (1977) 'Collectivism, Regionalism and Feminism: Health Visiting and British Social Policy 1850–1975', *Journal of Social Policy*, 6, pp. 291–315.

D. V. Donnison (1978) 'Feminism's Second Wave and Supplementary Benefits', *Political Quarterly*, 49:3, pp. 271–6.

Jean Donnison (1977) *Midwives and Medical Men: A History of Inter-Professional Rivalries and Women's Rights*, Heinemann, London.

J. W. B. Douglas (1967) *The Home and the School*, Panther, London.

Lesley Doyal with Imogen Pennell (1979) *The Political Economy of Health*, Pluto Press, London.

Lesley Doyal and Mary Ann Elston (1983) 'Health and Medicine', Unit 15, Course U221, *The Changing Experience of Women*, Open University, Milton Keynes.

Lesley Doyal, G. Hunt and Y. Mellor (1981) 'Your Life in Their Hands', *Critical Social Policy*, Vol. 1, No. 2.

D. Duman (1979) 'The Creation and Diffusion of a Professional Ideology in Nineteenth Century England', *Sociological Review*, 27, pp. 113–38.

S. Duncan (1976) *The Housing Crisis and the Structure of the Housing Market*, University of Sussex Working Paper, Department of Urban and Regional Studies.

Patrick Dunleavy (1981) *The Politics of Mass Housing in Britain, 1945–1975*, Clarendon Press, Oxford.

J. R. Eames, J. A. Jamieson and J. Hall (1971) 'A General-Practitioner Survey of the Abortion Act, 1967', *Practitioner*, 206, p. 227.

Wendy Edmonds and Suzie Fleming (eds) (1975) *All Work and No Pay: Women, Housework and the Wages Due*, Power of Women collective and Falling Wall Press, Bristol.

B. Ehrenreich and J. Ehrenreich (1978) 'Medicine and Social Control' in J. Ehrenreich, *The Cultural Crisis of Modern Medicine*, Monthly Review Press, London.

Barbara Ehrenreich and Deirdre English (1973) *Complaints and Disorders: The Sexual Politics of Sickness*, Feminist Press, New York.

Barbara Ehrenreich and Deirdre English (1974) *Witches, Midwives and Nurses: History of Women Healers*, Feminist Press, New York.

Barbara Ehrenreich and Deirdre English (1979) *For Her Own Good: 150 Years of the Experts' Advice to Women*, Pluto, London.

P. Elliott (1972) *The Sociology of the Professions*, Macmillan, London.

M. A. Elston (1977) 'Women in the Medical Profession: Whose Problem?', in M. Stacey *et al.* (eds) *op. cit.*

Equal Opportunities Commission (1978) *It's Not Your Business: It's How the Society Works – the Experience of Married Applicants for Joint Mortgages*, EOC, Manchester.

Equal Opportunities Commission (1979) *Response to the DHSS Discussion Document 'A Happier Old Age'*, EOC, Manchester.

Equal Opportunities Commission (1982a) *Caring for the Elderly and Handicapped: Community Care Policies and Women's Lives*, EOC, Manchester.

Equal Opportunities Commission (1978) *It's Not Your Business: It's How the Society Works – the Experience of Married Applicants for Joint Mortgages*, EOC, Manchester.

*and Processes*, Tavistock, London.

Zoë Fairbairns (1976) 'The Economics of the Argument in the Great Wages for Housework Debate', *Leveller* 1 (1).

J. Fairhall (1979) 'Shining Bright at All – in Schools', *The Guardian*, 27 April.

Family Policy Studies Centre (1984), *The Forgotten Army: Family Care and Elderly People*, Family Policy Studies Centre, London.

Elizabeth Fee (1975) 'Women and Health Care: A Comparison of

266    *Bibliography*

Theories', *International Journal of Health Services*, Vol. 5, No. 3.

Frank Field (1982) *Poverty and Politics: the Inside Story of the CPAG Campaigns in the 1970s*, Heinemann, London.

Janet Finch and Dulcie Groves (eds) (1983) *A Labour of Love: Women, Work and Caring*, Routledge & Kegan Paul, London.

Finer Report (1974) *Report of the Committee on One-Parent Families*, Cmnd 5629, HMSO, London.

D. Finn, N. Grant and R. Johnson (1978) 'Social Democracy, Education and the Crisis', in Centre for Contemporary Cultural Studies, *On Ideology*, Hutchinson, London.

Shulamith Firestone (1979) *The Dialectic of Sex*, The Women's Press, London.

R. A. Fisher (1932) *'Family Allowances in the Contemporary Situation*, Address to the Eugenic Society, 12 April.

Tony Fitzgerald (1983) 'The New Right and the Family', in Martin Loney *et al.* (eds) *Social Policy and Social Welfare*, Open University Press, Milton Keynes.

Suzie Fleming (1973) *The Family Allowance Under Attack*, The Falling Wall Press, Bristol.

Annis Flew (1980) 'Looking after Granny: the Reality of Community Care', *New Society*, 54 (934).

Caroline Freeman (1980) 'When is a Wage not a Wage?', in Ellen Malos (ed.) *The Politics of Housework*, Allison & Busby, London.

Marilyn French (1978) *The Women's Room*, Sphere Books, London.

Betty Friedan (1963) *The Feminine Mystique*, Penguin, Harmondsworth.

Jean Gaffin and David Thoms (1983) *Caring and Sharing: the Centenary History of the Co-operative Women's Build*, Co-operative Union, Manchester.

Eva Gamarnikow (1978) 'Sexual Division of Labour: the Case of Nursing', in Annette Kuhn and Ann Marie Wolpe (eds) *Feminism and Materialism*, Routledge & Kegan Paul, London.

Katy Gardner (1981) 'Well Woman Clinics: a Positive Approach to Women's Health', in H. Roberts (ed.) *op. cit.*

Norman Ginsburg (1979) *Class, Capital and Social Policy*, Macmillan, London.

Elizabeth Gittus (1976) *Flats, Families and the Under Fives*, Routledge & Kegan Paul, London.

D. V. Glass (1936) *The Struggle for Population*, Oxford University Press, Oxford.

Linda Gordon (1975) 'The Politics of Birth Control, 1920–1940, The Impacts of Professionals', *International Journal of Health Services*, 5, pp. 253–77.

Linda Gordon (1977) *Woman's Body, Woman's Right: A Social History of Birth Control in America*, Penguin, Harmondsworth.

Ian Gough (1980) 'Thatcherism and the Welfare State', *Marxism Today*, July, pp. 7–12.

Ian Gough (1979) *The Political Economy of the Welfare State*, Macmillan, London.

A. Gray (1927) *Family Endowment: A Critical Analysis*, Benn, London.

Anne Gray (1979) 'The Working Class Family as an Economic Unit', in Chris Harris *et al.* (eds) *The Sociology of the Family: New Directions for Britain*, Sociological Review Monograph, 28 University of Keele, Keele.

Fred Gray (1979), Chapter 8 of Stephen Merrett, *op. cit.*

Majorie Green (1938) *Family Allowances*, Children's Minimum Council.

Karen Greenwood and Lucy King (1981) 'Contraception and Abortion', in Cambridge Women's Studies Group, *Women in Society: Interdisciplinary Essays*, Virago, London.

Victoria Greenwood and Jock Young (1976) *Abortion in Demand*, Pluto Press, London.

Germaine Greer (1979) *The Obstacle Race*, Secker & Warburg, London.

John Greve (1964) *London's Homeless*, Bell, London.

John Greve, Dilys Page and Stella Greve (1971) *Homelessness in London*, Scottish Academic Press, Edinburgh.

M. Griffiths (1980) 'Women in Higher Education – a Case Study of the Open University', in R. Deem (ed.) *Schooling for Women's Work*, Routledge & Kegan Paul, London.

Dulcie Groves and Janet Finch (1983) 'Natural Selection: Perspectives on Entitlement to the Invalid Care Allowance', in Janet Finch and Dulcie Groves (eds) *A Labour of Love: Women, Work and Caring*, Routledge & Kegan Paul, London.

Roger Hadley (1978) 'Retrenchment or Participation: A Choice for the Social Services in Developed Countries' in S. K. Sharma (ed.) *The Dynamics of Development: An International Perspective*, Vol. II, Concept Publishing Company, Delhi.

A. H. Halsey, A. F. Heath and J. M. Ridge (1980) *Origins and Destinations: Family Class and Education in Modern Britain*, Clarendon Press, Oxford.

Lyn Hamill (1976) *Wives as Sole and Joint Breadwinners*, Economic Advisers' Office, DHSS, London.

Jalna Hanmer (1977) 'Violence and the Social Control of Women', in G. Littlejohn, B. Small, J. Wakeford and N. Yural-Davies (eds) *Power and the State*, Croom Helm, London.

W. Hannington (1936) *Unemployed Struggles 1919–1936*, Lawrence & Wishart, London.

Valerie Hannon (1976) 'Education for Sex Equality: What's the Problem?', in D. Rubinstein (ed.) *Education and Equality*, Penguin, Harmondsworth.

Elizabeth J. Harman (1983) 'Capitalism, Patriarchy and the City', in Cora V. Baldock and Bettina Cass, *Women, Social Welfare and the State in Australia*, Allen & Unwin, Syndey and London.

Stephen Hatch (ed.) (1983) *Volunteers: Patterns, Meanings and Motives*, The Volunteer Centre, Berkhamsted.

Dolores Hayden (1981) *The Grand Domestic Revolution: A History of Feminist Designs for American Homes, Neighbourhoods, and Cities*, The MIT Press, Cambridge, Massachusetts and London.

Richard Hoggart (1956) *The Uses of Literacy: Aspects of Working Class Life*, Chatto & Windus, London.

Home Office (1974) *Equality for Women*, Cmnd 5724, HMSO, London.

G. Horobin (ed.) (1973) *Experience with Abortion: A Case Study of North-East Scotland*, Cambridge University Press, Cambridge.

House of Commons (1973) *Select Committee on Tax-Credit*, Vols I–III, No. 341 – I, II, III.

House of Commons (1975–6) *Select Committee on the Abortion (Amendent) Bill* Vol. I (HC 573–1); Vol. II (HC 573–II); *Report* (HC 737) HMSO, London.

Geoffrey Howe (1978) Report of a speech given by Sir Geoffrey Howe, *The Yorkshire Post*, 25 May 1978.

M. G. R. Hull, C. Gordon and R. W. Beard (1974) 'The Organisation and Results of a Pregnancy Termination Service in a NHS Hospital', *Journal of Obstetrics and Gynaecology of the British Commonwealth*, 81, 577.

Jane Humphries (1982) 'The Working-Class Family: a Marxist perspective', in Jean Bethke Elshtain (ed.) *The Family in Political Thought*, Harvester, Brighton.

Audrey Hunt (1978) *The Elderly at Home: A Study of People aged 65 and over Living in the Community in England in 1976*, Social Survey Division, OPCS, HMSO, London.

Bridget Hutter and Gillian Williams (eds) (1981) *Controlling Women: The Normal and the Deviant*, Croom Helm, London.

C. Ingham and M. Simms (1972) 'Study of Applicants for Abortion at the Royal Northern Hospital, London', *Journal of Biosocial Science*, 4, 351.

I. M. Ingram (1971) 'Abortion Games: an Inquiry into the Working of the Act', *Lancet*, ii, 1197.

James Report (1972) *Teacher Education and Training*, report of the DES Committee of Enquiry, HMSO, London.

T. N. A. Jeffcoate and P. Foot (1970) *Morals and Medicine*, BBC, London.

Bob Jessop (1980) 'The State in Post-War Britain', in R. Scase (ed.) *The State in Western Europe*, Croom Helm, London.

K. Jones, J. Brown and J. Bradshaw (1978) *Issues in Social Policy*, Routledge & Kegan Paul, London.

Ken Judge (1978) *Rationing Social services*, Heinemann, London.

A. Kadushin (1976) 'Men in a Women's Profession', *Social Work*, 21, pp. 440–7.

J. M. Keynes (1940) *How to Pay for the War*, Macmillan, London.

Jill Knight (1980) interviewed by A. Hamilton, *The Guardian*, 27 August.

D. Kravetz (1976) 'Sexism in a Women's Profession', *Social Work*, 21, pp. 421–6.

A. Kushlick (1967) 'The Wessex Experiment: Comprehensive Care for the Mentally Subnormal', *British Hospital Journal and Social Services Review*, 6 October 1967.

Labour Party and TUC (1922) *Motherhood and Child Endowment*, Interim Report prepared by the Advisory Committee of the Joint Research and Information Department of the Labour Party and TUC.

Labour Party and TUC (1929) *Majority Report of the Joint Committee on the Living Wage*.

Hilary Land (1975) 'The Myth of the Male Breadwinner', *New Society*, 9 October 1975.

Hilary Land (1976) 'Women: Supporters or Supported?', in D. L. Barker and S. Allen (eds) *Sexual Divisions and Society: Process and Change*, Tavistock, London.

Hilary Land (1977a) 'The Child Benefit Fiasco', *The Year Book of Social Policy in Britain 1976*, Routledge & Kegan Paul, London.

Hilary Land (1977b) 'Social Security and the Division of Unpaid Work in the Home and Paid Employment in the Labour Market', *Social Security Research*, papers presented at a DHSS seminar, 1976, HMSO, London.

Hilary Land (1978) 'Who Cares for the Family?', *Journal of Social Policy*, 7(3).

Hilary Land (1980) 'The Family Wage', *Feminist Review*, No. 6.

Hilary Land (1981) *Parity Begins at Home: Women's and Men's Work in the Home and its Effects on their Paid Employment*, EOC/SSRC, Manchester.

Hilary Land and Roy Parker (1978) 'The United Kingdom', in S. B. Kamerman and A. J. Kahn, *Family Policies: Government and Family in Fourteen Countries*, Columbia University Press, New York.

The Lane Report (1974) *Report of the Committee of the Abortion Act* (Chairman: The Hon. Mrs Justice Lane), Vol. I *Report*; Vol. II, *Statistical Volume*, HMSO, London.

Joyce Leeson and Judith Gray (1978) *Women and Medicine*, Tavistock, London.

Jane Lewis (1980) *The Politics of Motherhood: Child and Maternal Welfare in England, 1900–1939*, Croom Helm, London.

S. C. Lewis, S. Lal, B. M. Branch and R. O. Beard (1971) 'Outpatient Termination of Pregnancy', *British Medical Journal*, 4, 606.

T. L. T. Lewis (1969) 'The Abortion Act', *British Medical Journal*, 1, 341.

Ruth Lister (1973) *As Man and Wife*, Child Poverty Action Group, London.

Ruth Lister (1980) *The Great Child Benefit U-turn?*, Poverty Pamphlet 45, February 1980, CPAG, London.

Ramsay MacDonald (1909) *Socialism and Government*, Vol. II, ILP, London.

W. McDougall (1921) *National Welfare and National Decay*, Methuen, London.

D. MacGillivray and J. Dennis (1973) 'Gynaecological Aspects', in G. Horobin, *op. cit.*

Sally Macintyre (1973) 'The Medical Profession and the 1967 Abortion Act in Britain', *Social Science and Medicine*, 7(2) pp. 121–34.

Sally Macintyre (1976) 'To Have or Have Not: Promotion and Prevention of Childbirth in Gynaecological Work', in M. Stacey (ed.) *The Sociology of the NHS*, Sociological Review Monograph 22, University of Keele.

Sally Macintyre (1977) 'Old Age as a Social Problem', in R. Dingwall, C. Heath, M. Reid and M. Stacey *Health Care and Health Knowledge*, Croom Helm, London.

L. Mackie and P. Pattullo (1977) *Women at Work*, Tavistock, London.

John Macnicol (1980) *The Movement for Family Allowances 1918–45*, Heinemann, London.

Jen McClelland (1982) *A Little Pride and Dignity: the Importance of Child Benefit*, Poverty Pamphlet 54, January 1982, CPAG, London.

Linda McDowell (1983) 'City and Home: Urban Housing and the Sexual Division of Space', in Mary Evans and Clare Ungerson (eds) *op. cit.*

Mary McIntosh (1979) 'The Welfare State and the Needs of the Dependent Family', in Sandra Burman (ed.) *op. cit.*

Mary McIntosh (1981) 'Feminism and Social Policy', *Critical Social Policy*, Vol. 1, No. 1.

Ellen Malos (ed.) (1980) *The Politics of Housework*, Allison & Busby, London.

Jean Martin and Ceridwen Roberts (1984) *Women and Employment: a Lifetime Perspective*, Department of Employment/OPCS, HMSO, London.

J. Manton (1965) *Elizabeth Garrett Anderson*, Dutton, New York.

M. Maresh, N. Barber, D. Adshead and S. Rowlands (1974) 'Why Admit Abortion Patients?', *Lancet*, ii, 888.

David Marsh and Joanna Chambers (1981) *Abortion Politics*, Junction Books, London.

Matrix (1984) *Making Space: Women and the man-made environment*, Pluto Press, London.

Mary Maynard (1985) 'The Response of Social Workers to Domestic Violence', in Jan Pahl (ed.) *Private Violence and Public Policy*, Routledge & Kegan Paul, London.

A. L. Mennerick (1975) 'Organizational Structuring of Sex Roles in a Non-Stereotyped Industry', *Administrative Science Quarterly*, 20, pp. 570–86.

Stephen Merrett (1979) *State Housing in Britain*, Routledge & Kegan Paul, London.

Ministry of Health (1921) *Poor Law Relief to Unemployed Persons*, Circular No. 240 to Boards of Guardians, 8 September.

Ministry of Labour (1924) *Report on National Unemployment Insurance to July 1923*, HMSO, London.

Maxine Molyneux (1979) 'Beyond the Domestic Labour Debate', *New Left Review*, No. 116.

R. M. Moroney (1976) *The Family and the State*, Longman, London.

National Children's Homes (1979) *Family Life*, Occasional Papers No. 1, National Children's Homes, London.

National Council for the Single Woman and her Dependants (NCSWD) (1975) *Single Women: Ten Years Later*, NCSWD, London.

National Union of Societies for Equal Citizenship (NUSEC) (1918) *Equal Pay and the Family: a Proposal for the National Endowment of Motherhood*.

National Union of Societies for Equal Citizenship (NUSEC) (1920) *National Family Endowment*.

Mica Nava (1980) 'Gender and Education', *Feminist Review*, No. 5.

Newsom Report (1963) *Half Our Future*, a report of the Central Advisory Council for Education, HMSO, London.

J. Newson and E. Newson (1968) *Four Years Old in an Urban Community*,

Allen & Unwin, London.

J. Newson and E. Newson (1976) *Seven Years Old in the Home Environment*, Allen & Unwin, London.

R. A. Nisbet (1967) *The Sociological Tradition*, Heinemann, London.

Ann Oakley (1974) *The Sociology of Housework*, Martin Robertson, Oxford.

Ann Oakley (1980) *Women Confined: Towards a Sociology of Childbirth*, Martin Robertson, Oxford.

Occupational Pensions Board (1976) *Equal Status for Men and Women in Occupational Pension Schemes*, Cmnd 6599, HMSO, London.

Katherine O'Donovan (1979) 'The Male Appendage – Legal Definitions of Women', in Sandra Burman (ed.) *op. cit.*

Office of Population Censuses and Surveys (OPCS) (1978a) *Demographic Review, 1977*, HMSO, London.

Office of Population Censuses and Surveys (OPCS) (1978b) *Marriage and Divorce Statistics: Review of the Registrar General on Marriages and Divorce in England and Wales, 1975*, HMSO, London.

Office of Population, Censuses and Surveys (1979) *Changing Patterns of Family Formation and Dissolution in England and Wales, 1964–76*, HMSO, London.

Jan Pahl (1978) *A Refuge for Battered Women*, for DHSS, HMSO, London.

Jan Pahl (1979) 'Refuges for Battered Women: Social Provision or Social Movement', *Journal of Voluntary Action Research*, Vol. 8, Nos 1–2, pp. 25–35.

Jan Pahl (1980) 'Patterns of Money Management Within Marriage', *Journal of Social Policy*, Vol. 9, No. 3.

Jan Pahl (1983) 'The Allocation of Money and the Restructuring of Inequality Within Marriage', *the Sociological Review*, Vol. 31, No. 2.

N. Parry and J. Parry (1976) *The Rise of the Medical Profession*, Croom Helm, London.

A. Parry Jones and M. R. Grimoldby (1973) 'Abortion Act in Somerset', *British Medical Journal*, 3 (90).

Talcott Parsons (1939) 'The Professions and Social Structure', *Social Forces*, 17, pp. 457–67.

Talcott Parsons (1951) 'Social Structure and Dynamic Process: the Case of Modern Medical Practice', in *The Social System*, Glencoe Free Press.

G. Pearson (1975) *The Deviant Imagination*, Macmillan, London.

Phillips Report (1954) *Report of the Committee on the Economic and Financial Problems of the Provision for Old Age*, Cmnd 9333, HMSO, London.

Angela Phillips and Ruth Wallsgrove (1978) 'Payment for Staying Put', *Spare Rib*, p. 11.

Erin Pizzey (1975) *Scream Quietly or the Neighbours Will Hear*, Penguin, Harmondsworth.

Plowden Report (1967) *Children and their Primary Schools*, a report of the Central Advisory Council for Education, HMSO, London.

Politics of Health Group (PHG) (1980) *Cuts in the NHS*, PHG, London.

Politics of Health Group (PHG) (1982) *Going Private*, PHG, London.

Ruth Popplestone (1980) 'Top Jobs for Women: Are the Cards Stacked Against Them?', *Social Work Today*, Vol. 12, No. 4.

F. K. Prochaska (1980) *Women and Philanthropy in 19th Century England*, Clarendon Press, Oxford.

Eleanor Rathbone (1917) 'The Remuneration of Women's Services', *Economic Journal*, Vol. 27, Man. 1917.

Eleanor Rathbone (1940) *The Case for Family Allowances*, Penguin, Harmondsworth.

Eleanor Rathbone (1949) *Family Allowances*, 2nd Edition, Allen & Unwin, London.

W. J. Reader (1966) *Professional Men: the Rise of the Professional Classes in Nineteenth Century England*, Weidenfeld & Nicholson, London.

Robbins Report (1963) *Higher Education*, a report of the Committee on Higher Education, HMSO, London.

Helen Roberts (ed.) (1981) *Women, Health and Reproduction*, Routledge & Kegan Paul, London.

J. A. S. Robertson and J. M. Briggs (1979) 'Part-Time Working in Great Britain', *Department of Employment Gazette*, 87 (7), pp. 671–7.

Hilary Rose (1971a) *Rights, Participation and Conflict*, Poverty Pamphlet No. 5, CPAG, London.

Hilary Rose (1971b) 'Up Against the Welfare State', in R. Miliband and J. Saville, *The Socialist Register*, Merlin, London.

Hilary Rose and Steven Rose (1982) 'Moving Right Out of Welfare – and the Way Back', *Critical Social Policy*, Vol. 2, No. 1, pp. 7–18.

A. Rosenblatt, E. M. Turner, A. R. Patterson and C. K. Rollosson (1970) 'Predominance of Male Authors in Social Work Publications', *Social Casework*, 51, pp. 421–30.

Sheila Rowbotham (1973) *Hidden from History*, Pluto, London.

B. Seebohm Rowntree (1918) *The Human Needs of Labour*, Nelson, London.

Royal Commission on Income tax (1920) *Report*, Cmd 615, HMSO, London.

Royal Commission on the Distribution of Income and Wealth (1978), *Lower Incomes, Report No. 6* (Cmnd 7175), HMSO, London.

Russell Report (1973) *Adult Education: a Plan for Development*, Report of a Committee of Enquiry, HMSO, London.

Susan Saegert (1981) 'Masculine Cities and Feminine Suburbs: Polarized Ideas, Contradictory Realities', in Catherine R. Stimpson *et al.*, *Women and the American City*, University of Chicago Press, Chicago and London.

Eric Sainsbury (1977) *The Personal Social Services*, Pitman, London.

Duncan Sandys (1937) *Report of the Conservative and Unionist Party Conference*.

Janet Sayers (1982) *Biological Politics*, Tavistock, London.

C. B. Scotch (1971) 'Sex Status in Social Work – Grist for Women's Lib', *Social Work*, 16, pp. 5–11.

Hilda Scott (1976) *Women and Socialism: Experiences from Eastern*

*Europe*, Allison & Busby, London.

Seebohm Report (1968) *Report of the Committee on Local Authority and Allied Personal Social Services*, Cmnd 3703, HMSO, London.

Jenny Shaw (1980) 'Education and the Individual; Schooling for Girls, or Mixed Schooling – a Mixed Blessing', in R. Deem (ed.) *Schooling for Women's Work*. Routledge & Kegan Paul, London.

Skeffington Report (1969) *People and Planning: Report of the Committee on Public Participation* (MOHLG, Scottish Development Department), HMSO, London.

Carol Smart and Barry Smart (eds) (1978) *Women, Sexuality and Social Control*, Routledge & Kegan Paul, London.

Social and Community Planning Research (1977) *Interviewers' Manual*, SCPR, London.

Social Survey Division, OPCS (1979) *General Household Survey, 1977*, HMSO, London.

Social Survey Division, OPCS (1981) *General Household Survey 1979*, HMSO, London.

Social Survey Division, OPCS (1982) *General Household Survey 1980*, HMSO, London.

Dale Spender and Elizabeth Sarah (eds) (1980) *Learning to Lose: Sexism and Education*, The Women's Press, London.

Dale Spender (ed.) (1981) *Men's Studies Modified: the Impact of Feminism on the Academic Disciplines*, Pergamon Press, Oxford.

Margaret Stacey *et al.* (eds) (1977) *Health and the Division of Labour*, Croom Helm, London.

Margaret Stacey (1982) *Who Are the Health Workers: Patients and Other Unpaid Workers in Health Care*, paper presented at World Congress of Sociology, Mexico, 1982.

Daphne Statham (1978) *Radicals in Social Work*, Routledge & Kegan Paul, London.

Gareth Stedman Jones (1971) *Outcast London*, Clarendon Press, Oxford.

Mary Stocks (1949) *Eleanor Rathbone*, Gollancz, London.

Hugh Stretton (1974) *Housing and Government*, Australian Broadcasting Commission.

Hugh Stretton (1975) 'Ownership and Alienation: Some Social and Economic Implications of Michael Young and Peter Wilmott, *The Symmetrical Family*', *World Development* Vol. 3, Nos. 11 and 12, pp. 785–798.

Supplementary Benefits Commission (1976) *Living Together as Husband and Wife*, Administration Paper No. 5, DHSS, London.

J. Taylor (1977) 'Hidden Labour and the NHS', in M. Stacey *et al.*, *op.cit.*

Jane Thompson (1983) *Learning Liberation: Women's Response to Men's Education*, Croom Helm, London.

R. M. Titmuss (1938) *Poverty and Population*, Macmillan, London.

R. M. Titmuss (1968) *Commitment to Welfare*, Allen & Unwin, London.

A. Theodore (ed.) (1971) *The Professional Woman*, Schenkman, Cambridge, Mass.

Noel Timms (1964) *Psychiatric Social Work in Great Britain, 1939–1962*,

Routledge & Kegan Paul, London.

N. A. Todd (1971) 'Psychiatric Experience of the Abortion Act', *British Journal of Psychiatry*, 119, 489.

J. Todd and L. Jones (1972) *Matrimonal Property* (Social Survey Division, Office of Population, Censuses and Surveys) HMSO, London.

Peter Townsend (1956) 'Women and Social Security', in P. Townsend (1976) *Sociology and Social Policy* Allen Lane, London.

Peter Townsend (1979) *Poverty in the United Kingdom: A Survey of Household Resources and Standards of Living*, Penguin, Harmondsworth.

J. Tucker (1976) *Honourable Estates*, Gollancz, London.

Trades Union Congress/London Trades Council/Social Democratic Federation (1905) *Report of the National Labour Congress on the State Maintenance of Children.*

Clare Ungerson (1971) *Moving Home: A Study of the Redevelopment Process in Two London Boroughs*, Bell, London.

Clare Ungerson (1983) 'Women and Caring: Skills, Tasks and Taboos', in Eva Gamarnikow *et al.* (eds) *The Public and the Private*, Heinemann, London.

Clare Ungerson (1985) 'Paid and Unpaid Caring: a Problem for Women or the State?', in Paul Close and Rosemary Collins (eds) *Family and Economy in Modern Society*, Macmillan, London.

M. C. Versluysen (1981) 'Midwives, Medical Men and "Poor Women Labouring of Child": Lying-in Hospitals in Eighteenth Century England', in H. Roberts (ed.) *op. cit.*

Stephen Walker and Len Barton (eds) (1983) *Gender, Class and Education*, The Falmer Press, Sussex.

Ronald G. Walton (1975) *Women in Social Work*, Routledge & Kegan Paul, London.

Beatrice Webb (1919) Contribution to *Report of the War Cabinet Committee on Women in Industry*, CMD 135, HMSO, London.

Sidney Webb (1907) *The Decline in the Birth rate*, Fabian Tract, No. 131.

David Wilkin (1979) *Caring for the Mentally Handicapped Child*, Croom Helm, London.

Margaret Wilkin (1982) 'Educational Opportunity and Achievement', in Ivan Reid and Eileen Wormald (eds) *Sex Differences in Britain*, Grant McIntyre, London.

J. Williamson (1972) 'The Problem of Abortion', *Journal of the Royal Society of Health*, 2 (85).

Elizabeth Wilson (1977) *Women and the Welfare State*, Tavistock, London.

Elizabeth Wilson (1980) 'Feminism and Social Work', in R. Bailey and M. Brake (eds) *Radical Social Work and Practices*, Edward Arnold, London.

Wolfenden Report (1978) *The Future of Voluntary Organisations*, Croom Helm, London.

Women and Geography Study Group of the IBG (1984) *Geography and Gender: an Introduction to Feminist Geography*, Hutchinson, in association with the Explorations in Feminism Collective, London.

Virginia Woolf (1938) *Three Guineas*, Hogarth Press, London.

# Index